CREATING AMERICA

George Horace Lorimer

CREATING AMERICA

George Horace Lorimer and
the *Saturday Evening Post*

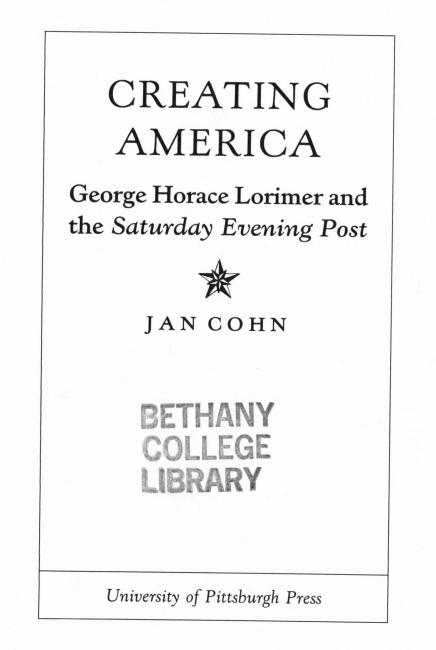

JAN COHN

University of Pittsburgh Press

Published by the University of Pittsburgh Press, Pittsburgh, Pa. 15260
Copyright © 1989, University of Pittsburgh Press
Baker & Taylor International, London
Manufactured in the United States of America

Library of Congress Cataloging-in-Publication Data

Cohn, Jan, 1933–
    Creating America: George Horace Lorimer and the Saturday evening post / Jan
Cohn.
    p.   cm.
    Includes index.
    ISBN 0-8229-3609-7
    1. Lorimer, George Horace, 1869–1937.   2. Saturday evening post—History.   3.
Corporate culture—United States—History—20th century.   4. American peri-
odicals—History—20th century.   5. United States—Social conditions.   6. United
States—Intellectual life—20th century.   7. United States—Social life and customs
—20th century.   I. Title.
PN4900.S3C64 1989
051—dc19   88-28083
                                                                                                    CIP

Quotations from the following collections are published by permission: The Max
Eastman Collection in Lilly Library, Indiana University, Bloomington, Indiana. The
Hal G. Evarts, Sr., Papers, in the University of Oregon Library. The George Horace
Lorimer Papers in the Historical Society of Pennsylvania. The Mary Roberts Rinehart
Collection in the Special Collections Department of the University of Pittsburgh
Libraries. The Kenneth Roberts Papers in the Special Collections Department of
Dartmouth College Library. The Reminiscences of Boris Shishkin (1957) in the Oral
History Collection of Columbia University. The Julian Street Papers and the Booth
Tarkington Papers in the Princeton University Library. Thanks to Mrs. Frederick
Rinehart for permission to quote from the letters of Mary Roberts Rinehart, and to
Hal G. Evarts, Jr., for permission to quote from the letters of Hal G. Evarts. Quota-
tions from two letters by William Faulkner are reprinted by permission of W.W.
Norton & Co., Inc. Illustrations from the Saturday Evening Post are reprinted with
the permission of the Saturday Evening Post © Curtis Publishing Company.

This book is dedicated
to Bill, for the history,
and David, for the technology.

Contents

Acknowledgments

For me this book will always recall long days in the main reading room of the Library of Congress, days spent with the files of the *Saturday Evening Post*. But if working on the story of Lorimer and the *Post* seemed at times like taking up residence in the LC, the book that has emerged depends as well on the resources of a number of other libraries. For the help they provided me in finding important materials, I wish to express my appreciation to Rebecca Campbell Cape, Mark Clark, Philip N. Cronenwett, Hilary Cumings, Peter Parker, and John Verso. The Curtis Archive in Indianapolis has been another particularly rich source of documents; for their assistance with this project, I am grateful to archivist Steve Pettinga and to his predecessor, Carol Brown McShane. For the kind of insight that can only be provided by personal reminiscence, I am indebted to the late Mr. Graeme Lorimer, and to his widow Mrs. Sarah Lorimer, for a long and pleasant afternoon spent recalling his father, George Horace Lorimer.

In many ways the writing of this book has been a long and difficult process. The scope alone was daunting. I might not have undertaken the project and surely would not have persevered in it without the encouragement and the patience of Fred Hetzel. My background in historical information and historical thinking often seemed to me inadequate. Colleagues in history helped out. Roy Rosenzweig provided a rich, indeed a formidable, bibliography. Methodology and theory for dealing in historical, and in literary-cultural, terms with mass-market journalism are extremely ill-developed. Jack Censer, whose research on prerevolutionary French journalism has forced him to confront many of the same problems I faced, offered constant encouragement and criticism. Richard

Ohmann, whose own work on mass-market journalism is among the most sophisticated, read the manuscript and gave me thoughtful comment and criticism.

It is customary to thank members of one's family for their moral and emotional support, but in my case the support was a good deal more concrete, and my thanks are therefore a good deal more particular. Among the sophisticated and instructive historians I have turned to I count first my husband, Bill Cohn. And I count him, too, among my readers and critics, amazed in retrospect that anyone could so patiently and thoughtfully read so many drafts so many times. My son, David Solomon, a card-carrying member of the computer generation, recognized early my need for a data base. When no appropriate software was available, he created a program himself, and while he battled the bugs, I learned to shape my notes to the rigorous logic the computer demands. Later he discovered "Nut-shell," the most flexible and friendly of database systems, in which the old *Post* files now reside, ordered and logical and accessible.

Finally, I am grateful to George Mason University for a faculty research leave that allowed me the time to complete the research and begin the writing for this book.

CREATING AMERICA

Introduction

This book is a study of one of America's great mass magazines, perhaps its greatest. My subject is the *Saturday Evening Post,* acquired by Cyrus H. Curtis in 1897 and, by 1899, placed under the editorship of George Horace Lorimer. Under Lorimer's direction the *Post* grew and prospered, through the years of Progressivism and war and economic boom; it survived the Great Depression as well, though Lorimer did not, resigning at the end of 1936 and dying less than a year later. It is Lorimer's *Post* this book investigates, the thirty-eight years of his editorship.

It is useful to make clear at the outset, however, what this book is not. It is not a biography of George Horace Lorimer, although biographical materials are used from time to time, for Lorimer's significant life story can be read in the files of the *Post.*[1] As he and others reported, nothing went into the pages of the magazine that he had not personally read and approved. His role, of course, was considerably more dynamic than mere approval: he set the tone and the purpose of the *Post,* he sought out writers, he developed ideas for stories and articles for many of those writers, he established a network of important political and business connec- tions as sources for information and ideas, and he wrote material as well—in the early days, serialized business fiction, and always, editorials. Against the deep personal imprint he left on the *Post,* most other personal information becomes, with time, insignificant.

Nor is this book simply a record of the development of the *Post,* a list of its fairly remarkable successes in the publishing of fiction, a review of the significant men and women who chose to print their ideas or policies or memoirs in the magazine, a record of the well-known staff writers whose views on economics or politics or technology served as a medium of education and acculturation for millions of Americans. This record exists in the admirable work of Frank Luther Mott, whose study of the *Saturday Evening Post* in *A History of American Magazines* remains the fullest and most authoritative such account.

This book is not intended to be a history of the rise and fall of a magazine giant within a publication empire. The Curtis Company is not my subject, nor is the larger field of magazine journalism within which the *Post* faced such feisty newcomers as *Time* and later *Life*, nor, beyond that, the even vaster field of mass media and the new technologies of radio, film, and television that would alter irrevocably the role of magazines in America. Studies of this kind are available, from histories of twentieth-century magazines to corporate accounts of the demise of the *Post* years after Lorimer himself had retired.

Finally, this book is not a review of mainstream American history as recorded, or told, or created by the *Saturday Evening Post;* nor is it a re-vision of American history told in counterpoint *against* the history the *Post* codified. Early twentieth-century America streams past in the pages of the *Post,* in illustration and story and advertisement as well as in articles on politics, business, agriculture, education, and the arts, but that history—that stream of events, profound and trivial—must remain, for this study, largely the background of occurrences before which the weekly issue of the magazine played out its own particular historical role.

To express most clearly just what this book *is,* it is useful to start with the question of why such a study should be done in the first place. What interest can the *Saturday Evening Post* have for us, living in late twentieth-century America, a world of high-speed electronic communications in which television brings us news as it happens and transmits wars live onto our home screens? The principal answer lies precisely in our contemporary world of mass communications and mass entertainment, for that was the world the *Post* set about shaping, and it remains a world we urgently need to understand. Mass society exists in an atmosphere of messages, inhales them like the air it breathes—unavoidably—yet we are only beginning to understand the social dynamics of mass communication.

Through the *Post* we can study this pervasive phenomenon at its roots, its inception. Moreover, we can study it in an fairly uncluttered laboratory. *Before* movies, *before* radio, *before* television, the *Post* delivered its version of America week after week to an audience of millions. By 1908, when one million copies a week were sold, reaching a total readership of four to five million, the magazine may well have been seen by one out of every nine American readers.[2] No single contemporary medium has anything like so powerful, because essentially unchallenged, a hold on mass society. The market dominance of the *Post* raises important questions: how did the *Post* achieve its success, what uses were made of its enormous power, what limits did that power have, and how did the *Post*—which is to say, George Horace Lorimer—understand that power, its limits, and its responsibilities?

It is the thesis of this book that George Horace Lorimer set out to create America in and through the pages of the *Saturday Evening Post*. Week after week he crafted the issues of his magazine as an image, an idea, a construct of America for his readers to share, a model against which they could shape their lives. Certainly, there were other magazines, other carriers of culture, and other visions of America, but for over a quarter of a century the *Post* was unrivaled in codifying the ground rules that explained and defined Americanism. Despite the vast changes in American society between 1899 and 1936, what the *Post* achieved was the fullest expression of a broad American consensual view. It can be argued, moveover, that the *Post* was instrumental in creating and continually reframing a set of attitudes and beliefs that, at least until the time of the New Deal, constituted an American ideology. And finally it is important to recognize that the *Saturday Evening Post* was not only a medium for the dissemination of ideology but in fact became itself an artifact of that ideology.

Stuart Hall, whose work on mass culture is constructed on his reading of Raymond Williams, Louis Althusser, and especially

Antonio Gramsci and his theory of hegemony,[3] has defined the principal functions of mass media, establishing as the primary function "the provision and the selective construction of *social knowledge,* of social imagery, through which we perceive the 'worlds,' the 'lived realities' of others, and imaginarily reconstruct their lives and ours into some intelligible 'world-of-the-whole,' some 'lived totality.'"[4] Although Hall is concerned with contemporary forms of mass media, "the whole gigantic complex sphere of public information, intercommunication and exchange," his definition encapsulates the mission Lorimer established for the *Post* nearly a century ago. Hall also defines the work of media as "actively ruling in and ruling out certain realities, offering maps and codes which mark out territories and assign problematic events and relations to explanatory contexts, helping us not simply to *know more* about 'the world' but to *make sense* of it."

Mapping the territory is an exercise in power. The "lived realities" presented in the *Post* were expressions of Lorimer's view of the world, an ideology constructed out of traditional values, an interpretation of the present, and a vision of the future. That ideology was shot through with contradictions, but there can be no doubt that the contradictions themselves, the pious weight of traditional values and the heady promise of the present and future, accounted for the initial success of the *Post* and, partly out of nostalgia, for its continuing media dominance in the 1920s and 1930s.

Lorimer, of course, saw all this through a different lens; he believed that he was creating an America that would become, though his agency, a reality. He set out to make the *Post* a medium of information and entertainment, an instrument to shape society. In the stories of the romance of business, in the upbeat polemics of leaders of the day, in the articles that told young men how to succeed, readers of the *Post* could discover an America mapped, intelligible, and full of promise.

Lorimer succeeded beyond his expectations, for the *Post* became not only the preeminent medium of its day but finally itself an artifact of American mass culture. It is probably possible, in fact, to speak of a "culture of the *Post*," meaning the entire construct of article, story, illustration, and advertising that replicated itself week after week, continually reifying its particular vision of America.

As an artifact of the culture, the *Post* expressed its ideology in article, story, editorial, and illustration. The stories and serials in the *Post* were entertaining, to be sure, but they were as well potent carriers of values. At the very least, *Post* fiction sanctioned, by codifying and celebrating, the popular values of the time—and of the magazine. Even those stories most innocent of "intention" were partners in the job of constructing America for the *Post* audience; westerns, historical romances, sports fiction were all spun out of the collective web of a comprehensible society, a society built on fair play and individual initiative and common sense.

The role of nonfiction was, of course, more directly informative, educational, or polemical. From the outset, Lorimer wanted prestige for his magazine and he wanted *authority*. Thus, he solicited articles from former President Cleveland, whether about the political responsibility of young men (no doubt Lorimer's idea) or the joys of fishing (without question, Cleveland's choice). He developed a long-term professional and personal relationship with Senator Albert Beveridge, who wrote about Manchuria, the Philippines, and the young man in America. He sought out politicians, civil servants, businessmen, theater producers to write about politics, government, business, the theater. Articles in the early years frequently carried a full description of the writer's official role, a guarantee of his authority.

But about a decade after he began editing the *Post*, Lorimer found a new source of authority in the journalist himself. Not any journalist, of course, but those whose names and styles and views would become familiar to the readers of the *Post*. At first, these men came to the magazine from careers fully established in other media, many from the *New York Sun*. By 1908 David Graham Phillips, Samuel G. Blythe, Isaac F. Marcosson, Will Irwin, and Irvin S. Cobb were essentially *Post* staffers. Later, once the mantle of authority was draped over the *Post* itself, the magazine could grow its talent at home—with men like Kenneth L. Roberts, Garet

Garrett, Edwin Lefevre. Thus, newer nonfiction writers, from early in their careers, were vested with the *Post*'s authority.

Those journalists were the Edward R. Murrows and Walter Cronkites of the day, the name on the article, the familiar style and tone, promising not only accuracy but also intelligence and good judgment. A number of these writers produced both fiction and nonfiction, allowing them a wide license for the expression of their views. And as time went on, a good number of them wrote personal essays as well, usually in a tone of bluff, manly humor. If Sam Blythe went on the wagon or Cobb was placed on a diet, it was the stuff of an informal piece, even a series of pieces. Such articles only enhanced a reader's sense of kinship to the spokesmen of authority.

The "culture of the *Post*" was the culture of the emerging world of business—business as it hovered between production and consumption and managed to live comfortably with the contradic-tion between traditional values and present realities. The great paradox of the *Saturday Evening Post* is that it remained an artifact of American culture *after* that period passed, maintaining its market dominance through the 1920s and 1930s. Lorimer and the *Post* are important because, among other things, their history traces the course of the dominance and subsequent disintegration of nineteenth-century bourgeois ideology in America.

Although Lorimer saw himself and the *Post* as the very breath of the contemporary, of the new twentieth century, traditional values inherited from the nineteenth century lay at the heart of Lorimer's ideology. Paradoxically, these values supplied the energy that fueled his belief in the promise of the new century. For Lorimer, that promise lay in business. Business as the American way of life with success as the promise of the future was erected on the foundations of hard work and thrift inherited, like the idea of progress itself, from the traditions of nineteenth-century thought. The problem was that Lorimer's nineteenth-century values had developed in support of a producer society and were, therefore, already anachronisms for the emerging consumer society of the early twentieth century.

Tradition, as Raymond Williams has noted, is a much more

active and powerful force than is customarily acknowledged. "[Tradition] is always more than an inert historicized segment; indeed it is the most powerful practical means of incorporation. What we have to see is not just 'a tradition' but a *selective tradition:* an intentionally selective version of a shaping past and a preshaped present, which is then powerfully operative in the process of social and cultural definition and identification."[5] As Williams makes clear, the use of tradition is selective. What Lorimer selected was the *idea* of worker virtues in themselves, detached from economic reality, and he simply transferred them to the businessman, and subsequently to the consumer, along with the success they promised. Those values, inherited and transmuted, were encapsulated in the three key terms that informed the *Post* throughout Lorimer's editorship: *American, businessman,* and *common sense.*

Lorimer was conscious from the outset of his editorial work that America was unformed as a nation; he saw the country as an unassimilated collection of regions and nationalities in which an overriding and unifying consciousness of Americanism had yet to be developed. The *Post* was conceived by both Lorimer and Curtis as the medium of an American consciousness. Geographically, as a national magazine, it was intended to transcend local markets dominated by newspapers. Intellectually, as a general-interest magazine printing both fiction and nonfiction on a wide variety of subjects, it was designed to reach audiences ignored by "highbrow" magazines like *Harper's* and the *Atlantic.* Commercially, as a magazine that carried national advertising and allied itself with the newest business economics of standardization and national distribution, the *Post* was created to echo and reinforce in its contents the emerging concept of America as a nation unified by the consumption of standardized commodities.[6]

The creation and dissemination of a transcendent American consciousness was the overriding mission of the *Post.* To that end, political and business articles, life stories of successful men, informational pieces on science and technology, and the editorial page offered a common education both in facts and in values. But perhaps even more effective in creating that mass consciousness were the storytellers and artists whose work became intimately associated with the *Post*. Readers *became* a national community as they came to know, to share in, and to talk to one another about familiar stories by familiar writers about familiar characters— Father Brown, Lawyer Tutt, Letitia Carberry, or Alexander W. Botts. The very appearance of another Rockwell or Leyendecker cover enriched and confirmed the culture of *Post* readership. To read the *Post* was to become American, to participate in the American experience.

The representative American, in Lorimer's view, was a compendium of nineteenth-century values; he worked hard, saved money, and assumed the duties of citizenship responsibly. The American was pragmatic and self-reliant, dedicated to his own social and economic betterment, but always within the constraints of law and decency. Because America was the land of opportunity, a land without fixed classes or social barriers, it was entirely possible to rise without abridging the rights or opportunities of others. Progress was limitless, both personally and nationally, and hard work and honesty the only prerequisites for success.

The enemy of progress was the idea of class, and Lorimer argued vehemently throughout his editorship that the United States had no class system. In the early years the threat of classism came from the idle rich. An editorial called "Rich Men's Handicaps" (July 25, 1903) spoke of the joys to be found on the road of labor and elicited from history the warning that "leisure breeds coarseness and mental deterioration." But the truly dangerous aspect of leisure was that it threatened to divide society into classes, into those who worked and those who did not. There are no classes in America, insisted Lorimer, save "the worthy and the unworthy."[7] The unworthy were excluded from the *Post*'s America, specifically the wealthy and idle, often expatriated, who sneered at a nation dedicated to work and to money. Lorimer, of course, posited his America on precisely that dedication. The great leveler was work; work united Americans, work and the promise of success. "The world has room for idlers—it has room for all sorts of people. But America has no room for them. That great workshop wants no idlers of whatever kind obstructing the aisles and hinder-ing toilers at their tasks. That will be a sorry day for America when the leisure class finds it an agreeable place of residence."[8]

If Lorimer believed he was creating America, we can see in retrospect that he was, in actuality, creating the culture of business. In Lorimer's lexicon the characteristics of the businessman were essentially those that constituted the American. Businessmen of whatever shape were hardworking, prudent, honest, self-reliant. They were practical not idealistic, well informed not intellectual. They were optimistic, trusting their future to America's future. And they were modern, for business "is the age itself."[9] The businessman was protean in the *Post*'s conception. His meta-morphoses ran from a Carnegie to a chicken farmer, and he turned up as well in professional shapes, as lawyer, doctor, even minister and artist. The businessman was, above all else, the antidote to the idle rich. He worked, his work promised success, and his success demonstrated the fluidity of American society, the absence of classes.

The businessman was defined and profiled, interviewed, ad-dressed and exhorted, finally made the subject of a new kind of literature—business fiction. Lorimer serialized Harold Frederic's *The Marketplace* and Frank Norris's *The Pit;* when he could not find enough business fiction, he wrote it himself. His anonymously serialized *Letters from a Self-Made Merchant to His Son* became a best-seller in 1902. In articles and fiction, the *Post* established and promulgated the cluster of primary values: its businessman was a family man, an informed and responsible citizen, a balanced man who exercised thrift toward a self-reliant old age on the one hand and on the other, consumed, with moderation, the newly available signs and tokens of upward mobility—travel, electrical appliances, or the new games of golf and contract bridge.

In the early years, the businessman Lorimer most assiduously addressed and courted and constructed was young. As subject and object of the magazine, this young man was malleable, educable; in his hands lay the future of America, the future of business, and the *Post* set out to create him in the image they held for that future. In the pages of the magazine in its first decade was everything that young man needed to know: a moral system of cleanliness and honesty, business information of the how-to sort on topics ranging from setting up law offices to succeeding as a salesman, a sense of political responsibility that went far beyond merely voting to encourage local involvement, housekeeping tips on how to set up a bachelor establishment in the new apartment-hotels, ideas for suitable, "manly" recreation like hunting and camping. As this youth matured and prospered, the *Post* helped him with investment information, primers on stocks and bonds, real estate and mortgages, life insurance and commodity markets. Much later, in the 1920s, when the young man had turned middle-aged, he could learn how to maintain his health and keep his figure; he could also learn how to spend his more considerable income—or, as Lorimer might have put it, whatever income was left to him after the confiscatory taxes exacted by the federal government—in antique collecting, European travel, and of course market investments.

As one studies the portrait of the businessman drawn in the early years of Lorimer's *Post* from the vantage point of three-quarters of a century, it becomes clear that Lorimer was in fact engaged in creating his own class revolution, although he would have rejected the term out of hand. He saw in the businessman America's new dominant class, a class replacing the aristocracies both of old money and the genteel professions. Again, he would have disavowed this language, for he believed that there was no question whatsoever of class and that his goal was a thorough democratizing of America.

The promise of democratization through business again depended on nineteenth-century values, specifically the belief in unlimited opportunity for hardworking, thrifty, honest, productive men. But in the early years of the *Post,* the contradiction between the old values associated with production and the emerging new realities of consumption was masked by an emphasis on the shadowy middle ground of distribution. Although Lorimer's businessman was conceived broadly enough to encompass the great majority of American men in all kinds of business, it was the salesman who appeared as the favored, representative type. The salesman was not only the go-getter, the energetic emblem of business, he was as well the agent of distribution.[10]

With the boom of the twenties, when consumption replaced production as the economic basis for continued prosperity, Lorimer had to face the contradictions in his world view. Although business articles in the *Post* acceded to the new economics of consumption, editorials anxiously rehearsed the old values of thrift and self-denial. As consumption was fueled by the bull market of the late 1920s, the contradictions became even sharper, for hard work and thrift had nothing to do with a prosperity founded on speculation and spending.

The stock market crash seemed to resolve the contradictions; the old values had been proved correct. Lorimer rehearsed them to what he hoped was a chastened American people, and when the Depression settled over America he rehearsed those values again in the expectation that they would provide models of behavior and sources of hope. Instead, Lorimer found Americans turning away from the last of the quintessential characteristics of Americanism. The nation had abandoned hard work and thrift in the boom years; under the New Deal it jettisoned self-reliance.

As Lorimer witnessed it, the New Deal threatened to destroy the American nation and the American character. Lorimer, who had set out to create America, now found himself trying to save America. The ideology of the *Post* remained consistent, but it was no longer the voice of the hegemony, or more accurately, it was now one of a number of competing voices in a society in crisis. Driven to rescue America from the New Deal, Lorimer attacked on every front, but more and more frequently he had recourse to the most potent of his key terms: common sense.

Gramsci has called common sense "the 'philosophy of non-philosophers.'" It is "the conception of the world which is uncritically absorbed by the various social and cultural environments in which the moral individuality of the average man is developed."[11] Common sense, moreover, carries its own history, what Stuart Hall calls "the debris and traces of previous, more developed ideological systems," referring "to what passes, without exception, as the wisdom of *our* particular age and society, overcast with the glow of traditionalism."[12]

Lorimer used common sense as a talisman against the complex economic reality of the Depression and thus as a means of prevent-ing despair: "Courage and common sense will conquer situations that look desperate to the timid," Lorimer declared.[13] Common sense was also the mark of those whose sober good judgment set them off from dangerous extremists: "The air is full of cries of the Radical Reds and the Conservative Whites. The Commonsense Blues, the great majority of inarticulate moderate men who retain their sanity, view with bewilderment a world apparently gone mad."[14] Common sense would be the hallmark of a new party as well, a party neither of the right or left, but one "founded on the simple principles of common honesty and common sense."[15] FDR and the New Deal were, of course, the antithesis of common sense; to the cry "Is everybody happy?" Lorimer sourly responded, "No . . . not those who hold fast to old-fashioned, commonsense ideas of thrift, economy, good faith and personal liberty."[16]

The enemy of common sense was the intelligentsia, a word Lorimer discovered shortly after the war. *Intelligentsia* neatly summed up everything that the *Post* opposed, from liberal-radical political opinions to avant-garde art forms. Because the term *intel-ligentsia* was, like radical thinking and experimental art, itself an import from Europe, it served as a scornful shorthand for all that was alien and un-American. Common sense, of course, was quintes-sentially American, and that was so because what common sense expressed was precisely what constituted America for Lorimer. America was the realization of the set of values referenced by the single magical phrase *common sense*. In common sense resided the ideology of Lorimer's America.

Although the traditional values inherited from nineteenth-century bourgeois America had by the mid-1930s become increas-ingly distant from social reality, those values remained potent, even if only as nostalgia, if only as a means of escape. The *Post*, by this time a weekly ritual celebrating an outworn ideology, maintained its audience, but—as Lorimer discovered—it had lost whatever political power it might once have wielded. Lorimer's long and fevered campaign against Roosevelt's reelection in 1936 demonstrated how strenuously Lorimer believed in the power of the *Post*. Roosevelt's landslide reelection demonstrated the limits of that power.

If the *Post* did not command political power, it did continue to influence the ways in which Americans thought, or at least preferred to think, about themselves and their country. And if *Post* ideology had become, in terms of practical affairs, a matter of nostalgia, no doubt *Post* readers found comfort in a weekly reconstitution of that vanished world. Certainly, that was not Lorimer's purpose. He intended to recall the values of that traditional world in order to change the present situation; he had no intention that the *Post* become an artifact of nostalgia.

But thirty-seven years had passed since Lorimer began to create his America in the pages of the *Post,* and it is easy to see with hindsight that it would have been impossible to construct a version of America in 1899 that could possibly hold good for 1936. When Lorimer took over as editor of the *Post,* the Spanish-American War was under way, Teddy Roosevelt was charging up San Juan Hill, and a good many people—including George Lorimer—were worried about incipient American imperialism in our Philippine adventure. When Lorimer retired, Franklin Delano Roosevelt had just been reelected, Hitler had retaken the Rhineland, and a good many people—again including George Lorimer—were deeply concerned lest America be drawn again into another European war. Nevertheless, a foundation of unchanging values undergirded the continuous alterations, the remodeling, of the *Post's* America, and those values, no matter how anomalous, remained dear to the readers of the *Post.*

Indeed, the argument for the influence of the *Saturday Evening Post* rests most convincingly on its success, on the fact that week after week, year after year, and decade after decade, millions and millions of Americans bought and read it. For these millions it provided a major source of fiction, of imaginative narrative, at least until the time of the movies. And it provided as well a major source of information about the world they lived in. Even for those who did not necessarily believe everything they read, the sheer volume of material, of information, all essentially based on the same premises about America and the world, would ultimately have its cumulative effect. That kind of influence remains elusive, unmeasurable, un-provable; nevertheless, it is my belief that the *Saturday Evening Post* exerted precisely such influence, and on that belief this study is premised.

Throughout I have been speaking about Lorimer as a man who consciously shaped the ideology of the *Post* and my emphasis has been intentional. Although the products of mass culture are gener-ally understood as reproductions and reprocessings of elements of ideology rather than as the works of individual minds, the case of Lorimer's *Post* cannot be adequately described in those terms.[17] To be sure, the *Post* was financially dependent on advertising; the famous nickel it cost did not begin to support the editorial side. It would be naive to suppose that great national advertisers would have placed ads in the *Post* had it espoused an ideology hostile to business and consumption. But this does not mean that any particu-lar serial, story, or article had to compete, as television shows do today, for sponsorship. Lorimer, not the advertiser, determined the contents of the magazine; the contents sold the magazine to a vast audience; the advertisers sought that audience as a potential market.

To the extent that it is possible for a mass medium to be the expression of one man, the *Post* was the expression of George Horace Lorimer and of his ideology. But to understand Lorimer is to see that he was a man of his time, specifically a man of the first fifteen years of the twentieth century. The ideas and values he held—that mixed bag of traditional and contemporary views and beliefs—were those of a great many young, aggressive, and optimistic Americans. That was his genius and his good fortune. He had no recourse to commit-tees; he did not trim his ideas to fit some market survey.

The materials for this book are preeminently the files of the *Saturday Evening Post*. In reading through thirty-eight years, fifty-two issues a year, I have tried to recapture the experience of imme-diacy the reader of each issue would have had. As a result, some sense, faulty though it may be, has come through of the press of passing events, of the fascination with the new—new ideas or styles, new songs or sports, new heroes and celebrities, and the delight in the familiar—another Earthworm Tractor story, another political article by Blythe, another war report by Cobb.

At the same time, that research itself raises a difficult, and probably unanswerable, question. It is one thing to discover what messages the *Post* was encoding and sending, quite another to know what messages were received and how they were decoded. Even more basically, it is impossible to know just what material in the magazine was even read by its enormous audience. After all, the *Saturday Evening Post* cost only a nickel, and when it swelled to 200 pages and over, many might have felt they more than got their nickel's worth merely in reading the fiction.

In the face of unanswerable questions, I have decided to read the *Post* as if it had been read in its entirety by at least a majority of its audience. In the first place, there is no other reasonable approach to a study of a print document so widely disseminated; and second, the primary emphasis of my work is on the magazine itself and only secondarily, and by implication, on its audience. Moreover, while proof is out of the question, common sense—as Lorimer might have said—is on the side of postulating a fairly thorough reading of each issue. After all, an issue would have typically remained in the house for at least a week, at least until it was replaced by the next one. In homes without television, and for many years of the *Post*'s history without radio, it is probable that an issue was picked up several times by one family member or another, seated in an easy chair after dinner.

As Robert Darnton has written in *The Great Cat Massacre,* it is finally impossible to relive the experience of someone in the past face to face with the text one now studies from the different vantage point of our own contemporary society, with our own particular and equally distinct signs and codes. But as Darnton eloquently demonstrates, the attempt must be made in the hope of coming ever closer to the lost experience of the past; there is, after all, no other way to reclaim the past, and it is the past, in the form of Lorimer's America, that this book sets out to discover.

Beyond the basic, insurmountable problem of the pastness of the past, my work on the *Saturday Evening Post* runs into another difficulty that must be acknowledged. Despite all the ways in which one works to assure objectivity, no study like this can honestly claim it. I have read through nearly 2,000 issues of the *Post,* and with the reading of every issue, as with every subsequent phrase of this work, it has been necessary to determine which articles and stories, which editorials and departments to read, which to skim, which merely to note, which to ignore, which to quote in this book, which to analyze, which to cite, which to omit altogether—in short, from that great sea of print what great amounts of material to leave out. I have tried throughout to let the pages of the *Post,* rather than my own predilections, inform me about what is significant or representative. Still, it is, finally, my own reconstruction of the *Post* that appears in this book.

Beyond the files of the *Post* I have had available to me other various, scattered, but highly useful primary materials. Lorimer left no archive of correspondence save a collection, now in the Historical Society of Pennsylvania, of several hundred representative letters from several hundred *Post* contributors. Lorimer intended these as an *aide-mémoire* in the writing of a projected autobiography; to the researcher they are too fragmentary to serve as more than autographs. Included with the Lorimer Papers are those of Adelaide Neall, who joined the *Post* in 1909, becoming an associate editor who worked closely with Lorimer and many major contributors. Wesley Stout, who followed Lorimer as *Post* editor, also saved some significant correspondence, now in the Library of Congress. Other archives, as well, preserve some Lorimer letters, principally the Albert Beveridge archive at the Library of Congress and the Mary Roberts Rinehart collection at the University of Pittsburgh Library. The archives of Booth Tarkington and Julian Street at Princeton and of Kenneth Roberts at Dartmouth also include Lorimer correspondence, and a few letters remain among the

Robert Herrick papers at the University of Chicago Library and those of Hal G. Evarts at the University of Oregon. All these letters are valuable in recreating Lorimer's tone as a businessman-editor and as a friend, and some are particularly useful in outlining his position on one issue or another.

The Curtis Company, now located in Indianapolis, preserves a *Post* archive, though it does not hold the masses of information one might hope for; letters from readers, editors' reports on manuscripts, internal memos—all are gone. There is an abstract of the minutes of the Curtis Company's meetings over two decades, as well as a small number of long memos on company policy in the face of economic hard times; both are invaluable in allowing me to reconstruct something of the business side of the *Post*. Similarly, a remarkable archive at the University of Oregon preserves the business correspondence received by Victor Pelz, a wildly successful young *Post* boy in Seattle early in the century; from that correspondence one can learn a great deal about the workings of the *Post*'s system of circulation through networks of boys in every American city.

George Horace Lorimer was thirty-one years old when Cyrus Curtis made him editor of the *Saturday Evening Post*. If it seems quite a gamble to have given so responsible a position to so young a man, it is useful to understand that there was little to lose; Curtis was putting his money on the future. Lorimer realized that future, creating the magazine that, for a significant percentage of the American public, created the world they lived in. This book, then, represents an attempt at reconstructing the world the *Post* created, at reconstructing Lorimer's America.

Courtesy UPI/Bettmann Newsphotos

Cyrus Curtis

"The Greatest Weekly Magazine in the World"

The story of the early years of the modern *Saturday Evening Post* has become a legend of American journalism and the hero of the legend is Cyrus H. K. Curtis.[1] In August 1897, when Cyrus Curtis bought the *Saturday Evening Post* for $1,000, the failing periodical had neither circulation, advertising, nor major writers to recommend it. A cut-and-paste job of sentimental fiction and worse poetry, with about 2,000 subscribers, the *Post* was scarcely a promising acquisition for the Curtis Company, not even at $1,000.

Accepted wisdom in the magazine business asserted that weeklies had seen their day, but Curtis, who had already made a considerable success of the *Ladies' Home Journal,* was entirely prepared to pour the profits of the monthly magazine for women into his new weekly, energetically promoting it with a series of advertising campaigns that eventually cost close to a million dollars. The trade periodical *Printers' Ink,* watching Curtis sink *Journal* profits into the moribund *Post,* predicted disaster.[2] Nevertheless, with the capital supplied by *Journal* profits, supplemented by bank loans and a line of credit with the N. W. Ayer advertising agency, Curtis set about establishing his new weekly magazine.

What precisely had Curtis bought and what was he prepared to back to the tune of a million dollars? In hard fact, he had acquired a periodical with no obvious assets. But with some liberties as to dates and a little historic imagination, he could be said to have bought himself Benjamin Franklin. A complicated and tenuous genealogy of the *Post* claimed its founding father in Franklin's *Pennsylvania Gazette,* and to bolster that claim the *Post* suddenly aged a hundred years. In the January 22, 1898, issue, the founding date of the *Saturday Evening Post* was given as 1821. On January 29, the masthead pushed that date back to 1728, the year Franklin's *Gazette* began. By 1899 the name of the magazine on the inside cover was dignified by the statement: "Founded A⁰ Dⁱ 1728 by Benj. Franklin," and Franklin's face became a permanent part of the logo on the editorial page. And, as if to seal this ancestry, for several years a special Franklin issue appeared on Ben's birthday. The new *Post* would soon claim itself as quintessentially American; the Franklin legacy was the first article in the assertion.

Franklin was a powerful symbolic ancestor, but what the *Post* needed it could not gain through inheritance. Whether as a jour-nalistic endeavor or a business proposition, or both, the magazine Curtis purchased was a disaster. The January 1, 1898, issue was typical—sixteen oversize pages poorly printed and laid out in a four-column format without illustrations. Poems and very short stories, signed only with initials and reprinted from other peri-odicals, alternated over the first few pages, continuing on through the book interspersed with regular departments and random filler of such banality as to give it a kind of perverse fascination. Readers could learn that the czar attended church on Sundays, that beating one's cow reduced its milk flow, and that four and a half billion needles were manufactured annually in Aix-la-Chapelle. A readers' column served to pose and answer inquiries—where might one find a grammar for Erse? who was Saint Hubert?—and departments for women talked of fashion and provided recipes both medicinal (a turpentine poultice) and gastronomic (prune pie).

Curtis recognized that his new acquisition needed to be made over entirely. In order to gain circulation and thereby encourage advertisers, the format and the editorial content of the *Post* would have to be wholly recreated. Within six months, considerable physi-cal improvements had been carried out. By July 1898, the printing was far cleaner and the front page was now laid out in two columns, with a masthead and a large black-and-white illustration. Stories, too, were illustrated and articles decorated; all the pieces were now signed. But physical improvements in the *Post* far out-stripped gains on the editorial side. A good deal of the material and nearly all the fiction still consisted of reprints; and the magazine looked better, but it offered little reading of interest.

Curtis, meanwhile, turned his attention to promotion, investing heavily in advertising his magazine. His optimism in its future was shared with N. W. Ayer and Son, the advertising company that essentially underwrote Curtis's *Post* promotion for nearly five years. Through Ayer, Curtis advertised in major and minor cities all over America, buying cards in railway and elevated cars and space in newspapers and magazines. In December 1899, for example, Curtis had Ayer take two ads in all the newspapers in forty-four cities. In mid-January 1900, he bought six-inch ads in seventy-five weekly magazines. These campaigns continued unremittingly, until by January 1900, Curtis had an outstanding debt to Ayer of $83,172.50.[3]

Meanwhile, the majority of the 2,000 subscribers, apparently content with information about the czar's sabbath activities and needle production in Aix-la-Chapelle, canceled their orders. Nevertheless, the figures on circulation showed improvement, reflecting gains that were altogether misleading, since quantities of magazines were being given away as part of Curtis's advertising effort. Thus, in December 1898, when there were five issues of the *Post*, the circulation average reached an astonishing 250,000 a week, for hundreds of thousands of copies of the *Post* had been given away that month; some were sent out on a special "ten-cent offer," some went to *Journal* subscribers, over 1,000 to "advertisers" and more than 26,000 to "possible advertisers." Another 12,375 were mailed to the offices of doctors and dentists.[4]

Although the *Post* legend has been frequently retold, the most eloquent record of its financial situation in the first years can be found not in histories of journalism but in the minutes of the Curtis Company Board and particularly in the increasingly despondent voice of the company treasurer. At the outset, the figures reported were almost comically inconsequential. At the December 1897 meeting the board heard, "The Saturday Evening Post reports 67 subscriptions received, 30 complaints and 22 samples sent out. Monthly cash expense was $70.70 with no receipts." But as Curtis continued his campaign for the *Post*, losses mounted along with the treasurer's despair. By October 1898, "the Treasurer re-port[ed] cost of the Post to date as $57,454." Ten months later, costs had risen to $302,567, and by September 1899 "total unpaid obligations," including bank loans and the debt to N. W. Ayer, reached $734,086.[5]

The giveaway circulation succeeded in affording the *Post* more exposure, but it provided no revenue. Advertising was crucial for the magazine's solvency, but at this time Curtis was buying adver-tising, not selling it. The Ayer agency continued to support Curtis's advertising for the *Post*; unfortunately, it was proving difficult to find advertisers whose faith in the magazine met Curtis's own. The January 1 issue for 1898, nearly six months after Curtis had acquired the *Post*, carried only nine advertisements, seven of them for the *Ladies' Home Journal*. The two non-Curtis Company ads offered patent medicines, Dr. D. Jayne's Expectorant and Hall's Catarrh Cure.

The situation had not improved greatly by the middle of the year. The *Post* aimed ambitiously at national circulation and national advertising, and while Curtis would make his magazines a major force in the development of national advertising, it was very slow going in the first few years. The issue for July 16, 1898, carried only two advertisements, and while they were somewhat larger than the patent medicine advertisements in the January 1 issue, the advertisers were very local indeed, both Philadelphia firms: Straw-bridge and Clothier, and Smith, Kline and French, the latter a manufacturer of Eskay baby food, whose ad pointed out that they were located "Next door to The Saturday Evening Post."

The advertisements for patent medicines had disappeared by July 1898 because Curtis and his editors refused to carry them. The *Post* might be hurtling toward a million-dollar loss, but Curtis's belief in the significance of advertising and in the potentially inti-mate—and therefore profitable—relationship between a magazine and an audience that trusted it to provide judgment and credibility equally in editorial and advertising content led to stringent rules: no patent medicines, no investment opportunities, no liquor, and—until many years later—no cigarettes.

In October 1898 there was finally some good news from the advertising end; the *Post* had sold its first advertising contract, for 5,000 lines, to the Singer Sewing Machine Company. This lone success encouraged the optimistic Curtis Company to double the *Post* line rate from fifty cents to a dollar.[6] In the December 3 issue for that year, the Singer Sewing Machine ad, illustrated with a line drawing, stretched across the bottom of three of the magazine's four columns. There were eleven other advertisers as well, although they took much smaller spaces, making a total of about two and a half columns of advertising in the sixteen-page issue, or a meager 4 percent of the book.

The annual report of the Curtis Company for July 1899–June 1900 showed an average weekly circulation of 193,544, as well as notable gains in advertising, but losses on the *Saturday Evening Post* for the three-year period of Curtis's ownership had mounted to over $900,000, an amount roughly equal to more than $11 million today.[7]

Cyrus Curtis was certainly a determined man. Perhaps only a combination of stubbornness and boundless optimism could have survived the depressive effect of the treasurer's reports.[8] Certainly he believed in the possibilities of a weekly magazine and, with his own confidence in advertising, saw his weekly as a potentially profitable medium for that young but burgeoning industry. Whether Curtis's determination sprang from any particular editorial mission he had in mind for the *Post* is an open question.[9] What he did know was that he needed an editor.

Curtis had learned from his experience with the *Ladies' Home Journal* the importance of a first-rate editor. Edward Bok had succeeded splendidly with the *Journal* and Curtis knew he had to find an equally remarkable man for the *Post*. He had no illusions about himself as an editor; he was a magazine publisher, a businessman, and his real genius lay in his instinct for finding brilliant editors and then allowing them an entirely free hand to do their editing work. As Bok put it, "'Make good or hang yourself,' is [Curtis's] motto with his men, and every resource of moral and financial support is put back of the man."[10] For that reason, while the legend of the *Post* has Curtis for its hero, the history of the magazine is the story of George Horace Lorimer's editorship.

Lorimer's life provides one of America's many model biographies of success, but not the formulaic story of rags to riches. In Lorimer's history we find instead a restless search for some appropriate enterprise, some arena for his considerable abilities. He discovered that arena in the *Saturday Evening Post*.

Born in Louisville in 1867, the son of a famous Baptist minister, Lorimer grew up in Boston and Chicago and entered Yale in 1888. In the summer of 1889, Philip D. Armour, one of his father's parishioners, convinced him to leave college and come into the meatpacking business. Married in 1892 to Alma Ennis of Chicago, Lorimer was rapidly achieving success: by 1896 he was heading a department and earning the very considerable salary of $5,000 a year.

Then Lorimer decided to go into business for himself and failed. At that point he turned to newspaper work; he moved to Boston and worked as a reporter for a few months before returning to college, this time to Colby, believing he needed more education and particularly more work in writing. From Colby he went back to Boston, reporting first for the Boston *Post* and then the *Herald*. In 1898, as the story has been told, Lorimer read of Curtis's purchase of the *Saturday Evening Post* over the wire in the *Herald* office and immediately sent his own wire, asking for a job. Curtis met with him the next week in Boston and after a few minutes of conversation hired him as literary editor at an annual salary of $1,000. In fact, Curtis had already heard about Lorimer, whose famous father had met Curtis at a resort and had filed a strong endorsement of his son with the publisher.[11]

It would have been impossible to predict Lorimer's future brilliance as *Post* editor from his first signed work in the magazine. For the Christmas issue for 1898, Lorimer wrote a piece called "Legends of the Child Who Is King" (December 24, 1898), consisting of two pious, quasi-medieval stories rendered in a style itself an unconscious parody of the medieval: "Wroth was the King that one, the meanest of his serfs, had been preferred to him. . . . And stooping in his anger o'er the lad, he thought to break in roughly on his dreams and ask what he did there." From whatever misguided model Lorimer forged this prose, he entirely belied his own style and voice, and he addressed a subject both Lorimer and the *Post* would conscientiously avoid in the years ahead.

In March 1899, Lorimer received a pro tem promotion to acting editor, succeeding William George Jordan who had been brought over temporarily from the *Journal*. At that time, Curtis was eager to hire Arthur Sherburne Hardy as *Post* editor. Hardy, formerly with *Cosmopolitan,* was now minister to Persia, and Curtis sailed to Europe to talk with him. But Lorimer knew this was his real chance, and he poured his energy into the issues that were his to edit. When Curtis received a set of current *Posts* in Paris, he was so pleased with them that he abandoned his search for Hardy and named Lorimer editor. Lorimer's name first appeared on the masthead of the *Saturday Evening Post* on June 10, 1899.

In mid-1899 when he took over as editor of the *Saturday Evening Post*, Lorimer had little to start with but Curtis's moral and financial support and his own extraordinary energy and ambition. His days were typically spent in the office, overseeing the editorial side. In the evenings he spent at home, he read manuscripts; otherwise he took a late afternoon train to New York or Washington to meet contributors or traveled to the homes and offices of famous men he hoped to bring to the pages of the *Post*.

From the very beginning, Lorimer set the direction of his magazine, writing countless letters urging writers to take up favored subject matter, slowly setting about collecting a staff of dependable writers on business, politics, and science, composing editorials and promotional material, and even writing a number of full-length novels for *Post* publication. And nothing—not a story or an article or a piece of filler—appeared in the pages of the *Post* that Lorimer had not read and approved.

And from the beginning, he had a remarkably clear sense of his audience and his purpose. Although in 1899 the *Saturday Evening Post* had no identity, no voice, and no focus, Lorimer remedied this with astonishing sureness and speed. He knew what he wanted the *Post* to become and he knew how to sell that idea to America. He intended to create a national magazine by appealing to the average American; he would, in fact, *invent* the average American—some compound of nineteenth-century values and twentieth-century opportunities. In the construction of this American and in the complementary creation of America itself, Lorimer and the *Post* played their most significant role in the development of a mass national consciousness.

Lorimer's first portrait of the American appeared on December 30, 1899. After only six months as editor, Lorimer announced the "Post's Plans for 1900" in a two-page advertisement. The ad asserted that the *Post* was neither a local publication nor a "news weekly," but a "magazine [whose] appeal is national." Much more than a come-on for potential subscribers, the ad boldly asserted intention and boasted of success. Promising continual improvements, it claimed the *Post* would "become the indispensable magazine." The premise on which that success lay was the character of the "average American." "[He] is an omnivorous reader. His range of interests is wider than that of the citizen of any other country, and so it is necessary for a magazine that will met his needs to be of the broadest scope possible."

Fiction, the ad promised, would appeal to the wholesome tastes of this average American: "The public knows what sort of stories it likes, and the Post will continue to satisfy a healthy appetite rather than attempt to create an abnormal one." And in fiction and nonfiction alike, readers would reap the rewards of the *Post*'s untiring efforts to "secure the greatest living writers." Lists of names followed, scores of them, including both famous writers and men of affairs and relatively unknown persons whose significance lay in their credentials as experts in one or another field.

Having promised the American audience fiction by the greatest living writers, Lorimer had to prove his word good. He genuinely wanted the best in fiction, as he judged it, and he set out to get it by providing much more favorable terms than any other magazine offered. The *Post* guaranteed to read stories within seventy-two hours of receipt and to pay on acceptance rather than on publication. Understandably, these policies paid off handsomely. By 1900, in the place of undistinguished fiction reprinted from other magazines, the *Post* was carrying stories by Joel Chandler Harris, Hamlin Garland, Bret Harte, Rebecca Harding Davis, and Paul Laurence Dunbar. By any contemporary standards, this was a distinguished list; to have gathered writers of this quality within a year as *Post* editor was an extraordinary achievement.

Nonfiction required different tactics. For one thing, the names of nonfiction writers did not automatically attract loyal audiences as fiction writers' names did. For another, Lorimer had some very definite ideas about the subjects he wanted the *Post* to address and equally clear ideas about how those subjects should be presented. What the *Post* needed was a cadre of writers on key subjects, writers capable of making complex ideas simple and even entertaining, and writers whose names would be connected with the *Post*. Before too long, Lorimer would have a staff of writers intimately associated with the *Post* who became its collective voice. And as the *Post* prospered and its influence grew, it would come to carry sufficient authority of its own, authority it could bestow on the writers who appeared in its pages. But at the turn of the century the fledgling weekly had to borrow whatever prestige it could from the men who wrote for it. In these early years, therefore, Lorimer filled the pages of the *Post* with the work of notable men and certified experts.

The biggest fish among the notables was Grover Cleveland; a former president, even if a Democrat, was a splendid acquisition. As Lorimer wrote to his friend, Albert J. Beveridge, the young senator from Indiana, he had "induced" Cleveland to write for the *Post*, adding, perhaps as a political aside, that "with all his faults, there are a good many of us who still feel a sneaking affection for him." [12] He was also hot on the trail of Benjamin Harrison, but that former president died before Lorimer could sign him up. Again, he reported to Beveridge: "I saw General Harrison two weeks before his death; he was very kind in his manner and was not such a 'frost' as he has been written up. I was to have something from him for the Post."13

Realizing the potential of the Post as Lorimer imagined it, however, required much more than simply finding writers, even famous writers, to fill its pages. It demanded that he shape and focus the magazine around his conception of the American. The "average American" for whom the Post was being published was no vague abstraction for Lorimer; he was a responsible, hardworking, practical, and patriotic man. And he was quintessentially a businessman, as Lorimer shaped and defined that term. Lorimer found the principal focus for the Post in the idea of business, and the intended audience in the businessman, especially the younger man out to make his way in an America Lorimer believed would discover and create itself through business in the century that lay ahead.

As business became the Post's principal theme, the businessman became both subject matter and intended audience for the magazine. The Post ran scores of articles and stories for and about him. Fiction, to be sure, was hard to come by, for few novelists found business an appealing or exciting source. But as early as 1899, while still literary editor, Lorimer had managed to serialize Harold Frederic's The Market-Place, and by 1901 the Post carried Merwin Webster's Calumet "K" and The End of the Deal by Will Payne, who was to have a long association with the Post.14

Nonfiction on various business topics was easier to find than fiction, but Lorimer's problem was to discover and shape the kind of information and approach that would prove most useful and attractive. By no means did Lorimer intend the Post to be a specialized periodical; indeed, he did not conceive of the businessman himself as a specialized type, but rather as the average and even the quintessential American. The Post was always intended for general circulation, with the understanding that this implied a white, American-born, middle-class, and, at this time, essentially male audience. Such readers would obviously appeal to advertisers, but beyond that they represented the "real" America to Lorimer, men who would work hard, vote intelligently, and shape the future.

To these men George Horace Lorimer gave the label "business man." It is not too much to say, in fact, that Lorimer virtually created the idea of the businessman. By this term he did not mean "man of business" or "man of affairs" in the nineteenth-century sense, but something a good deal more inclusive, embracing the established professions to include lawyers, doctors, and even clergy-men, and reaching down to absorb drummers, clerks, and even men who raised chickens for sale in their backyards. The term busi-nessman was at once a great leveler, denying any European specter of classes, and a powerful incentive, for to be a businessman of even the most meager sort held out the promise of becoming a busi-nessman who achieved great success.

For the majority of hardworking American men, of course, success would be at best modest, and whatever the glamour of fiction or biography about the very rich, Lorimer knew that it was the great majority of "average Americans" who would comprise the *Post*'s readership. They were harder to write about directly, for their lives and work lacked romance and adventure, but they could be addressed in informational articles about getting ahead through hard work, new ideas, and even modest investments. In a few years, such information would become a mainstay of the *Post* in regular back-of-the-book departments, but at the turn of the century Lorimer had not yet discovered this approach. The ordinary man making his ordinary way through the world could find his portrait, or his interests, presented directly only rarely. One of those rare presentations, however, appeared in 1900, and it attempted to define Lorimer's American.

Though the expression "a plain business man" may not be exact enough to suit the stickler for scientific accuracy, it certainly is sufficiently descrip-tive to be generally understood. As I shall use it in this paper, and as it is commonly understood by the public at large, it describes the man of affairs who has had his own way to make, and has gained a fair degree of material success without having had the time or opportunity to gloss over his attainments with the "rubbed finish" of bookishness and ripe culture. He is a product of the common schools, not of the college, and his special training has been picked up in the store, the shop, the office or the factory instead of in the classroom. His equipment, in short, is that of the average Western business man of to-day who has reached middle life.[15]

This portrait of the "plain business man" was not a perfect likeness, but it was close enough. It probably served as a fairly accurate picture of the targeted *Post* audience, but this businessman was, at middle age, too old to represent the reader Lorimer wanted most to influence. The *Post* was a young magazine in a new century; it wanted to speak with special urgency to young men.

Young men were addressed in articles that dangled the lure of great financial success or offered specific advice about the practical side of starting out in business life. A series of articles in 1899, called "How I Made My First $1000," featured stories of giants like Andrew Carnegie and Russell Sage.[16] Harlow Higinbotham turned to more modest ambitions in "The Making of a Merchant" (beginning June 3, 1899), as did series on "The Choice of a Profession" and "The Choice of a Business."

Despite the headiness of a new century and a youthful audience, the values instilled by *Post* business articles remained rooted in nineteenth-century virtues. In several brief pieces on the subject of "Why Young Men Fail," successful businessmen explained that failure plagued those who ignored the American values of diligence, honesty, and thrift, falling prey to dishonesty and intemperance, as well as lack of thoroughness, indifference to detail, or "the time-serving spirit." Old-fashioned virtues gained fresh authority from the impressive titles of the writers whom Lorimer had cajoled or flattered into contributing to his magazine: president of the Delaware, Lackawanna, and Western Railroad; superintendent of the American District Telegraph Company; president of the Chicago, Milwaukee, and St. Paul Railroad; and William A. Pinkerton himself, who warned against the evils of gambling.[17]

By 1900, with Lorimer fully in editorial control, the emphasis on the young man in business increased. Frank G. Carpenter traveled through the Orient for the *Post* and sent back a series on

"Chances for Young Men" in China, Japan, the Philippines, and Hawaii. These articles provided very practical information and advice. Japan, for example, offered good chances for young men with brains, "nerve," and capital for manufacturing. The import business, however, was not recommended because the Japanese were quick to copy imported articles and, since labor was so cheap, to undersell the competition.[18] Young men without capital could profit from a study of William H. Maher's articles on "The Clerk Who Makes Friends" or "The Clerk Who Reads." Advice about reading might *seem* to touch on the less practical aspects of succeeding but, as Maher argued, that was not the case: "My object in writing this is to show that [reading] will pay in dollars and cents; a clerk is measured by his intelligence, and now, as in every year since the world began, Knowledge is Power."[19]

Knowledge being Power, the *Saturday Evening Post* also occasionally set out to educate its readers about business in more general ways, to inform them about "How Trusts Affect Trade" or about "The Onward March of American Trade."[20] But it would be a few years before Lorimer found himself the men who could write informative and engaging articles about a wide variety of business matters, and until that time pieces featuring either advice to the young or exemplary tales of success would dominate the *Post*.

Without question, the most engaging and the most popular exemplary tale published in the first years of the *Post* was Lorimer's own *Letters from a Self-Made Merchant to His Son,* appearing anonymously in 1901–1902. The first installment (August 3, 1901), printed on the op-ed page, was illustrated by Martin Justice with a drawing of John Graham, the self-made pork-packer, dictating a letter to his son Pierrepont, just enrolled as a freshman at Harvard. This letter and those following trace through Graham's eyes the follies and extravagances of his son while at college and during his first years with his father's firm. The letters allow full scope to Graham's voice—uncultivated and unsophisticated, but direct and wry and "American"—as he showers his son with advice and bolsters advice with anecdotes from his own small-town youth. Nothing could be further from the false and mincing style of Lorimer's 1898 Christmas piece.

Chicago, October 1, 189–

Dear Pierrepont: Your Ma got back safe this morning and she wants me to be sure to tell you not to over-study, and I want to tell you to be sure not to under-study. What we're really sending you to Harvard for is to get a little of the education that's so good and plenty there. When it's passed around you don't want to be bashful, but reach right out and take a big helping every time, for I want you to get your share. You'll find that education's about the only thing lying around loose in this world, and that it's about the only thing a fellow can have as much of as he's willing to haul away. Everything else is screwed down tight and the screwdriver lost.[21]

In John Graham, known as "Old Gorgon Graham," and his son Pierrepont, alias "Piggy," Lorimer was creating two characters who stood for competing sets of values in a society undergoing rapid change, especially in the world of business. John Graham is entirely a self-made man, educated only by his experiences in life and particularly in work, and strong enough in his rural upbringing and consequent moral values to withstand the lures of "society." He is self-made, but he is not nouveau riche. His values are very much those Lorimer respected: hard work, simplicity, ambition, honesty, and common sense. "It's good business, when a fellow hasn't much behind his forehead, to throw out his chest and attract attention to his shirt-front. But as you begin to meet the men who have done something that makes them worth meeting you will find that there are no 'keep off the grass' or 'beware of the dog' signs around their premises, and that they don't motion to the orchestra to play slow music while they talk."[22]

But Lorimer knew perfectly well that old Graham's day was passing, that business itself was changing, and that a new kind of businessman was appearing in America. Like Pierrepont, that new man might be indulged with a fancy name and a fancy education, and in that case he needed a good deal of help if he were to succeed and, more to the point, if his success were not entirely to corrupt

American values with borrowed notions of class, elegance, leisure, and too much money expended in supporting such "European" vanities. A Harvard education was a mixed blessing in Lorimer's eyes, as in Graham's, and it needed to be counteracted with strong doses of other forms of learning. That was the purpose of Graham's letters and a mission to which Lorimer would devote the *Saturday Evening Post.*

"The first thing that any education ought to give a man is character [wrote Graham], and the second thing is education. That is where I am a little skittish about this college business." Lorimer, too, was "skittish," not only about "this college business," but about the larger prospect of a generation of businessmen who did not need to start at the bottom. "I didn't have your advantages when I was a boy, and you can't have mine. Some men learn the value of money by not having any and starting out to pry a few dollars loose from the odd millions that are lying around; and some learn it by having fifty thousand or so left to them and starting out to spend it as if it were fifty thousand a year."23

Lorimer's fiction was an instant success. Between August 3, when it began serialization, and the end of the year, the *Post* received 5,000 letters in response to Old Gorgon Graham. In 1902 *Letters from a Self-Made Merchant* was published as a book that became a best-seller here and abroad. According to John Tebbel, *Letters* was translated into more languages than any American work since *Uncle Tom's Cabin.*24

Lorimer was not a romantic trapped in nostalgia for some trumped-up vision of the past. He believed in America and he believed in the future; most of all he believed in business. But if business was to be the expression of America in the twentieth century, there was much it could carry with it from a world that was fast disappearing.

For Lorimer, it was business that translated into concrete terms the nineteenth-century belief in progress and held out that promise to America as a whole and to individual men who, through business, could realize their personal ambitions. He was not, however, dedicated to preserving the nineteenth century intact. His campaign in favor of business and the businessman necessarily included a kind of social revolution in which the glamour and prestige associated with the older professions of law and medicine would be transferred to the new "calling" of business. It was not merely that business, in the terms of a 1903 editorial, was "the age itself, with all of its abounding activities and energies," but that "business proclaims itself boldly and exceeds all other callings. It has gained ascendancy and has vaunted its dignity."[25] The ascendancy of business would mean a true democratizing of America. An editorial celebrating the rising number of college graduates in fields other than medicine and law made this point. "One happy result of the new condition is the realignment of the social order. The professional men no longer monopolize the inner circle of culture and aristocracy. The man who does things has taken a place higher than the man who simply belongs to a profession. . . . A big lot of nonsense has been kicked out of society."[26]

Since Lorimer argued that the day of the professional elite was ending, he insisted concomitantly that the kind of education offered by the elite eastern colleges, the kind of education he believed served to foster and maintain an aristocracy of professionals, was no longer appropriate for America. Of course, it was perfectly obvious to Lorimer that for businessmen to rise to real eminence in American society they would have to be college-educated; therefore, the traditional kind of college education would have to be supplanted by something at once more practical and more democratic. Arising from the *Post*'s thematic focus on business, especially when allied with the emphasis on youth, education developed into an important issue in the magazine from the outset. Two major questions dominated these discussions: should all boys receive a college education, and what are the appropriate subjects for the college curriculum?

Lorimer approached the question of a college education for all somewhat disingenuously. While he recognized that a college education was going to be a prerequisite for real success in America, he also understood that many American boys were unlikely to attend college; many families could not afford it, and others would continue to send their sons out to make a living as soon as possible. Even more to the point, perhaps, was the fact that business did not especially require or even want college-educated men to fill most jobs. Lorimer's belief in business and his sense of mission toward the young man in America necessarily came into conflict on this issue. The *Post* was often ambivalent or downright confused over it.

In 1900 former President Cleveland took on the problem in a lead article called "Does a College Education Pay?" (May 26, 1900). Cleveland floundered, sometimes on one and sometimes the other side of the issue. He testified vaguely to the value of liberal education and charged those opposing it with a "sullen, sodden hatred of all education above the lowest." Even the "so-called self-made men . . . posted behind the infirm defense of the things they have achieved" failed to see that the world was changing and that change would favor the educated man. On the other hand, he pointed out, college men were frequently either too studious or not studious enough, and they suffered from being cut off from the outside world.

For the same issue, Lorimer asked a small number of college presidents to contribute to an article on "The Problems and Prospects of College Men as Seen by Their Presidents." Not surprisingly, the presidents of Princeton, Michigan, and the University of California all argued for the benefits of a college education, and President Patton of Princeton even took the opportunity to urge all parents to educate their sons.[27]

Quite another point of view, however, was supplied by business itself in the person of the president of the Metropolitan Street Railway Company of New York. In "The Young Man's Opportunity in the New Business Order" (March 23, 1901), Herbert Vreeland urged the benefits of a street railway career, promising high wages and the opportunity for advancement. He specifically pointed out that a college education was unnecessary and probably detrimental, since a boy who knew nothing could start out at a salary of $3.50 a week and, if he applied himself, be worth something in six or seven years when he would be the same age as a college graduate who only thought he knew something. College men were a problem in another way, Vreeland pointed out; having made social connections in college, they wanted to keep them up and therefore needed to take time off. Social relaxation, he added darkly, was a very bad thing early in a man's career.

On the subject of the appropriate college curriculum, however, Lorimer had no doubts and suffered no ambivalence. Traditional education, the liberal arts, was out of date, tied to the elite world of the professions, and entirely inappropriate for the American youth determined to make his way in business. Lorimer very much admired some of the new kinds of colleges and schools that were starting up, dedicated to science or applied science or business. When the University of Wisconsin opened a School of Commerce in 1900–1901, Dean William A. Scott wrote an article for the *Post* that was little more than raw promotion. Scott did not feel it at all necessary to defend his school against the claims of liberal educa-tion; the only important matter was whether the education offered by the School of Commerce matched that provided by real experi-ence in the business world, and the dean ruefully admitted it could not "take the place of actual business experience."[28]

Post editorials frequently mounted attacks on the traditional college curriculum, arguing that young men no longer needed to learn "to make quotations from Horace," since the purpose of a college education was no longer "to produce a parasitic intellectual aristocracy."[29] The *Post* was deeply in the American tradition here, as its championship of business over the established professions led to a position of deep distrust and even contempt for the intellectual. But Lorimer was not merely a naysayer; he was prepared to be constructive. In a 1904 editorial he laid down the "four pillars" of a college education appropriate to the American twentieth century:

Thinking and writing clearly in the English language.

A knowledge of the history of democracy or the emancipation of man.

A knowledge of taxation—the great fundamental of human society.

A knowledge of the mechanism of business—how commodities are produced, distributed and consumed.

However skewed and impoverished this curriculum, the editorial assured *Post* readers that "a man with such an education would be both competent and cultured."[30]

The *Saturday Evening Post* did not limit its influence on education to the expression of views in articles and editorials. Through a circulation plan devised by the Curtis Company, it was able to carry out a practical program of business education for the benefit of an extensive network of young magazine salesmen known as *Post* boys.

Although the system of boy salesmen was always a business proposition for the Curtis Company, it fitted perfectly with the values the *Post* espoused editorially. First, it put boys to work, and the *Post* always celebrated work as the activity that defined one as a man, and especially as an American man. The *Post* subscribed fully to the nineteenth-century belief that boys who worked and saved their earnings were being properly trained for a life of diligence and thrift. But beyond that, work as a *Post* boy offered special kinds of training that were directly applicable to the world of business, even specifically to the world of monopoly capitalism.

The Curtis Company first began to sell the *Post* through boys some time in 1899. In October the plan was still too new to be properly evaluated, but a comment in the board minutes helps explain why it was put into operation in the first place: that month 179,900 copies of the *Post* had been shipped to news dealers and 57,473 were returned.[31] If dealers were returning one-third of their copies, it was clear that the Curtis Company had to find some other means of distribution.

The plan the Curtis Company devised was to sell the five-cent *Post* to boys at three and a half cents a copy, allowing for a penny and a half profit on each copy sold. The first week's supply of ten copies was sent free, but after that all orders had to be prepaid. Moreover, with the horrible example of the news dealers before them, the company set a ceiling of 15 percent on returns.[32] The plan was, at least on the level of ten copies a week, both simple and modest, but the Curtis Company did not expect to sell hundreds of thousands of copies of the *Saturday Evening Post* in job lots of ten. What it anticipated and what it set out to do was to encourage boys to order and sell larger and larger numbers of magazines, and to that end a system of prizes was set up, with awards up to $10 and later $25 for the boys who sold the greatest number.

A major advertising campaign began in the pages of the *Post* to gather the army of young salesmen. A typical ad featured the photograph of a successful boy with an account of his success story, emphasizing pluck, ambition, and business acumen and featuring headlines with exciting business allusions. In the case of Jay Johns from western Pennsylvania, the theme was monopoly: "From the neighboring city of Pittsburgh he has apparently absorbed some of the spirit of its gigantic business combinations." Although he had to contend with five other young salesmen in his town, Jay kept increasing his order, from ten to fifteen to thirty copies, and soon three of his competitors grew discouraged and quit. Having won $25 in prize money, so the account went, he used his capital to insure his monopoly, writing to the *Post* to explain, "Today I bought out the other two boys by giving them fifty cents apiece. These little fellows only spoil the business." He asked that the town be made his exclusive territory: "If you will agree not to appoint anybody else so long as I sell a lot of copies, you can credit this $25.00 to my account and send me 100 copies for next week and 125 copies each week thereafter."[33]

Such an ad might well fire the ambitions of other American boys, imagining that the considerable sum of $25 could be theirs for selling about 100 copies of the *Post*. This was not by any means the case; in fact, selling 100 copies at a cent and a half profit each would have earned Jay Johns exactly $1.50. Boys who were winning substantial prizes were boys who were selling well over 1,000 or even 1,500 copies a week.[34]

Even at Curtis no one really expected ten-year-old boys in knickers and caps to sell thousands of copies of the *Post* each week

Jay Johns of Western Pennsylvania—a Post ad for Post boys

single-handed, and that was precisely what all the exciting, if somewhat vague, talk of business combinations was really about. When the company discovered a particularly ambitious boy, they encouraged him to undertake an "Exclusive Agency," which gave him a more or less assured local monopoly on *Post* sales by boys and allowed him to hire his own subagents. A boy with an exclusive agency could buy the *Post* for three cents and resell it to his own agents at the standard three and a half; his profit was cut to half a cent, but his volume increase more than made up for that. Moreover, all the subagents' sales went to the account of the boy with the exclusive agency in the figuring for prizes, and the only real chance to make money lay in winning the top money prizes.

Despite the apparent attractiveness of the exclusive agency, there were substantial pitfalls awaiting the ambitious boy. For one thing, it was not long before the Curtis Company figured out that prizes given for *increases* in sales were much more effective prods than prizes given for total sales. Thus, in order to win prizes a boy had to increase his sales continually and that meant continually increasing his weekly orders and his weekly prepayment. A boy selling 1,000 copies a week would prepay $30 and, when he sold them to his subagents, take in $35. If all the issues were sold, he made a profit of $5. An increase to 1,200 copies, however, would require a prepayment of $36, absorbing the entire profit and requiring an additional $1—or the profits on 200 more magazines.

Real problems arose when a boy did not sell all his copies. Curtis would accept 15 percent returns, but that meant a boy could earn a profit on only 85 percent of his order, and if fewer than 85 percent were sold, he had to absorb the loss. A boy who persistently increased his order so as to compete for prizes was sooner or later going to find himself with hundreds of unsold copies, inadequate funds for prepayment, and a notification from the Curtis Company that he was in arrears for an amount representing returns above 15 percent.

The pitfalls of monopoly capitalism notwithstanding, ten of thousands of American boys over the next four decades would become salesmen for the *Saturday Evening Post*. On its part, the

Curtis Company was intensely proud of what it had done for American youth. Years later, facing the problems of the Great Depression, the company reviewed its situation and decided the best plan lay in strengthening still further the organization of boy salesmen. In 1933, an in-house memo noted that the plan of selling the *Post* through boys had maintained the same two aims for thirty-four years:

It must produce sound circulation—the kind of circulation of maximum value to the advertiser.

It must teach boys sound business methods—namely, to sell a product on its merits, to be accurate in accounting, to be honest, energetic and thrifty.[35]

The Curtis Company was sincere about teaching "business methods" to the boys. It published lively illustrated pamphlets encouraging neatness and proper demeanor in their young salesmen and laying out the basics of the hard sell.[36] Moreover, in 1902 it added to the list of awards a college scholarship, an award that was "non-competitive," meaning that scholarships could be won by a large number of boys rather than only by the single most successful one. By 1904, however, in keeping with the editorial line of the *Saturday Evening Post,* the company restricted the scholarship offer, limiting it to "a complete, commercial training at the *business* college of your choice."[37]

The progress Lorimer made in his first years as *Post* editor was remarkable, in less than four years more than fulfilling the promise—or boast—expressed in the December 30, 1899, advertisment. Lorimer was succeeding personally as well. In October 1903, he received a pay increase, from $10,000 to $12,000. By April 1905, he was earning $18,000 and in October of that year received another raise to the very substantial salary of $25,000. In 1903 he had also been elected to the board of directors, becoming a part of the small group of men responsible for the major financial and policy decisions affecting the Curtis magazines.[38]

The move to the board was particularly significant in that it placed Lorimer on a more or less equal footing with *Journal* editor

Bok. Understandably, Bok had not been pleased to watch the prof-its on his magazine poured into the insatiable, and desperately unprofitable, *Post*. It is clear from the records of the Curtis Com-pany that from the time Lorimer took over as *Post* editor one board member continually insisted on making the point that *Post* "costs to date" were not at all the same thing as *Post* "deficits." Those "defi-cits" included costs *plus* unpaid obligations to the *Journal,* presum-ably for advertising. Moreover, even the deficits did not reflect the *Post*'s entire indebtedness, for the new magazine was not being charged for machinery or overhead.[39] Surely Bok was the dis-gruntled board member insisting on a full accounting of the *Post*'s profligacy.

Lorimer was spending money. To be sure, Curtis ran up much more spectacular bills with his unflagging advertising campaigns, but Lorimer was spending freely to buy the kind of editorial mate-rial he wanted. For the four issues in January 1899, contributors, including illlustrators, were paid over $13,000. Apparently, that was too much, for in June 1900 comparable costs were just over $8,600, and in November they were down to $7,600. Despite some pulling back here, the *Post*'s financial statement for the fiscal year, July 1899 to June 1900—Lorimer's first year as editor—indicates that combined editorial and illustration costs came to approxi-mately $180,000, exceeding the income from subscriptions and sales by $10,000. At the same time, advertising expenses of nearly $285,000 were more than three times as great as advertising reve-nues. The *Post*'s losses for Lorimer's first year as editor came to $444,992.54. The total loss to date reached $923,564.06. There was also, the treasurer added, no doubt at Bok's insistence, an obligation to the *Journal* of $646,843.85.[40]

Deficits, losses, and obligations notwithstanding, Lorimer and the *Post* were making some headway. Average circulation, in no small part due to the boy agents, rose from 108,000 in December 1899 to 153,000 in May 1900, establishing a consistent upward surge. Advertising revenue increased as well; in October 1900 the treasurer could report for the first time, "Receipts this month exceed payments by $11,016.42."[41]

The promise of future solvency for the *Post* did not assuage Bok. In the spring of 1901 he made some kind of direct challenge to Lorimer's authority over the *Saturday Evening Post*. The incident arose after Curtis had hired a business manager who apparently had some difficulty sorting out the chain of command, especially difficult in the case of Bok, who was not only editor of the *Journal* but also a vice-president of the Curtis Company and Curtis's son-in-law. Whatever the specific incident, it caused Curtis to write the new man a letter explaining that his position as business manager gave him no editoral control whatever over the Curtis magazines. Furthermore, in Curtis's absence, when vice-president Bok was in charge, even he had no authority over the editorial decisions of any magazine but his own.

Despite the explicitness of Curtis's letter to the business manager, another incident occurred. Most likely, the business manager, acting under Bok's orders, refused some request of Lorimer's. Lorimer was angry enough to write a formal letter of complaint to Curtis demanding a full statement of lines of authority over the *Saturday Evening Post*. Lorimer's letter does not survive, but Curtis's reply, in its insistent repetitions, to say nothing of its military diction, provides a fair sense of what Lorimer understood to be at stake.

My dear Mr. Lorimer,

To clearly define the jurisdiction of the Editor's office of The Saturday Evening Post, permit me to say that I expect you to continue as in the past in supreme editorial command of The Saturday Evening Post, and as such you are not under the jurisdiction of the Business Manager, nor of the Vice-President of this Company, nor of the Editor of The Ladies' Home Journal, nor anyone connected with The Curtis Publishing Company except myself as President, and no one has any right to interfere with you in any way or to issue any order concerning the editorial content of The Saturday Evening Post. . . . I don't think any one has ever intended to give the impression that any one else should have anything to say concerning the Post editorially, but I think it wise to put this in black and white and make it as strong as English words can make it: that no one has or ever shall have any authority whatever to dictate to you in any way concerning the Post, and that it is absolutely under your supreme control and command editorially. It is your right and you have the authority to issue commands from the Business Office, just as much as Mr. Bok has the same right concerning The Ladies' Home Journal. Your editorial position with this Company is exactly on the same and equal basis with that of Mr. Bok.[42]

No further questions about the jurisdiction over the *Post* arose during Lorimer's editorship. And, by the end of the decade, Curtis gave more than lip service to the equal basis that existed between Lorimer and Bok. In 1909 he raised both their salaries, paying them for the first time the same amount of money. In 1909, Lorimer was earning $50,000 a year.

The December 1899 advertisement had asserted that the *Post* would become "indispensable" to the average American. In 1903, Senator Beveridge claimed that it had already succeeded in becoming an integral part of American life. Beveridge, campaigning in Indiana, wrote to Lorimer to tell him this. "It is certainly worth your while to know that the common people are coming to have a positive affection for the Saturday Evening Post. It is taken for the family amusement, recreation and guide. . . . I tell you this that you may know how your work is appreciated at the firesides of your vast constituency. I should think you would be proud of it. I would surely be proud of it were I the creating brain of this most remarkable magazine that has yet appeared in the history of American magazine making."[43] Senator Beveridge's style was never particularly restrained, nor was he a disinterested observer, having written articles for the *Post* since 1900; nevertheless, his congratulations were sincere, and they reflected accurately the rising power and influence of the *Saturday Evening Post*.

By 1903 Lorimer had succeeded in creating a handsome magazine with a real identity. It could boast of first-class writing, a circulation of over half a million, and advertising that filled up to 45 percent of some issues.[44] The *Post* now had a cover, in two colors, with beautifully drawn illustrations by leading artist-illustrators of the day, including the great J. C. Leyendecker, as well as Harrison Fisher and Henry Hutt, both known for their elegant pictures of women, and Charles Livingston Bull, naturalist and master animal painter. Fine illustrations and decorations accompanied all stories and articles, and the layout, now in three columns through the front of the book, was clean and appealing. Issues were typically twenty-four or thirty-two pages, but occasionally the book grew to as many as fifty-six. Articles and fiction appeared in the front of each issue up to the editorial and op-ed pages. Only after that did the magazine revert to four columns, allowing space for advertising as the front material tailed through to the end. Major advertisers were given space on the inside front cover and, occasionally in color, on the back cover, the first space to be sold for full-page ads.

Lorimer had also dramatically improved the editorial content of the *Post*. Public figures regularly contributed articles, including young Senator Beveridge, providing a series (beginning January 28, 1903) on "Americans of To-Day and To-Morrow," and William Allen White, whose "What's the Matter with Kansas?" had catapulted him into the national spotlight in 1901, sending articles from Washington on the Senate and the House as well as on the nation's favorite topic, President Teddy Roosevelt.[45] Former President Grover Cleveland continued to write occasionally, on politics or on fishing,[46] and Charles Emory Smith, formerly minister to Russia, explained "Russian Diplomacy" to *Post* readers (December 26, 1903).

Fiction was another strong suit, and serialized fiction for 1903 was distinguished by Frank Norris's *The Pit* and Alfred Henry Lewis's political novel, *The Boss*. The *Post* also ran two novels by David Graham Phillips that year, *The Golden Fleece* and *The Cost*, a story of business and politics with a hero based on Senator Beveridge, with whom Phillips had attended college. Jack London's *Call of the Wild* appeared in 1903, as well as George Ade's *Tales of a Country Town*. The most popular serial in 1903 was *Old Gorgon Graham*, Lorimer's anonymous sequel to *Letters from a Self-Made Merchant to His Son*.[47]

Beveridge wrote congratulations to Lorimer on the new serial, ironically complaining that his "jealousy was deeply aroused" at its

Albert Beveridge

success and comparing it to his own lofty series on "Americans of To-Day and To-Morrow:" "Here I am writing the great and eternal things, and here is the editor with his bloody old pork-packing wisdom actually getting famous."[48]

The relationship between Lorimer and Beveridge was the first significant tie formed between the *Post* and the centers of power in America. An especially deep and enduring friendship arose between the editor and the senator, and along with novelist David Graham Phillips, they made a threesome of young, energetic, and powerful men, with different talents and dedicated to different fields, but all bent on reshaping America along upbeat Progressivist lines. But preceding and coexisting with the close personal ties between Beveridge and Lorimer were a sense of mutual respect and an awareness of the mutual advantages they could bring one another. Beveridge provided Lorimer an entree to government power. Lorimer provided Beveridge a major platform from which to reach a wide audience.

The junior senator from Indiana was a very attractive *Post* contributor both as a respresentative of the Progressive Republican movement in Congress and as the hero of his own life story which, by 1900, seemed written straight out of the most cherished American mythology. Born in Ohio in 1862, "he began life without opportunities," as a *Post* promotion piece explained. He experienced considerable hardship as a boy, rising at 3:00 A.M. to plow for local farmers and "welcom[ing] rainy days" when he could remain at home reading the history of Greece, Rome, and America. From plowboy, Beveridge went on to work as a section hand, a teamster, and a logger until he was finally able to enter high school at the age of sixteen. A fifty-dollar loan enabled him to attend DePauw University (then Asbury College), where he rose at four in the morning to take a cold bath and exercise, setting to work by six. When he graduated in 1885, he was the top man in his class.[49] In 1887 he entered law in Indianapolis and the same year he married Katherine Langsdale.

Elected to the Senate in 1899, at the age of thirty-six, Beveridge was youthful, handsome, forceful, and idealistic. Another piece in the *Post* described him as he rose to speak in the Senate, with "a thick mane of hair which he parts in the middle, and his face beneath the hair . . . quite all that it should be: pale, thin, intelligent, and the face of the orator."[50] He soon became dedicated to Progressivist reforms that would make him a leader in the Republican insurgency and ally him closely to Teddy Roosevelt. Those ties eventually spelled the end of Beveridge's political career. Reelected to the Senate in 1905, he was defeated in 1911 through a coalition of Democrats and conservative Stand Pat Republicans. In 1912 he bolted to the Progressives with Roosevelt and ran unsuc-cessfully for governor of Indiana. In 1914 he was again defeated in the Senate race. Although Beveridge did run once more in 1922, again unsuccessfully, his time was now devoted principally to writ-ing. He published his major work, a biography of Chief Justice Marshall, in 1916 and 1919, and when he died in 1927 he was working on a biography of Lincoln.

In 1900, however, Albert J. Beveridge looked very much like the future of America incarnate. In him Lorimer could see the self-made western man, triumphing over hardship and poverty, dedicat-ing himself to the good of his country. Beyond that, Beveridge was an investigator, a fact-finder; like Lorimer's "average American," he needed to know about a great many things, but in Beveridge's case the knowledge he gained could be brought to bear directly on the future of the nation.

Before assuming his seat in the Senate, Beveridge went to the Philippines to get a first-hand look at the situation there. The infor-mation he brought back not only served him in the Senate but introduced him as well to the readers of the *Saturday Evening Post*. Lorimer met with Senator Beveridge at the end of January 1900, and the two reached an agreement about a series of articles on the American soldier in the Philippines. Lorimer agreed to buy six essays, 3,000 or more words each, for $1,000 apiece.[51]

The first installment appeared on March 17, following a flurry of letters over matters of promotion and presentation. Lorimer was accommodating and respectful to the young senator: "[I am] deeply . . . sensible and appreciative of your great personal kindness and courtesy to me in this whole matter."[52] He promised to watch the promotional material with the greatest care, "so that nothing detrimental to your best interests may creep in," and when, despite Lorimer's care, Beveridge found the biographical sketch prepared for the *Post* unacceptable, the editor wired to say "that the sketch [would] be duly 'killed.'"[53]

Beveridge was very concerned about the cover illustration for his article and about prepublicity, and Lorimer kept assuring him on this score: "Advance notices of the first article have appeared in about five thousand newspapers, dailies and weeklies, and we are leaving nothing undone at this end in order to call the attention of the public to the articles." A few days later he wrote again to say, "Before the first article makes its appearance it will have been announced in fully ten thousand dailies and weeklies."[54] Lorimer had found an important contributor for the *Post* and Curtis was providing the requisite financial support.

Although at the outset Lorimer's relations with Beveridge were formal and businesslike and his letters respectful of Beveridge's position as a senator, there were some issues about which the editor of the *Saturday Evening Post* was entirely adamant— with Beveridge in 1900 as with contributors of all kinds in the years ahead. Beveridge wanted a second extensive campaign of newspaper advertising in April; Lorimer had other ideas, insisting, "Returns from . . . newspaper advertising have been disappointing," turning out to be much less effective than "the millions of circulars and booklets which are being placed right in the hands of prospective buyers by our agents."[55]

Money was another issue on which Lorimer could not be bullied. Beveridge wrote suggesting that he receive more than the agreed-upon $1,000 for one of the pieces because it was somewhat longer than the others.[56] Lorimer declined. At the same time, he was interested in having Beveridge continue to write for the *Post,* suggesting as a topic something on the young man in politics and sketching out the general ideas. Beveridge preferred to write about contemporary great men, but wanted the same arrangement as he had for the articles on the Philippines. From

Lorimer's point of view, contemporary great men were not worth that much money.[57]

The subject of "young men" returned, however, in 1901, when Beveridge wrote to say that while he was not enthusiastic about writing anything at the present time, he would do it for the money. Lorimer replied, "If it is, as you say, simply a question of money I do not believe we could go high enough on them to overcome your distaste for writing." He suggested that they wait for "a subject of wide timely importance, which would possess special advertising value. . . . I do not, however, want to use a thirteen inch gun for knocking over a hen house."[58]

The subject of "wide timely importance" was quickly discovered. Beveridge was to visit the Far East for the particular purpose of learning about the competition posed by Germany and Russia to the United States' interests in the China market. Apparently, the two men met to discuss the trip and the articles that might come out of it. Lorimer was enthusiastic: "My sleep over that plan of yours confirms my impression that the only place where those articles should appear is in The Saturday Evening Post. Roughly, and without going into details; we would be willing to pay ten thousand dollars ($10,000) for the serial rights of the book—say about fifty thousand words, divided into ten or twelve articles, as the material best splits up."[59]

Beveridge's series began in the *Post* on November 16, 1901, and under the title "The White Invasion of China" appeared as the lead article for three successive weeks, subsequently continuing on into 1902. The February 8, 1902, installment was called "The Coming War Between Russia and Japan," and in it Beveridge predicted, to the subsequent delight of the *Post,* the war that was to break out a year and a half later. Beveridge was very pleased by his prescience:

Things are coming along in the Far East in the exact time fixed by my schedule. You see I am the great scheduler of events and the Saturday Evening Post is the announcer thereof. You fellows ought to have an editorial upon this thing, calling attention to the fact that you . . . were the first to give the word—and two years in advance . . . [at a time] when the rest of the American press was saying that the whole thing was tommy-rot and our distinguished Secretary of State—(who by the way between you and me "don't know a little bit" about foreign affairs)—was declaring that Russia would not permanently occupy Manchuria at all, at all, at all.[60]

By 1902 the formal business relationship between Lorimer and Beveridge was turning into a close friendship born of mutual respect, shared values, and a kind of western bonhomie that enlivened their long-term correspondence. Friendship never impinged, however, on the rules of business, and Lorimer continued just as firmly as before to hold down the line on prices for articles or on requests for additional money. On the other hand, friendship made it possible for the two men to serve one another's interests in important ways. Lorimer, for example, could ask Beveridge to meet with Jesse Lynch Williams whom the *Post* was sending to Washington to do "some special work" or to arrange for State Department letters of introduction to the United States ambassadors in St. Petersburg and Rome "for our Paris correspondent, Vance Thompson."[61]

For his part, Beveridge needed some favorable press on matters up before the Senate. Late in 1902 he was working to force a subcommittee of the Committee on Territories to visit Oklahoma and New Mexico in order to investigate these territories at first hand before the statehood question was brought before Congress. Beveridge, who was by no means free of racism, felt strongly that New Mexico should be denied statehood, since about half of the small population consisted of "Spanish speaking Mexicans"; more- over, very little of the land was cultivatable. He knew he faced a fight and thought it "of the most enormous importance" to have "the public opinion of the country with us." "What can you do in that line?" he asked Lorimer, at the same time making clear that the question finally remained one for the *Post* editor's own political conscience. "If you believe in us, help us out. If you don't believe in us, why lambaste us. But whether you help us or lambaste us, I nevertheless will continue to hold you in my heart and affection."[62] On February 16, 1901, "Publick Occurrences," the regular public affairs department, printed a statement of opposition to proposed statehood for Arizona, New Mexico, and Oklahoma.

Lorimer's relationship with Senator Beveridge was beginning to open certain avenues of power to him, with resulting advantages and responsibilities. The advantages mounted early in 1903 when Beveridge determined to bring about a meeting between Lorimer and President Teddy Roosevelt, who, reported the senator, "very thoroughly appreciates the good work the Post is doing for him to which his attention has been called right along."[63] In February Beveridge telephoned with an invitation: "The President expects you to lunch with him next Wednesday at one o'clock."

Beveridge continued over the next few years to cultivate the Roosevelt-Lorimer relationship. In 1906 he wrote to say he had dined with the president: "Repeatedly—at least a dozen times—the President said: 'Get Lorimer down here. I want to talk to him.' . . . The President is very anxious to talk over the whole situation through the United States with you, very anxious indeed." Two weeks later Beveridge wrote on the subject again, saying the president had asked him whether he had invited Lorimer to Washington: "I told him you thought the president should invite you and he said: 'By George, I will.'"[64]

Lorimer met occasionally with Roosevelt and they corresponded. All this attention from the head of state was decidedly flattering to the editor and his magazine, but Lorimer managed to keep his head. Early in 1907 he dropped a note to Beveridge just before leaving for Chicago. "I'm just about to start West for a week, but I have no doubt that Theodore will be able to bear up without me during my absence. If, however, the Japanese question should become acute while I am away and he really feels in need of my advice tell him that a telegram to the Auditorium Annex will find me. The Union must and shall be preserved."[65]

The Post was certainly a supporter of TR, but Lorimer was careful to maintain the magazine's political independence, or at least the appearance of independence. At the outset, he had determined on an appropriate political stance for the Post: it would carry out its public role, especially in the area of domestic politics, by keeping its readers informed and, when significant issues arose, by providing a forum for the presentation of responsible points of view. None of this is meant to suggest that the *Post* was politically disinterested and certainly not that it was free of ideology. Nevertheless, in asserting its character as an American magazine, Lorimer intended to keep the *Post* free of any obvious political or party affiliations.[66]

Still, TR got good press in the *Saturday Evening Post*. Even back when Roosevelt was nominated as McKinley's running mate—an effort on the part of conservative Republicans to remove him from the public eye as well as from the governorship of New York—a *Post* editorial, in Lorimer's wry style, commented that this would not eventuate in Roosevelt's political death: "He is the last man a cautious undertaker should attempt to bury without his full consent."[67] Lorimer printed a number of articles on TR after he became president, beginning with a reminiscence of his Harvard years by Owen Wister and including an essay on Roosevelt's Oyster Bay home as well as some very favorable pieces by William Allen White.[68]

By the time of the 1904 election, Lorimer was able to bring a number of authorities and personages to the pages of the *Post* for the purpose of laying out the claims of both parties and both presidential candidates, establishing what would be a permanent feature of election-year coverage. Grover Cleveland acted as principal spokesman for the "Democracy," as the Democratic party was then termed, with Beveridge, assisted by Alfred Henry Lewis, supporting the Republicans. The political articles for 1904 culminated with a pair of October pieces: Beveridge's "Why Young Men Should Vote the Republican Ticket" (October 1, 1904) and Cleveland's "Why Young Men Should Vote the Democratic Ticket" (October 8, 1904). Then, as if bending over backward to demonstrate his disinterestedness, Lorimer gave space late in the month to William Jennings Bryan for a campaign plea called "Why the Democrats of 1896 and 1900 Should Support Parker & Davis in 1904" (October 22, 1904).[69]

By 1904 Lorimer had established the *Post* as a forum for political debate carried on by major political figures. He exploited the forum model again in 1907 when Wall Street attacked Roosevelt as the cause of the recent financial panic. On November 23 the *Post* ran a pair of articles called "Is Roosevelt a Menace to Business?" The articles consisted of short statements by leading businessmen who took both sides of the issue, from "Dishonest Financiers, not Roosevelt, Responsible" to "He Has Strained Public Confidence to the Breaking Point."[70] The articles aroused sufficient interest so that the *Saturday Evening Post* invited readers to send in their responses to the question. By early December the *Post* had received 5,000 letters. An editorial noted, if the letters "mean anything, the President is stronger with the country to-day than he has ever been."[71] Readers' letters on the question continued, in the back of the book, well into 1908.

The whole question of the panic, however, and the attempt to fix blame on the president, or for that matter on J. P. Morgan, was too important for the *Post* to leave entirely in the hands of representative businessmen and interested readers. Lorimer took a hand in it himself, with an op-ed piece called "The ABC of Confidence" signed by "Uncle Bill Spurlock" (November 30, 1907).[72] The article was fairly evenhanded. Although it made clear that "no panic ever has been, or, from its very nature, ever can be, *started* except by the stronger party," which in this case meant Wall Street, it also made the point, dear to Lorimer's heart, that greedy and overly optimistic speculators were no more than sheep for the shearing. And as far as Teddy was concerned, Uncle Bill Spurlock said, "Don't blame Roosevelt." If he was not "the great and only three-ringed President, surpassing all other rulers and lawgivers in a bewildering and kaleidoscopic series of marvelous and stupendous acts of statesmanship," he was still "an earnest, able man, often right, often wrong, whose efforts to do right atone for many errors of judgment, and whose ability is doubled in effectiveness by its use for honest purposes."

Lorimer, whether in his own character or that of Uncle Bill Spurlock, did not believe Roosevelt was anything like a menace to business. As he wrote to Beveridge, a great deal depended on what one's definition of business happened to be. "It is a curious and significant thing that all the men who are stock gamblers, or who are engaged in financing stock gambling, without exception, come out unequivocally—in private, not over their own signatures—and say that Teddy is a terror for trade. But all the merchants and manufacturers I have approached, the people who are concerned with the real industries, say that he hasn't anything more to do with it than a little child." [73]

The panic and resulting depression had no effect whatsoever on the fortunes of the *Post;* in fact, during the latter part of 1907 the magazine added 90,000 to its circulation. [74] A major advertising campaign was again under way, on which Beveridge congratulated Lorimer, but as far as the senator was concerned, increases in circulation were the obvious effect of a magazine that was "better, brighter, fresher now than it [had] ever been." [75] Beveridge was an acute observer; as strong as the *Post* had been in 1903, it was stronger by far in 1907, principally because a major change had taken place in the contributors.

One of Lorimer's boasts was that the *Post* had no staff of writers and that no one's work was automatically accepted for publication. As far as fiction was concerned, this was by and large the case, but the situation was somewhat different with nonfiction. Lorimer always retained and exercised absolute authority to accept or reject material, [76] but that did not mean he failed to encourage contributors to write on certain topics or that he hesitated to collect a group of writers whose work he admired and made arrangements for them that would guarantee a certain annual income by writing articles for the *Post.*

David Graham Phillips came to the *Post* on the strength of such a guarantee. In 1902 he was working for Joseph Pulitzer's New York *World* and eager to leave newspaper journalism except for his timidity "about separating himself from the weekly pay envelope." Beveridge arranged for Phillips to meet with Lorimer, already predisposed in Phillips's favor from having read his novel *The Great God Success.* The terms Lorimer offered did not promise publication of all Phillips's work; what he did guarantee was that Phillips "would make as much out of writing for the *Saturday Evening Post* during the first year as he was then earning on the *World*."[77]

Other writers, too, were being collected as *Post* regulars, their voices beginning to be identified with the magazine's. Some men were first brought in to undertake a specific assignment and subsequently turned to various subjects. Emerson Hough, who first appeared in the *Post* as a fiction writer, was hired in 1905 to handle the "OutofDoors" department; he stayed on to cover widely different topics.[78] The great political writer Sam Blythe, another graduate of Pulitzer's *World*, first appeared in the *Post* with "The Senator's Secretary," an anonymous record of political life in Washington. In 1907 he took on "Who's Who and Why," an update of an earlier department featuring personalities that Lorimer had continually tried to enliven. With Blythe he succeeded in more than invigorating a weekly department; Blythe became a mainstay of the magazine—particularly, but not exclusively, as an observer of American politics.

Under whatever kind of arrangement, a staff was being assembled in the first seven or eight years of Lorimer's editorship and by 1907, Lorimer had gathered together a group of firstclass writers for the *Saturday Evening Post*: Sam Blythe, James H. Collins, Emerson Hough, Edwin Lefevre, Isaac Marcosson, Will Payne, David Graham Phillips. With these men writing for him, Lorimer was able to turn away from a dependence on articles by celebrated men and authoritative experts in favor of articles by writers whose knowledge of a field came not from working in it but from observing it from the outside. The development of a staff of writers did not, of course, mean that the *Post* no longer carried material by famous men and women; that was certainly not the case. What it did mean, and this was of central importance to the development of the *Post*'s style, voice, and even public strategy, was that a number of men and women became associated in the public mind with particular areas of interest and, most important, with the identity of the *Saturday Evening Post*.

Thus, by the end of 1907, the *Post* had assumed an identity, begun to wield power, brought circulation to a weekly average of 725,000, and succeeded in attracting sufficient national advertising to have altered the format and given pages 1 and 2, as well as the inside covers and back cover, to full-page advertisements.[79] And in December, the Curtis Company was sufficiently solvent for the board to approve the plans for the ambitious new Curtis Building.

Back in the middle of 1903, Beveridge, having received a letter from India in response to one of his *Post* articles, had written to Lorimer on the great success of his magazine. "Thunder and Mars! Are you like Alexander sighing for more world's [*sic*] to conquer? Are you not satisfied with America as your field? Are you like the fervid and fervent missionary who says 'the world is my field?' Do you intend to make the Saturday Evening Post march in militant triumph all around the globe?"[80]

Lorimer had answered in the same spirit, boasting that the *Post* had "'done marched' in a humble way," with readers in Hawaii, the Philippines, China, and Russia. And with the ebullience of success, he added that even in the United Kingdom there was "quite an aggregation of rooters for the greatest weekly magazine in the world."[81] That may have been an empty boast in 1903; it was looking like the real thing by the end of 1907.

"More Than a Million a Week"

The December 12, 1908, cover of the *Saturday Evening Post* featured one of Harrison Fisher's beautiful drawings of elegant women, in this instance hanging mistletoe to strike a seasonal note. Above the picture a bold headline announced that the *Post* had attained "MORE THAN A MILLION A WEEK CIRCULATION."

Weekly circulation of a million copies was more than a quantitative achievement for Curtis and Lorimer. There was magic in the number, the magnitude of such a readership somehow demonstrating the *Post*'s authority to speak to and for America. From the time when the *Post* stopped operating in the red, the magic of a million circulation took on a special fascination for both Curtis and Lorimer. Circulation exceeded half a million by early 1903 and for two more years it maintained a steady climb. In the summer of 1904, a sanguine Lorimer wrote to Curtis, away on vacation, "I hope to have eight hundred thousand of that million safely salted down this year."[1] But it took a little longer than Lorimer had hoped; not until in the spring of 1905 did circulation reach 800,000. Moreover, that success was temporary; the trajectory had stalled. In 1907 average circulation was still only three-quarters of a million. A year later, the Curtis Company decided to mount a full-scale campaign to carry *Post* circulation over a million.

While Lorimer addressed the problem of circulation by modestly reshaping the *Post* to attract new readers, Curtis, true to type, turned to advertising, placing large ads in hundreds of daily papers. A typical advertisement spread across the newspaper page, three columns wide and half a page high. Under a bust of Franklin and the *Saturday Evening Post* logo, the number "904,050" stood in headline-size type. "This is, by far, the largest circulation ever achieved by any weekly magazine in this country," the ad declared, going on to praise George Horace Lorimer who, in his nine years as "Editor-in-Chief" had overseen "an average increase in [*Post*] circulation of a hundred thousand copies a year."[2]

Curtis was not averse to drumming up some free advertising as well. The accolades for Lorimer in the newspaper ads were tied to a scheme to publicize the *Post* free of charge. Curtis had a piece on Lorimer written up and set about trying to place it in various magazines, first in general-circulation periodicals and, when that failed, in trade publications. General-circulation magazines were courteous, but definitely not hospitable. Walter H. Page, editor of *World's Work,* returned the essay to Curtis, with the vague promise that his magazine might "do up" Lorimer "in a little while." But, he wrote, "this piece won't do it. It is too direct and too full of mere praise for the man and too empty of interesting stories about him."[3]

The trade journal *Printers' Ink* was more receptive, commenting, "The matter is intrinsically interesting to our readers." Not that the editor was really comfortable about publishing so overtly promotional a piece: "I can see where it is going to make a whole lot of trouble for Printers' Ink, because there are a lot of other publishers who would like to have their editors written up in the same style." But Curtis was too much of a power in the magazine world to be turned down. The editor conceded that Lorimer was certainly "a subject of general interest" and requested a photograph of the *Post* editor to go with the story.[4]

The campaign succeeded within a matter of months. But while selling a million copies a week represented a milestone, neither Curtis or Lorimer was satisfied to rest on that achievement. Within the next five years circulation doubled, and on January 15, 1913, the *Post* could trumpet another new high of over two million copies a week.[5] The years between 1908 and 1913 witnessed other evidences of success as well. In 1908 a typical issue was thirty-two pages and might fill between 35 and 40 percent of those pages with advertising. Five years later issues as small as thirty-two pages had disappeared; by 1913 nearly a third of the issues were seventy pages or more. Advertising in these larger issues often ran as high as 45 and even 50 percent, and during this five-year period, advertising revenue increased by almost 600 percent.[6]

The extraordinary commercial success of the Curtis Corporation found its physical expression in its splendid new building on Philadelphia's Independence Square. As early as 1907 the economic success of both the *Saturday Evening Post* and the *Ladies' Home Journal* had been more than adequate for the Curtis board to approve plans for a new Curtis Building. Planning and construction took four years and when the building was completed the Curtis Company could take possession of a property that signified its great power and prestige. Early in 1912 the *Architectural Record* published two articles describing the new building, one a technical discussion of its engineering and architecture, the other a descriptive piece. The emphasis throughout was on scale, in the building itself as in the Curtis magazine empire.

The Curtis Building was very grand and very modern. Grandeur was for the publisher and his editors, in the offices, board room, and private dining room, or what the *Architectural Record* called the "state apartments." The board room boasted ornate moldings, wall panels, and sconces as a setting for the Louis XIV chairs, sofas, and conference table. The major offices were somewhat simpler, but nonetheless costly, large, and imposing, with fine furnishings, paintings, fireplaces. The offices represented authority.

The modern aspect of the Curtis Building lay in the facilities provided for the 3,500 workers Curtis employed. In addition to such amenities as a pleasant, clean, and efficient lunch room, the employees enjoyed rooms set aside for recreation, notably a lounge for women workers connecting with a promenade terrace. There was even a small hospital. The concern for the comfort and well-being of employees was much admired by the *Architectural Record,* which shared Lorimer's belief that enlightened paternalism on the

The Curtis Building, Philadelphia

part of management would eliminate any need for labor to organize in its own interests or even for labor to see itself as a distinct class with interests different from those of management. Amenities like those offered in the new Curtis Building, explained the *Architectural Record,* were effective means to "discourage the anarchistic sentiments" and "to constitute as effective a safeguard as could well be named . . . against the formation of class-feeling, against hatred, envy, malice and all uncharitableness."[7]

When the Curtis Building was completed, the circulation of both the *Ladies' Home Journal* and the *Saturday Evening Post* was about a million and three quarters, and the *Architectural Record* was fascinated by the kinds of numbers involved in producing magazines in such quantities. If a single edition of any one magazine were stacked up, the writer marveled, it would reach a height of 29,100 feet, an elevation fifty-two times that of the Washington Monument. And should that edition be laid out side by side, it would extend around the world one and one-fifth times. Curtis presses were turning out 27,860,000 pages every day to produce 125,000,000 magazines a year. A single edition of either the *Ladies' Home Journal* or the *Saturday Evening Post* consumed four square miles of paper and 60,000 pounds of ink and required sixty-five railway cars to distribute it.[8] This was the magazine business on a colossal—which is to say, an American—scale.

The Curtis Company did not fail to see, or to use, its new building as an emblem. It was, in fact, possible to use the Curtis Building to express a variety of meanings. It could represent the great reach of its publications and its consequent power as an American institution. At the same time, as the *Architectural Record* made clear, it stood as a symbol of business progress and of a classless society of mutually dependent and mutually supportive owners and workers. The multivalent structure was also called on for more specialized messages. When Curtis began a major initiative to increase *Post* advertising in 1915, he had a brochure published that opened with a photograph of the Curtis Building, captioned "*An Institution Built on Faith.*" "This building in Independence Square," the copy intoned, "represents an institution built on faith—faith in the power of advertising."[9]

The business success of the *Post,* its power to attract advertisers, depended, of course, on circulation, and circulation in turn depended upon the editorial side. Advertising, circulation, and editorial were never seen as separate phenomena by Curtis, or indeed by Lorimer, but it was Lorimer's chief responsibility to create the magazine that would attract and keep the widest possible circulation among middle-class Americans.

Between 1908 and 1913, Lorimer succeeded fully in that task, turning his still developing weekly into a magazine with a fully realized and entirely unmistakable identity. By 1908 he had already collected the nonfiction writers who would explicate American business, politics, and society to *Post* readers. Over the next few years he would discover a group of fiction writers whose stories and characters would become intimately familiar to *Post* readers and deeply identified with the *Saturday Evening*

Post. The *Post*'s cover artists contributed to its identity as well. Although there were nearly sixty different illustrators whose work appeared on the *Post* between 1908 and 1913, more than 60 percent of the covers in these years were the work of only six different artists, and of those six, two—J. C. Leyendecker and Harrison Fisher—were responsible for fully 40 percent of all the cover art.[10]

And it was at this time that Lorimer first flexed his muscles a bit, testing the political power of his magazine. He discovered just what he could accomplish and, in the 1912 presidential election, precisely what he could not.

Finally, it was during these heady and prosperous years that Lorimer set out to refine his definition of the *Post* reader, to fill in the sketch of the businessman he had begun with. The young businessman had now progressed a bit in life, had become upwardly mobile, a confirmed consumer, even a potential investor. And for the first time the young businessman who read the *Post* appeared to have taken a wife: on June 28, 1908, as part of its circulation campaign, the *Post* suddenly announced that it was "Not for Men Only." The decision to turn the *Post* from a weekly for men into a magazine that appealed as well to women illustrates fully the symbiotic relationship among advertising, circulation, and editorial projects that characterized the rise of the *Post* to its position of media dominance. That decision was, like Curtis's advertising campaign, a part of the drive to push circulation to a million.

In 1908, the *Post* was typically using the center columns of page 2 for an editorial advertisement promoting the contents of the forthcoming issue. On June 28, this space was used to announce two upcoming articles of interest to women: "The Complexities of the Complexion" by medical writer Woods Hutchinson and "Frauds and Deceptions in Precious Stones" by "Tiffany's expert in precious stones." If the titles did not in themselves send out a call to women readers, the headline, "Jewels and the Complexion," helped to make the point, as did a second headline: "Not for Men Only."

"Who says that the SATURDAY EVENING POST is for men only? . . . we number women readers not by tens but by hundreds of thousands" (June 20, 1908).

The idea of claiming, or more likely creating, a female readership was certainly part of Curtis's circulation campaign, but it was not simply a matter of gaining new readers. It is, in fact, unlikely that there was any significant population of single, adult women seen as constituting a potential market for *Post* subscriptions, or that among this population there were any large numbers whose financial situation made them an attractive audience for *Post* advertisers. Thus, while circulation remained a dominant factor in decisions made about the *Post* in 1908, the determination to make an overt appeal to women rested on a more complex set of considerations having to do with advertising, new consumer products, and potential new consumers. The *Post* was after a million in circulation, but the million had to be made up of people with middle-class values, middle-class tastes, and some amount of discretionary income.

Cyrus Curtis had developed two brilliantly successful magazines during the infancy of modern advertising. His own belief in the power of advertising had carried the *Post* through its first unsuccessful years, and he intended both the *Post* and the *Journal* to be powerful advertising media. In fact, from Curtis's point of view as publisher, his magazines were nothing other than advertising media. He once told a meeting of advertisers that the idea that the *Journal* was published for "the benefit of American women" was "an illusion" of the editor's. "But I will tell you the real reason," Curtis continued, "the publisher's reason, is to give you people who manufacture things that American women want and buy a chance to tell them about your products."[11]

Nor, from Curtis's point of view, were the reasons for publishing the *Post* any different. However, as the *Post* grew in prestige as a magazine for men, something of a problem began to arise. While men were certainly the principal money-earners and money-holders at the turn of the century, their wives had the chief responsibility for purchasing the goods and services needed in the home.[12] At the same time, the kinds and varieties of these goods and services were increasing. Packaged and canned foods, small electrical appliances, and materials and substances for cleaning and hygiene are notable examples, as are all products intended for children and child care. Moreover, magazine advertisers were growing more canny about matching their products with the audience of the magazine. The *Post,* like the *Journal,* was the messenger of consumerism, but in the case of the *Post,* the messenger was delivering the news to the wrong audience.

Ironically, it was precisely Lorimer's success in creating his subject and his audience that by 1908 had begun to curtail the kinds of advertising the *Post* was carrying. In the first few years of his editorship, before the magazine was fully defined and shaped for an audience of businessmen, ads for products for women and for domestic goods had shared the choice and more expensive advertising positions more or less equally with ads for products appealing to men. But even as advertising percentages and profits increased in the *Post,* it became clear that its share of the potential advertising market was becoming a good deal narrower.

The September 30, 1899, issue, for example, reflects the eclecticism of *Post* advertising at the outset. Major advertisers—Quaker Oats, Edison Phonograph, Rogers Brothers silverplate, the Encyclopedia Britannica, and a company selling health underwear for the whole family—appealed to women, especially as consumers of products for the household. Only one of the larger ads, for Whiting Paper, directly addressed the businessman. A year and a half later, on February 9, 1901, the situation remained essentially unchanged, with major ads for Ralston Purina, Pearline Soap, Edison Phonograph, Ivers and Pond Piano, and Welsbach Reading Lamp. Again, only one larger ad appealed exclusively to the businessman, in this case for Remington Typewriter.

To be sure, little of the advertising in the earliest *Post* years was either extensive or sophisticated. Most companies were satisfied with column-ads or even fractions of columns. Still, the early success with the Singer Sewing Machine Company indicated that

In a sophisticated early ad, Oldsmobile lets the picture talk.

national advertisers did not see the *Post* as soliciting a predominantly male audience.

But by the beginning of 1903 the advertising situation had
altered markedly. In the January 3 issue, only one major advertisement for Ben Hur Flour appealed to the household market. All
other prominent ads addressed Lorimer's targeted audience, the upand-coming young man of business. These included Glenside Home
Sites, Globe-Wernicke Bookcases (with illustrations of office settings), Oldsmobile, the Chicago School of Advertising, and the
George T. Powell Correspondence School of Advertising.[13] Whatever increases the *Post* was realizing in advertising revenue, there
was no question but that it was losing out in products designed for
women and in the growing area of domestic goods and services. As
advertising began to become more self-conscious and sophisticated
in the first years of the century, and as advertisers gradually grew
shrewder about placing ads in relation to a magazine's probable
audience, a magazine addressed to men was increasingly unlikely to
attract advertisers for products designed to appeal to women.

The categories of products advertised in the *Post* became more
and more restricted over the next few years. The May 14, 1904,
issue sold a hefty 46 percent of all space for advertising, but showed
a distinct loss in the eclecticism of the advertising the *Post* had
previously enjoyed. Among the goods and services offered in the
issue were real estate, investment opportunities, travel, cars and
buggies, men's clothes and shoes, various kinds of business supplies,
some sporting equipment, and magazines, books, and correspondence courses on aspects of business. Such ads represented pretty
inclusively the categories of goods and services likely to appeal to
men. Ads addressed to women appeared as well, but there were
many fewer. Still, the categories into which such ads fell indicated
just where the *Post* was losing out; these categories included
women's shoes and clothes, beauty products, foods, health products, all goods offered for children, household supplies, furniture,
and kitchen appliances.

In the issue for June 20, 1908 (the issue announcing that
women were welcome as *Post* readers), the advertising situation,

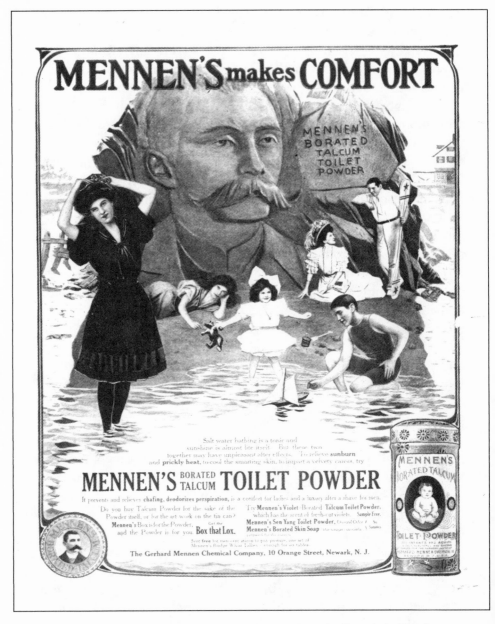

Mennen's takes the back cover with a product for the whole family.

like the circulation, had remained essentially unchanged over the four years since 1904. Advertising made up 42 percent of the thirty-two-page issue, with only about twenty-five of the approximately hundred and twenty-five ads offering goods for women or for households.[14] Moreover, in that issue only two of the four pages available for full-page ads had been sold as single ads: Mennen's Shaving Powder took the back cover and Packard the inside front cover. All other advertising pages carried multiple ads, even the inside back cover being made up of eight different advertisements—again, all for men.

The announcement of a coeducational *Post* apparently turned the trick, for a little over a year later, on October 9, 1909, considerable gains were apparent. In that fifty-six-page issue, thirty-four pages, over 60 percent of the magazine, were taken up by advertising. Advertisements for domestic products made the difference. Now, full-page ads appeared on the back cover, the inside front cover, and on pages 1 and 2, and the full-page advertisers included Ivory Soap and the Hoover Electric Suction Sweeper. There were also five two-page ads, three addressing the familiar male audience, but two offering relatively high-priced consumer goods for the household—the Mirrorscope Projector (a stereopticon) and the Western Electric telephone. All in all, a gender-free *Post* was turning out to be good business.[15]

It was one thing, however, to announce that the *Post* was hospitable to women readers; quite another to find appropriate content for this readership without either losing the magazine's established focus or trespassing on the *Journal*'s preserve. Between 1899 and 1908, articles on the subject of women had appeared very rarely in the *Post,* and articles addressed to women were virtually nonexistent. The little that was published tended to objectify women, treating them as something familiar in the (male) reader's environment, yet emotionally and intellectually remote from him.

Not that the *Post* took any unusual position toward women; in the mainstream of popular thought, it approved of good women—which is to say, dutiful wives and mothers—and disapproved of

Technology in an early ad: with Hoover these housewives do their own housework.

bad women—meaning extravagant or spoiled or headstrong or emancipated. But the *Post* did not present this banal position in the form of advice or counsel to women; instead, it presented observa-tions—to a presumed audience of nonwomen. In 1906, for example, Arthur Train, later the author of the famous Tutt and Mr. Tutt stories, wrote a pair of articles about women and the law, deploying a kind of ironic gallantry. "Our courts of law . . . are devised and organized, perhaps unfortunately, on the principle that testimony not apparently deduced from the observation of relevant fact by the syllogistic method is valueless, and hence woman at the outset is placed at a disadvantage and her usefulness as a probative force sadly crippled."[16] The irony was Train's, but the objectification of women was general and typical; nor was it confined to articles written by men. The few women who wrote about women for the *Post* were equally distanced from their subject and equally clear in their address to a male audience. In 1900, one Lady Jeune wrote about "Women in English Politics" (July 28, 1900) and strongly disapproved, noting that "their happiness and their career in life must always be in their homes." Lady Jeune's point of view is conventional; what is striking is her disinterested "their," which perfectly strikes the *Post* note.

Articles in which one might have expected to find advice specifically addressed to women turn out to be merely expository. In 1905, Mrs. Russell Sage wrote about "Women as Stock Gam-blers" (May 27, 1905), and rather than advice she provided objec-tive observation. The poor widow who happened to read this could, of course, have discovered that she lacked the "judgment" and "courage" to succeed, but the poor widow was not the in-tended audience.

Even women professionals adopted this stance in *Post* articles. Architect Josephine Wright Chapman wrote on "Women as Archi-tects" (March 30, 1901), expressing her disappointment at the lack of success women had achieved in her field, but she engaged neither in polemics against men nor in advice to women. Rather, with a distanced objectivity she explained that the trouble with women was an absence of seriousness that explained their failure to gain an adequate technical background as well as their susceptibility to the distractions of personal and home duties.

As for women in their conventional roles as wives and mothers, that subject belonged to Bok and the *Journal,* and its rare appearance in the *Post* was confined entirely to sour editorials repining over the lost virtues of grandmother's time. Like the occasional article on the subject, the rare *Post* editorial treated woman as object and other. One editorial turned to the subject of the emancipated woman—as the *Post* defined her. "Why Women Go to Seed" (December 10, 1904) explained that the emancipated woman was not one who was educated—or thought she was educated—but one whose husband's money freed her from work, leaving her in idleness, "destructive of character and degrading." The "idle, luxury-loving, work-despising, snob-breeding 'emancipated woman,'" moreover, lay "very near to the heart" of all current political and economic problems.

An editorial attack on Charlotte Perkins Gilman, titled "The Narrow-Minded Sex" (June 17, 1905), made it equally clear that the *Post* did not like the other kind of emancipated woman either. Citing biology and the differentiation of sex functions with evolution, the editorialist explained that male franchise "results from the fact that the affairs of the state are closely allied to those of the individual. Business and politics are two birds which the male citizen kills with the same stone." As for women, they are fortunate enough that the "latest result of the law of sex-differentiation has brought art, literature and drama, even science and philosophy" into their sphere.

The world of women in general, as far as the *Post* was concerned, was a world fallen sadly away from the nostalgic ideal of homemaker, wife, and mother. When some virago in Iowa "petitioned the authorities to close the high school, in order to leave some women in the town who were not unfitted by it for work in the house and kitchen," an editorial noted it and commented that it might not be such a joke as most of the country thought. "Has not the fine old art of homemaking fallen into disgrace among us simply because the popular education of women makes them despise the skilled trades of the needle and the kitchen range? After all, does the well-being of the nation depend on the skill of its women in cookery and baby-raising or on their knowledge of psychology and freehand drawing?"[17]

Despite the promissory "Not for Men Only," the June 20, 1908, invitation to women readers was premature, for that issue had nothing in particular to interest them, with the possible exception of some fiction. The nonfiction offered nothing that contemporary gender stereotypes, heavily marked in the promotional references to articles on jewels and the complexion, would assume appropriate to a female audience. That week, the magazine opened with an article on the American diplomatic corps and otherwise included pieces on speculation and business.[18]

Even the two future articles promised in the editorial advertisement were in fact parts of two ongoing series that predated the *Post*'s new appeal to a female readership. Woods Hutchinson's article on complexions provided the same kind of pop science and health he regularly contributed to the *Post,* and the article on jewels was the second in a series that began on June 13. In neither case was anything delivered like what the advertisement of June 20 had promised in its mawkish attempt at flattering copy: "a mere man suspects that every daughter of Eve is interested in jewels and that an article . . . written by Tiffany's expert in precious stones . . . will not be without appeal to the feminine heart."

It is in fact the very awkwardness of the June 20 editorial advertisement that is significant, for it demonstrated again the distance between the editorial writer and the mysterious world of women. The editorial, despite the fact that it purported to address a female readership, was in fact still talking *about* that readership. Lorimer's *Post* simply had no experience in talking *to* women for the very good reason that it had nothing to say to them.

It took about a year for Lorimer to find something to say, for it was not until 1909 that any real changes occurred in the *Post* reflecting its announced new attitude toward women. A small number of articles appealing to—and *addressed to*—a female readership appeared that year. "Adventures in Home-Making," a new series by Robert and Elizabeth Shackleton (beginning May 29, 1909), started out with instructive material on how to buy and redo a house. In June, the *Post* ran a two-part article called "A Woman's Rebellion," enthusiastically celebrating the "bloom" of the suffrage movement. Filler at the end of the first installment, with whatever good intentions, provided "Banking Don'ts for Women," explaining such matters as how to endorse checks properly.[19]

By 1910 a more significant change occurred when articles began to appear addressed to women in the work force, parallels to the kinds of articles the *Post* had provided from the beginning for young men in business. At first, these pieces acknowledged the working woman, but did so from the point of view of her male employer. Business writer James H. Collins, for example, wrote a series called "The Art of Managing Women." Two years later the focus had changed along with the sex of the writer. In 1912 the *Post* published the first-hand reports of successful women who offered their own experience to women readers: Anne Shannon Monroe, "Making a Business Woman," and Ann O'Neill, "The Woman on the Road."[20]

A good deal of the *Post*'s success in treating the subject of women from a new point of view and with a new sense of audience must be attributed to the writing of Maude Radford Warren, who began publishing with the *Post* in 1909. By 1910 Warren was providing series of articles on subjects like "The New Woman and Her Ways" and "Petticoat Professions." Despite its coy title, "Petticoat Professions" expressed Warren's passionate feminism. After presenting detailed and engaging information on the history and current status of women in law, teaching, and the arts, she concluded with the hope that the women of her time were preparing for a better world in the future: "Perhaps it is not a Utopian dream that the professional woman of today is blazing a trail for that possible woman who, in a readjusted world, may have not only a profession, but a husband and children too." The following year, Warren went west to interview women who had bought land and were farming it. In the last article in her series, "A Woman Pioneer," she encouraged other women to come west where they would be rewarded with more financial opportunity and less male prejudice.[21]

The editorial page, too, reflected the *Post*'s new attitude toward women, for Lorimer had found someone who could assist him in learning to address a female audience. In 1909 Adelaide Neall joined the staff of the *Post*. A 1906 graduate of Bryn Mawr, Adelaide Neall was working as secretary of the Bryn Mawr School in Baltimore in 1908 when art editor Harry A. Thompson wrote to tell her that Lorimer was considering her for a position that had opened up on Thompson's staff. Neall had met Lorimer previously when both were on vacation in the West. Now she wrote to him explaining that she was unable to leave her position immediately, but had decided to move home to Philadelphia the next year and would be looking for a job. "It seems only fair to remind you," she added, "that I am a graduate of Bryn Mawr College which, if I remember correctly, will count against rather than for me!"[22]

In March 1909 Neall accepted a position with the *Post*, planning to begin in the fall. Lorimer, however, asked her to start at Easter, promising her "a rather better opening then than in the Autumn—a position for which I think you are particularly well fitted and from which you will able to look down on the charwoman with scorn and contempt."[23] But, she replied, "Much as I should like to lord it over the charwoman!" she could not leave the Bryn Mawr School till the term ended.

Adelaide Neall joined the *Post* in August. She was to become one of Lorimer's trusted editorial lieutenants, along with Frederick S. Bigelow, who started in 1899, and Churchill ("Churchy") Williams, who was hired late in 1906. Williams and Neall were especially engaged over the years ahead in working closely with *Post* writers, handling their correspondence and often working with them on revisions. In time, it became Neall's job to close the book, making the final check of every issue before it went to the printer.[24] Adelaide Neall stayed with the *Post* until 1942, a tenure nearly as long as Lorimer's own.

When she joined the *Post*, Neall became a member of the

editorial staff. Before the completion of the Curtis Building, the editorial group worked in small offices in Arch Street, and they were, as Neall recalled, "a small organization where everybody on the staff did a little of everything." From the outset, she was "an all-round and general member . . . of the Post during the period of its great expansion and growth."[25] And from the outset, Neall did well with the *Post*. By June 1910 she had received a pay increase from $20 to $25 a week, and late in 1911, she was raised to $30. And while Adelaide Neall was never a radical feminist, she had strong views about women's suffrage and women's education. It seems no accident that with her arrival at the *Post* the editorial page abandoned the conservative view and the complacent irony that had previously marked its comments on women.

Early in 1909, the editorial page expressed a positive attitude toward women and the vote; an editorial, headed "Why Women Shouldn't Vote" (February 13, 1909), satirized arguments against female suffrage. But later that same year, the *Post* spoke out more strongly, pointing out the folly of denying the vote in an editorial that commented favorably on the appointment of a woman to the post of school superintendent in Chicago.[26]

By 1913, *Post* editorials were arguing in favor of increased wages for women workers, and in the place of laments over the passing of the self-sacrificing homemaker of grandmother's day, addressing the miseries of the average housewife's lot. Editorial irony had found a different target.

Probably it is high time to stop talking nonsense to women about their sphere. So long as it did impose on them it was, of course, perfectly justifiable, for a man is foolish to pay his cook wages if he can keep her cheerful and willing by flattering conversation.

Housework, as the ordinary small American household is conducted, is excessively stupid and irksome. No intelligent white man would submit to it a week without running amuck and shooting up the place. To see anything inspiring in mopping the floor, dusting the furniture, making the beds and washing the dishes requires a power of imagination that can not reasonably be expected of an ordinary female, since only a few extraordinary males have possessed it.

The *Post* had not prematurely espoused the gender revolution, however. Women did have the right to find interests outside the home, the same editorial argued, but only after the dishes were washed. "Food must be cooked, floors mopped, dishes washed, stockings darned. When this dull work falls to the wife it is adding insult to injury to tell her she should never think of doing anything else—that performing labor the relative value of which is measured by a wage of about six dollars a week is the highest usefulness she can possible find. When the dishes are done she ought to have interests outside the house, as different and as stimulating as possible."[27]

No editorial would have appeared, as no articles or fiction ever appeared in the *Post,* without Lorimer's approval. But the editorial is not Lorimer's; it is not his style. It is tempting to see this editorial as the work of Adelaide Neall.

Women, then, were making a place for themselves in the *Saturday Evening Post*—on the editorial staff as well as on the editorial page and in the articles the *Post* was publishing. There was one place in the *Post,* however, that had always belonged to women and that was the cover. In the nine years of Lorimer's editorship preceding the "Not for Men Only" promotion, the *Post* had printed 170 covers with pictures of women; no doubt this figure would be even larger but for much of this period the cover illustration was tied to the lead story or article. In the six years from 1908 to 1913, when covers had become entirely independent, 142 of 313 covers featured women. Often the illustrations simply depicted a beautiful woman; this was particularly true of artists Harrison Fisher and Henry Hutt. Sometimes romance was suggested with a picture of a handsome young couple; seasonal themes appeared with Valentine hearts or Easter flowers. There might be the implication of dramatic action with a fallen book, a mast and sail, a football pennant, even a tennis racquet. But the essential subject remained the same—the picture of a woman.

The women on the covers, of course, had nothing whatever to do with the women in the articles and editorials. They represented

THE SATURDAY EVENING POST

An Illustrated Weekly
Founded A° D! 1728 by Benj. Franklin

AUG. 5, 1911   5 cts. THE COPY

LOVE LYRICS

MORE THAN A MILLION AND THREE-QUARTERS CIRCULATION WEEKLY

A romantic Harrison Fisher cover

neither the pre-1908 object of curiosity or disparagement nor the later subject of articles about women and suffrage, women and work, women and the West. The lovely females on the covers of the *Post* were merely another expression of the objectification of women, here idealized as objects of beauty and allure. And in an oblique way they realized in line and color the women appealed to in the *Post* advertisements; they represented, in their passive elegance, in their splendid settings and costumes, even in the props of sailboats or tennis racquets that surrounded them, fetishes of consumerism.

Post covers that did not feature women favored two other subjects, children and old people. In some cases, the pictures of children, especially the little girls painted by Sarah S. Stilwell Weber, were simply whimsical and romantic idealizations, miniatures of the lovely cover women. Like them, Weber's little girls appeared in attitudes and settings designed to enhance their charm; they flew kites, watered roses, cuddled kittens, or merely stood in a fantasy field of autumn leaves or spring flowers, birds and butterflies.[28] Little boys, conversely, and the elderly were used to tell comic stories, an art that Norman Rockwell would perfect in the years ahead. Whether charming or comic, children and the elderly were objectified in their own way on the covers of the *Post,* and, where humor was intended, these covers presented subjects that tapped common sources of amusement among the *Post*'s mass audience.

One way the cover artists of the *Post* appealed to that audience and, more significantly, contributed to the magazine's increasingly established identity was through the use of recurring characters. The most familiar was J. C. Leyendecker's New Year's baby, appearing first on December 29, 1906, with a list of New Year's resolutions and reappearing every New Year through and beyond the period of Lorimer's editorship. For the first few years, Leyendecker's baby was not confined to the New Year's cover but would appear at various holidays. He, or she, might become a delivery boy bringing Easter flowers or a chef preparing to carve the Thanksgiving turkey; she could be seen trying on her Easter bon-

Robert Robinson's old codger tries out the movies.

net and he might leap away from an exploding Fourth of July fire-cracker.[29] The Leyendecker baby in whatever guise was a figure entirely identified with American celebrations, American traditions, and the quintessentially American magazine—the *Saturday Evening Post.*

Another familiar cover character from these years was Robert Robinson's old man, a rural type, an "old codger" or "geezer." The old fellow recorded the seasons for *Post* readers, unfreezing his well with water from a teakettle or wiping his brow with a printed handkerchief during a heat wave. Occasionally, he served as a comment on current events: a November 1910 cover showed a general store, a picture of TR on the wall, one old fellow snoozing away while the codger speechified about the election. And he could experiment with newfangledness, sneaking into the movies or speeding along in an automobile.[30] But whatever his forays into the age of technology, Robinson's old codger made a nostalgic appeal. He was a complex, even a contradictory sign of values held to be enduring though embodied in the aged and the rural.

The familiar, recurring characters that appeared on the covers of the *Saturday Evening Post* had their counterparts inside the pages of the magazine in the fiction that a score of new writers brought to the *Post* in these years. The enormous popularity of the *Post* has often been attributed to the fiction it printed, its stylishness, humor, and generally high quality as popular entertainment. Certainly, in a period that marked the heyday of popular short fiction, the *Post* had its pick of the best. But despite the variety of stories in Lorimer's magazine, a great number shared one overridingly important characteristic: they were built around a character who returned in story after story.

By 1911, half a dozen new writers had appeared in the *Post,* all bringing characters who would become part of the contemporary popular culture: Irvin S. Cobb's Judge Priest, Peter Kyne's Cappy Ricks, George R. Chester's Get-Rich-Quick Wallingford, Montgomery Glass's Potash and Perlmutter, Mary Roberts Rinehart's Tish, and G. K. Chesterton's Father Brown. Over the next years, they would be joined by Octavus Roy Cohen's Florian Slappey,

Published Weekly

The Curtis Publishing
Company
Independence Square
Philadelphia

London: 6, Henrietta Street
Covent Garden, W.C.

THE SATURDAY
EVENING POST
Founded A°D¹ 1728 by Benj. Franklin

Copyright, 1916
by The Curtis Publishing Company in
the United States and Great Britain

Entered at the Philadelphia Post-Office
as Second-Class Matter

Entered as Second-Class Matter at the
Post-Office Department
Ottawa, Canada

Volume 188   PHILADELPHIA, APRIL 1, 1916   Number 40

My Country Tish of Thee—

By MARY ROBERTS RINEHART
ILLUSTRATED BY MAY WILSON PRESTON

"The Outside Edge, by George!" Said Charlie Sands. "The Old Sport!"

WE HAD meant to go to Europe this last summer, and Tish would have gone anyhow, war or no war, if we had not switched her off onto something else. "Submarines fiddlesticks!" she said. "Give me a good life preserver, with a bottle of blackberry cordial fastened to it, and the sea has no terrors for me."

She all the proper way to do, in case the ship was torpedoed, was to go up on an upper deck, and let the vessel sink under one.

"Then without haste," she explained, "as the water rises about one, strike out calmly. The life belt supports one, but swim gently for the exercise. It will prevent chilling. With a waterproof bag of crackers, and mild weather, one could go on comfortably for a day or two."

I still remember the despairing face Aggie turned to me. It was December then, and very cold.

However, she said nothing more until January. Early in that month Charlie Sands came to Tish's to Sunday dinner, and we were all there. The subject came up then.

It was about the time Tish took up vegetarianism. I remember that, because the only way she could induce Charlie Sands to come to dinner was to have two chops for him. Personally I am not a vegetarian. I am not and never will be. I took a firm stand except when at Tish's house. But Aggie followed Tish's lead, of course, and I believe lived up to it as far as possible, although it is quite true that, stopping in one day unexpectedly to secure a new crochet pattern, I smelled broiling steak. But Aggie explained that she merely intended to use the juice from a small portion, having had one of her weak spells, the balance to go to the janitor's dog.

However, this is a digression.

"Europe!" said Charlie Sands. "Forget it! What in the name of the gastric juice is this I'm eating?"

It was a mixture of bran, raisins and chopped nuts, as I recall it, moistened with water and pressed into a compact form. It was Tish's own invention. She called it Bran-nut, and was talking of making it in large quantities for sale.

Charlie Sands gave it up with a feeble gesture.

"I'm sorry, Aunt Letitia," he said at last; "I'm a strong man ordinarily, but by the time I've got it masticated I'm too weak to swallow it. If—if one could have a stream of water playing on it while working, it would facilitate things."

"The Ostermaiers," said Aggie, "are going West."

"Good for the Ostermaiers," said Charlie Sands. "Great idea. See America first. My Country Tish of Thee, etc. Why don't you three try it?"

Tish relinquished Europe slowly. "One would think," Charlie Sands said, "that you were a German being asked to give up Belgium."

"What part of the West?" she demanded. "It's all civilized, isn't it?"

"The Rocky Mountains," said Charlie Sands, "will never be civilized."

Tish broke off a piece of Bran-nut, and when she thought no one was looking poured a little tea over it. There was a gleam in her eye that Aggie and I have learned to know.

"Mountains!" she said. "That ought to be good for Aggie's hay fever."

"I'd rather live with hay fever," Aggie put in sharply, "than cure it by falling over a precipice."

"You'll have to take a chance on that, of course," Charlie Sands said. "I'm not sure it will be safe, but I am sure it will be interesting." Oh, he knew Tish well enough.

Tell her a thing was dangerous, and no power could restrain her. I do not mind saying that I was not keen about the thing. I had my fortune told years ago, and the palmist said that if a certain line had had a bend in it I would have been hanged. But since it did not, to be careful of high places.

"It's a sporting chance," said Charlie Sands, although I was prodding him under the table. "With some good horses and a bag of this—or—concentrated food, you would have the time of your young lives."

This was figurative. We are all of us round fifty.

"The—the Bran-nut," he said, "would serve for both food and ammunition. I can see you riding along, now and then dropping a piece of it on the head of some unlucky mountain goat, and watching it topple over into eternity. I can see—"

"Riding!" said Aggie. "Then I'm not going. I have never been on a horse, and I never intend to be."

"Don't be a fool," Tish snapped. "If you've never been on a horse it's time and to spare you got on one."

Hannah had been clearing the table with her lips shut tight. Hannah is an old and privileged servant and has a most unfortunate habit of speaking her mind. So now she stopped beside Tish.

"You take my advice and go, Miss Tish," she said. "If you ride a horse round some and get an appetite, you'll go down on your knees and apologize to your Maker for the stuff we've been eating the last four weeks." She turned to Charlie Sands, and positively her chin was quivering. "I'm a healthy woman," she said, "and I work hard and need good nourishing food. When it's come to a point where I eat the cat's meat and let it go hungry," she said, "it's time either I lost my appetite or Miss Tish went away."

Well, Tish dismissed Hannah haughtily from the room, and the conversation went on. None of us had been far West, although Tish has a sister-in-law in Toledo, Ohio. But owing to a quarrel over a pair of andirons that had been in the family for a long time she had never visited her.

"You'll like it, all of you," Charlie Sands said as we waited for the baked apples. "Once get started with a good horse between your knees, and——"

"I hope," Tish interrupted him, "that you do not think we are going to ride astride!"

"I'm darned sure of it."

That was Charlie Sands' way of talking. He does not mean to be rude, and he is really a young man of splendid character. But, as Tish says, contact with the world, although it has not spoiled him, has roughened his speech.

"You see," he explained, "there are places out there where the horses have to climb like goats. It's only fair to them to distribute your weight equally. A side saddle is likely to turn and drop you a mile or two down a crack."

Aggie went rather white and sneezed violently. But Tish looked thoughtful.

"It sounds reasonable," she said. "I've felt for a long time that I'd be glad to discard skirts. Skirts," she said, "are badges of servitude, survivals of the harem, reminders of a time when nothing was expected of woman but parasitic leisure."

I tried to tell her that she was wrong about the skirts. Miss MacGillicuddy, our missionary in India, had certainly said that the women in harems wore bloomers. But Tish left the room abruptly, returning shortly after with a volume of the encyclopedia, and looked up the Rocky Mountains.

I remember it said that the highest ranges were, as compared with the size and shape of the earth, only as the corrugations on the skin of an orange. Either the man who wrote that had never seen an orange or he had never seen the Rocky Mountains.

3

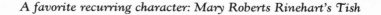

A favorite recurring character: Mary Roberts Rinehart's Tish

Arthur Train's Mr. Tutt, Ring Lardner's the Busher, and William Hazlett Upson's Earthworm Tractor salesman, Alexander W. Botts.

The idea of a series built around a recurring character was not, of course, new; Conan Doyle's Sherlock Holmes offers one striking earlier example. But in the pages of the *Post* this type of story flourished, virtually establishing a special subgenre in short fiction. Because stories built around a central, recurring character have become so familiar to us from radio and television, it requires an act of defamiliarization to comprehend how brilliantly the exploitation of this concept fitted Lorimer's plans for the *Post*. In the first place, he could manage at the same time both to steer clear of the contractual arrangements he so distrusted and yet be perfectly confident that stories about Judge Priest or Tish or Father Brown were stories that absolutely belonged in, even belonged *to*, the *Post*. It had been their birthplace and was consequently their natural place of residence. Beyond that, these stories and the characters they presented functioned like the *Post* covers to establish and maintain the *Post* identity. As early as 1910, they had become important enough for Lorimer to use them occasionally as leads, a position usually reserved for the first installments of serial fiction or major pieces of nonfiction.[31]

The recurring characters in *Post* fiction, like those on the *Post* covers, were woven out of stereotypes deeply embedded in American popular consciousness. As such, they reaffirmed popular attitudes and strengthened the values and prejudices of the broad middle-class, middlebrow community that made up the audience of the *Post*. While some of the characters presented were quasi-heroic, like Father Brown or even Rinehart's Tish, they were nearly always colored with a comedy that depended on stereotyping. Tish, for example, like Robert Robinson's old codger, was an elderly person essentially accepted as an object of fun. If Rinehart transcended the stereotype in a number of her stories, it nevertheless remained at the root of her character, at the very least the element against which ironic, and comic, triumphs could be counterpointed.

Some stereotypes were not so benign. Montgomery Glass's

Jewish businessmen and the comic black figures created by both Harris Dickson and Octavus Roy Cohen might have elicited a kind of comic affection from *Post* readers, but essentially they reinforced an ideology of white American supremacy. That ideology lay at the foundation of the *Post*'s dedication to the businessman and especially the young man making his way in America and the world, supported by the familiar cluster of businesslike virtues of industry, thrift, and ambition.

Whatever changes the appeal to women and the abundant new fiction brought to the *Post* in these years, the businessman remained the central focus and the principal audience. Lorimer continued to search for new ways to engage the interests and shape the attitudes of the businessman and, at the same time, revealed his own changing perception of this representative American.

Articles on the subject of business turned away from earlier themes, from exemplary life stories of self-made men and hortatory advice to young men starting out. New writers explored the world of business more objectively, explaining and analyzing a wide variety of subjects. While many of these articles remained essentially informative, offering advice and ideas, new rhetorical strategies were being discovered to package that information. Often an article would offer a hook to the reader, starting out with an extended anecdote, introducing characters, dialogue, and narrative so that fiction and nonfiction often seemed to blend into one another. This technique become so typical of nonfiction pieces in the Post as to become recognizably the *Post* style.

The *Post* found business everywhere. The arts became newly interesting when a business slant could be discovered; the *Post* published the views of syndicate owner Mark Claw and producer J. J. Schubert on the financial end of the theatrical syndicate. A how-to piece on "Making a Living by Literature" was offered anonymously. Sports, too, had a business aspect and B.B. Johnson, president of the American League, revealed the story of "The Business End of Baseball." Isaac Marcosson, one of the most important and versatile of *Post* writers, provided articles on the circus as a business proposition, and business writer James H. Collins managed to put together a whole series on "The Business Side of the Church." Collins explained away any seeming inappropriateness with entirely unintentional irony: "Poor business methods often begin with limited ideas about the functions of a church."[32]

Collins was the principal business writer for the *Post* at this time, as he would be for years to come. His forte was the series of articles built around a common idea: "The Buying End," "Your Relentless Competitors," "Interest—The Business Mainspring." A series on selling and salesmanship, always a key topic for *Post* business articles, included pieces that successfully incorporated the anecdote with practical advice: "Selling Without Samples," "Getting In— The Salesman's Entrance," "Getting Out—The Salesman's Exit."[33]

Collins did not have the business beat to himself. Isaac Marcosson handled larger financial and investment issues, especially the securities market. Forrest Crissey took on topics of more immediate interest to the reader looking for practical advice on a much smaller scale in articles like "Neglected Opportunities" or "Every Man His Own Merchant." Edwin Lefevre, another long-term *Post* writer, often contributed business articles, and like many of his *Post* colleagues showed considerable versatility, writing business fiction as well as a series on the question of securities and stock manipulation.[34] Investment—or speculation, depending on the writer's point of view—was an important problem after the panic of 1907, and with financier Roger Babson, who began to write for the *Post* in 1910, Lorimer found a man who could bring useful information on this subject to an audience of potential small-scale investors.

Babson's values, like Lorimer's, were profoundly those of nineteenth-century America; he believed "that *rewards* for industry, thrift and willingness to take risks are essential; while *punishment* for indolence, waste and cowardice is fundamental." But Babson had none of Lorimer's balance or judgment, and very little of what Lorimer himself would have called "common sense." He was immensely pleased with himself in the role of *Post* contributor, not precisely because it demonstrated the rewards due industry and thrift, but because the rewards themselves were so generous. His first piece, turned down by a financial magazine to which he had offered it free, earned $400 from the *Post*. In 1915, according to Babson, he earned over $20,000 for his *Post* contributions. More-over, looking back on what he called his "literary 'career,'" Babson was delighted to note, "Although I have since spent millions in paid advertising, none of it has equaled the efficiency of the space which has been given freely to me."[35]

Despite his ex post facto ebullience, the pieces Babson wrote for the *Post* were uncompromisingly educational and unremittingly sober: "When to Buy Stocks," "What Kinds of Bonds to Buy," "The Small Investor's Vocabulary" (November 5, 1910, April 1 and April 29, 1911). He took seriously indeed his responsibility to instruct about the equally serious subject of money. A more spe-cialized series of pieces in 1913 addressed the problem of small business loans; again, Babson carefully spelled out for the inex-perienced reader how to go about financing his business: "Do You Want More Money for Your Business?" and "How to Obtain Loans From Banks" (September 6 and 27, 1913). Babson was no master of the anecdote; probably he felt his subject too solemn for such levity. Moreover, he understood money and finance as responding to economic law with the same inexorableness with which *rewards* or *punishment* followed industry or indolence. In introducing the 1913 articles on business finance, he wrote, "In this series of articles I hope to show that the business man, however strong may be his intentions, can no more escape the laws of finance than he can the law of gravity."

Series like those by Babson reveal that the businessman, as implied audience for the *Post*, was undergoing change. At the out-set, Lorimer had emphasized the young man starting out and a considerable number of business articles had provided advice and general moral counsel to this neophyte. Now, the businessman the *Post* addressed was, like the *Post* itself, more successful, more estab-lished. As a result, a great many articles now emphasized practical information on matters like financing a business or on hiring and managing employees. Not that these articles were intended for the heads of great corporations, rather that the *Post*'s young businessman was beginning to get ahead, even if in a small way.

An important index to Lorimer's conception of his audience lies in the back-of-the-book departments the *Post* ran at this time. Between 1906 and 1913, six new departments were introduced offering information on business or investment. "Shop Talk," the first of these, was a readers' forum on business; the *Post* asked readers to send in their ideas, 500 words or fewer, adding, "What we accept we will pay well for." The result was an uneasy collection of practical advice and moral anecdote, ranging from "Collecting an Overdue Account" to "How I Lost My First Job" (July 28 and March 24, 1906). Whether practical or moral, "Shop Talk" contributions were distinctly small-time and seemed designed to bring to the *Post* audience the considerable population of workingmen whose occupations and incomes placed them marginally, if at all, in the middle class.

That same audience was addressed in "Thrift," beginning two years later in 1908 and offering anecdotes that demonstrated how the cardinal virtue of thrift could overcome all manner of obstacles on the way to success. Some stories were little more than wholesale adaptations of Horatio Alger. One, for example, told of a seventeen-year-old boy who earned $10 a month and saved a dollar a week. At the end of one year, he had saved $61 and spent $60 of it on a cow which he resold a few days later for $75. Improving on that experience, he bought and resold a horse and then a carriage. At nineteen he had $185 in the bank. Pluck was then rewarded with luck. The local newspaper printed his story and a reader, who had started in the same way, made him the proprietor of a chain of dairy lunchrooms.[36]

Most back-of-the-book departments, however, appealed to the somewhat more affluent, upwardly mobile young businessman. Departments like "Your Savings" and "The Forehanded Man" did continue to preach diligence and especially thrift, but they were clearly addressed to an audience for whom the exercise of thrift had already paid off in the accumulation of some capital.

These readers were now in a position to begin to invest the money they had saved.

"Your Savings" began in 1907 with an announcement that promised advice and information to would-be investors. "It is with the problem of the average man or woman with savings or other funds to invest that The Saturday Evening Post will now concern itself, and will publish each week a department that will endeavor to set forth, simply and concretely, the safest way to invest money to get the best possible return. This information will be gathered from the most reliable sources . . . and will aim to reach every class of conservative investment."[37] Lorimer was very serious about the "conservative investment," and particularly concerned to educate his readers away from unsound speculations.

The panic of 1907 had offered a moral lesson for investors; Lorimer summed it up in two words: "Don't speculate."[38] Very much a man of the nineteenth century in this regard, Lorimer believed a man's first responsibility was to earn a living and support his family, then to save enough to provide against emergency and support his old age, finally to invest with care whatever money he had over and above that necessary amount. Speculation, unlike investment, promised especially high returns and involved equally high risks, both of which stemmed from uncertain and often unsavory business methods.

Therefore, "Your Savings" offered a curriculum in conservative investment. Week after week it presented information on "Short-Term Notes and Bond Bargains," "Municipal Bonds as Investments," "Puts, Calls and Arbitrage," "The Facts About Receivers' Certificates."[39] As the American businessman grew more affluent, the Post was at his elbow with economic advice grounded in a blend of financial acumen and old-fashioned morality.

But sometimes the economic morality of "Your Savings" ran into conflict with that expounded in "Thrift." On August 13, 1910, "Your Savings" presented a piece on "Investing Your First Thousand Dollars," not an insignificant amount of money. A year and a half earlier, the same department had explained just how that first thousand might be got together; "How Money Grows" (January 30,

1909) carefully explained how thirty cents a day saved at 4 percent would grow to $1336.59 in ten years. Thirty cents a day does not seem an unreasonable amount to put aside each day, but for many *Post* readers it might have been impossible to do so. Those were the readers for whom "Thrift" explained how one could live "On Ten Dollars a Week" (October 22, 1910), but not how one could manage to save thirty cents a day, an amount that would have represented 20 percent of a ten-dollar-a-week salary. The *Post's* businessman was, generally, prospering, but old habits died hard.

The educational mission of the *Post* was directed first at business, but business was never a narrow concept for Lorimer. Almost always, it was inextricably intertwined with politics. In the most general way, Lorimer understood the role of the businessman as including and assuming that of the responsible and active citizen. Equally important was the way in which, for Lorimer, government—or more precisely, Republican government as he ideally imagined it—was the natural political reflection of a nation of businessmen, of the America his *Post* had set about creating. The American Lorimer addressed was the businessman, engaged in making his way, supporting himself, saving and investing. The America he was constructing was simply an aggregate of such businessmen, and the American government the necessary reflection of the aggregate: the government was responsible for making America's way in the world, expanding its markets and spreading its values, securing its future.

It was always Lorimer's public contention that the *Post* was nonpartisan. As early as 1904 he had established the convention of offering arguments in favor of each presidential candidate by leading spokesmen for the two major parties. That kind of evenhandedness supported Lorimer's representation of his magazine as a forum for competing ideas. Insofar as this "equal time" arrangement was concerned, the *Post* was indeed the partisan of neither party. In fact, the *Post*, like Lorimer, was Republican in outlook and ideology, sometimes progressive Republican and sometimes conservative Republican, but always Republican.

The contradiction between a Republican point of view and the *Post*'s much vaunted nonpartisanship was more complicated than it appears; it was not merely a question of speaking for one set of political values under the guise of political independence. The prob- lem was that the Republican party almost never satisfied Lorimer's own Republicanism. He especially decried the political machines that kept power locked in the hands of political bosses and, more often than not, was deeply disappointed in the presidential candi- dates those bosses managed to nominate. Nevertheless, in 1908 when Roosevelt declined to run, Lorimer swallowed his disappoint- ment and offered moderate support for Taft, despite his misgivings about the man.

But in 1910, when Beveridge ran for reelection to the Senate, Lorimer took a more determined stand. Not only were the men by now intimate friends who shared the deepest political convictions, but Beveridge's election was challenged in Indiana by Stand Pat Republicans led by organization politicians. The Indiana Senate race, moreover, was a rehearsal for the presidential election in 1912: Insurgents against entrenched Old Guard power and the machine. For all these reasons, and despite the fact that political endorsement was unprecedented in the *Post*, Lorimer endorsed Beveridge in a late September editorial. "The most important election to be held this fall is in Indiana, because nowhere else is the issue between popular and machine government quite so sharply drawn. Senator Beveridge broke with the organization of his own party when that became necessary in order faithfully to represent the people of his state."

The position that Lorimer was developing in the Beveridge editorial represented his first clear attack on the party system itself, an attack made on two fronts: political parties were dominated by bosses who ran the parties in their own self-interest, and neither major party represented anything like a coherent political point of view. Sometimes one argument and sometimes another dominated in the *Post*. In 1910, the bosses were the target; by 1912, both attacks would be mounted. In either case, the mission Lorimer set himself was to educate the voter away from party loyalty, lecturing him about his responsibility to stop cheering for parties and to start voting for accountable men. One of the chief problems with Taft, the *Post* argued, was precisely his party loyalty: "The very notion of a President as the servant of a party is repugnant."[40]

Lorimer's endorsement of Beveridge thus rested on his support of the interests of the people against party politics and the machine. The question the Indiana election would answer was "whether a majority of the people will recognize public service above party label." The voter who "believes in government for the people, instead of government for 'the interests' . . . knows from strenuous experience which side Senator Beveridge is on."[41]

When Beveridge lost, the *Post* put the best face it could on the election results, expressing its pleasure at seeing the number of Insurgents in the House doubled.[42] But what Lorimer learned was that the influence of his magazine had not been adequate to counter that of the organization politicians who worked for Beveridge's defeat. The Indiana election confirmed his contempt for party politics, corrupted by machines entirely under the control of self-interested bosses.

There was, as well, another issue at stake, the issue of precisely how much political power Lorimer and the *Post* actually wielded. The Beveridge election had proven the *Post* less effective than the party bosses, but that same year Lorimer, along with Curtis, had been successful in challenging the Taft administration when it proposed to reduce the postal deficit by charging higher rates for magazines. Facing this kind of financial threat, the *Post* and the Curtis Company led a coalition of periodicals in a political battle with the Taft administration. Cyrus Curtis allied with his colleagues in the Periodical Publishers' Association of America to defeat the rate increase, and as president of the association in 1910, he assumed a leading role in garnering support for the Carter bill, which sought to amend the postal laws so as to "place the Post Office Department on an efficient business basis."[43] Curtis was elected to the association presidency for three terms during this period, a responsibility he was willing to assume to see the postal campaign through.

Lorimer, meanwhile, used the pages of the *Post* for a barrage of editorials and articles aimed at attacking the administration and offering a solution to the postal deficit through the application of business methods to the Post Office Department. More generally he set about a counterattack that involved educating Americans about the true nature of the periodical and, equally, about the true nature of magazine advertising. Increased postal rates threatened the *Post* economically; when Lorimer finished his campaign, increased postal rates were seen as threatening America. In this campaign, as Lorimer explained to Beveridge, he would use his best weapon, his editorial pages.

I don't believe the [Post Office] department can put that postal increase across, once the country is educated up to the facts. But the average reader shares the ignorance of the Postmaster General about the publishing business.

We propose to start in on a little campaign of education, no matter what Congress may see fit to do.[44]

Lorimer set about alleviating the ignorance of the public. The government's contention was that higher postal rates were appropriate for magazines since they carried advertising.[45] That contention, Lorimer argued, made clear the government's "failure to understand the true significance and importance of advertising, not only to a magazine's readers, but to the business development of the whole country." Thus, the *Post* would explain the true nature of advertising. "Advertising is true pioneering. It is the great creator of new business, the great expander of old. The typical trust waits for some one else to create a new demand, to open a new market, and then it comes along with 'something just as good.' Advertising is today the mainstay of independent business: it is the bulwark of little business against big business; it is the one open path straight to the consumer; it is the small man's chance to win on the sheer merit of his goods and the brains that he puts into pushing them, against the brute strength of the most powerful trust."[46]

The brilliance of the editorial lay not only in the way it defended the magazines in their use of advertising but also in the way it implied an alliance between the Taft administration, particularly but of course not exclusively in the instance of the postal rates, with "big business" and the "typical trust." Against this Goliath were ranked the little guy, the small businessman, and his friend the *Saturday Evening Post*, which buttressed editorials with a piece on "That Postal Deficit" and followed with a series on "The Popular Magazines." Magazines, like the advertising they carried, were the friend of the economically powerless, "a potent force for the protection of the small investor," willing not only to refuse "unsafe, speculative and swindling [advertising] schemes," but to "maintain departments for the financial education of their readers along sound, conservative lines."[47]

The editorial on advertising spoke to the American as the independent businessman *and* as a Progressivist at heart, for behind the editorial lay Lorimer's own political beliefs as well as his conception of the American as a participant in the political process. The education provided by the *Post* was intended to serve the American in his double capacity as businessman and citizen. In his attack on the postal rate increase, Lorimer was not merely protecting the *Post* financially; he was mounting an attack on Old Guard Republicanism.

Lorimer's success in the postal rate battle strengthened his belief in the ability of the *Post* to shape American politics. That belief depended in part on the influence that a circulation of nearly 2 million and an estimated readership of nearly 10 million was assumed to wield. But it also depended on the way in which Lorimer saw politics as a necessary reflection of American life and values. He was neither an idealist nor naively optimistic, but he saw in the creation of a nation of businessmen the complementary creation of a nation of politically educated and politically active citizens. Against such a citizenry, weaned from party loyalty, the political machine would be powerless. The *Post*'s political responsibility, then, was to educate the businessman-citizen.

The 1912 campaign, promising a confrontation between Insurgent and Stand Pat Republicans for control of the party and the nomination, offered Lorimer another chance to teach his readers how to fight the bosses in the interest of Progressivism. But Roosevelt, by waiting too long before announcing his candidacy, lost ground, and as Beveridge wrote to Lorimer in May, Taft already had the convention delegates in his pocket.[48] Beveridge remained loyal, nonetheless, opening TR's campaign in Chicago and making speeches across the country in support of his nomination. Soon both he and Lorimer had talked themselves into a more optimistic frame of mind, based on what Beveridge believed to be the extent of popular support for TR in the Middle West. For a month before the Republican convention at the end of June, *Post* editorials were driving home the significance of the popular vote and attacking the evils of a convention system that allowed the organization politicos to ignore the voters' preferences and principles.[49]

Lorimer watched the convention closely, ready to bring the *Post* into action. Late in June, he told Beveridge he was waiting for the outcome of the convention "holding open both the Editorial page and the leading pages of the number which goes to press the last of the week. I felt I must handle the copy for these pages personally."[50] The editorial that followed Taft's nomination was savage about the victory of the party organization allied with the conservatives. The convention, Lorimer wrote, demonstrated that "we have here a true-blue Tory party, dedicated to the principle that the wise and right-minded minority should rule." But there was a bright side. Surely a new party would grow out of the debacle of this convention, "a clear-cut, out-and-out genuinely democratic and insurgent party."[51]

While Lorimer's editorials hammered away at the party system, political articles by Sam Blythe reported on the mood of the electorate. Blythe was an experienced political journalist whose stout figure and benign face belied his energy, intellectual penetration, and shrewd irony. A contemporary called him "the mounted police of literature, with his guns trained on pretense."[52] And Beveridge believed his conversation, "which [was] even better than his writing," made him "the American Sam Johnson."[53] Blythe was the *Post*'s star political writer, but with remarkable versatility he also contributed serial fiction, humorous articles, and, anonymously, regular features on Washington mores and personalities and a series of memoirs about his career in newspaper journalism.[54]

In 1912 Blythe toured the nation, as he would in election years throughout Lorimer's tenure at the *Post*. He was expert at getting the feel of the political situation in every region of the country and at writing articles that combined accurate reporting with shrewd editorializing. By the fall of 1912, however, with the Republican party split by the defection of the Progressives and a Democratic victory anticipated, Blythe was in the awkward position of having to write the kind of savvy analysis and prediction that had gained him his reputation and at the same time not throwing in the Roosevelt towel. This task was not made easier by the necessary time lag between writing and publication, a minimum of three weeks.

In mid-September Blythe wrote an article with a number of "conclusions," or predictions, principally forecasting that "Mr. Roosevelt's nomination makes the defeat of Mr. Taft almost certain," and that "Mr. Roosevelt's nomination makes the election of Mr. Wilson probable." Simple political logic supported these conclusions, but warned Blythe, "there is absolutely no basis for any political logic in this campaign. New conditions exist. A revolution is underway." Echoing Lorimer's views on the editorial page, Blythe promised a revolution that would emancipate the voter from party obligation; men would now cast their votes "for personal, independent, individual, constructive reasons."[55] In his final article before the election, however, Blythe was not so sanguine. He acknowledged Wilson's "seeming advantage" and could only promise that TR would "poll a tremendous vote."[56]

To the editorials and political articles in the *Post* during the 1912 campaign were added the requisite nonpartisan pieces in support of each candidate. But this year, these pieces were written, or at least signed, by the candidates themselves, a striking measure of the growing prestige of Lorimer's magazine. On October 19, the lead article featured William Howard Taft on the subject of "The Supreme Issue." After a series of paragraphs boasting of the history of the party that "freed the slaves," Taft attempted to rebut the

Progressives' claim that he had sold out to the entrenched Old Guard, especially in regard to his stand on the tariff, a stand he defended. Overall, he insisted, "I defy any man to prove that I have ever been false to my solemn responsibilities, have ever betrayed the trust reposed in me." But he was no radical; the "people," he proclaimed, were not only "the unfortunate and the weak," but all kinds of Americans. The "people," moreover, would not be swayed by "the sugar-coated nostrums of the third party."

Roosevelt led off the October 26 issue with "The Deceitful Red Herring," his characterization of the tariff issue. The real issue was "social and industrial justice." The Progressive platform was a "covenant with the people," and TR pledged to fulfill the promise of that platform in areas like industrial accidents, occupational safety, and health standards. Action was the keynote of the Roosevelt article and the writing itself bristled with energy as compared with the bluster of the Taft piece.

Woodrow Wilson wrote with cool reason, filling only the half page below the conclusion of Roosevelt's piece. The Democrats were longtime progressives, a party that opposed the idea of a government "that dispenses special favors, and that is always controlled by those to whom the special favors are dispensed." The tariff was an issue only because it protected privilege. Finally, Wilson pointed out, the Democrats were "not embarrassed by alliances." He had won the nomination in defiance of the party bosses, as *Post* editorials had noted, and could state, therefore, that he was "absolutely free." [57]

The presidential election may have been a foregone conclusion, but that was not the case with the governor's race in Indiana, in which Beveridge was running on the Progressive ticket. As Lorimer had broken precedent with his 1910 editorial endorsement for Beveridge, he now broke his own editorial rules by sending Beveridge an advance copy of a piece supporting his candidacy. "Here's a little editorial about you which we are going to run in our October 19th issue," Lorimer wrote. "Tear it up after you have read it, as it is against our rules here to slip out any advance stuff." [58] The editorial, titled "Beveridge in Indiana" (October 19, 1912), called for the people of that state to "perform a service to the nation, as well as to themselves" by returning Beveridge to public life.

Beveridge lost again, and his defeat was more of a blow than Roosevelt's anticipated loss to Wilson. Lorimer made the best of the situation by announcing the death of the Republican party, now no more than "a historic name." He prophesied a similar fate for the Democrats and the consequent birth of new parties based on real political differences.[59] These predictions were echoed in an article by Beveridge in the last issue of the year. "The Future of the Progressive Party" (December 28, 1912) argued that the Progressives were now "the minority party, the second party in numbers." Moreover, the Progressives would not reunite with the Republicans to form a single party; rather, they would continue to represent the liberal force in American politics. And when a new conservative party arose, America would have an honorable political system, no longer marked by the "sham battles" of the present.

By most measures the *Saturday Evening Post* had shown itself to advantage during the 1912 election. Lorimer's editorials were pungent and incisive, and Blythe's articles racy, tough, informative; beyond that, the candidates had appeared in person in the pages of the magazines. But by the measure of political effectiveness, the election year had demonstrated all too clearly the limits of the *Post*'s power and influence. Despite the *Post,* Taft was nominated as the Republican candidate, and despite the *Post,* Roosevelt could not poll a majority of the vote, nor could Beveridge win the gubernatorial race in Indiana. It was extremely unlikely, to be sure, that any medium, no matter how popular, could have effected these outcomes; still, that was what Lorimer had been aiming at and, in failing, had discovered the limits of his power. It was a lesson he failed to profit from.

"A Great Social Influence"

World War I was the great watershed for Lorimer's *Saturday Evening Post*. A buoyant and optimistic magazine in 1914, by 1918 the *Post* had grown suspicious and defensive, expounding a shrill and virulent nativism. The change was permanent, and though in good times Lorimer might modulate his intensity, this new attitude and tone characterized the *Post* for the remaining years of his editorship. The dramatic shift in the *Post* can be traced through Lorimer's responses to the war, through his own move from neutrality to belligerence.

Lorimer's stand on neutrality was an expression of his vigorous patriotism. The America he created in the pages of his magazine represented the future and celebrated manly competition, progress, and common sense. War was unnecessary, outmoded—in fact, unthinkable. War bled the treasuries and depleted the resources of a nation, resources necessary for business and industrial progress, therefore for national progress as a whole. America had geography, history, and destiny to protect it from war; to join the conflict would be to march backward into Old World barbarism.[1]

Nor was Lorimer especially in sympathy with Europe. Europe, a victim of its "tangled alliances," now revealed itself as retrograde. War was evidence enough, but in addition, the very alliances forged by war gave further proof that Europe had turned back the calendar, denying the twentieth century itself and the progress of civilization. Particularly insofar as progress was reflected in political systems, European alliances seemed forged by a perverse illogic. France and Germany, nations that led "the van of civilization," should be the "staunchest allies." Instead, due to festering old hostilities, each had turned against the other and joined forces with a retrograde nation, France with "Cossack Russia" and Germany with "Bourbon Austria."[2] The result could be nothing but economic ruin, and the victims, "commonplace" families. Wars, the *Post* determined, would continue until such families learned to tell their political and military leaders, "Excuse me! I have no sons to be shot in a game of statecraft. If you want to maintain, by force of arms, a theory about balance of power, go do the fighting yourself!"[3]

Moreover, Lorimer personally had little if any sentimental affection for European art and culture; the culture of the Old World had as little allure for him as did its politics. It was not until 1913 that the prosperous Lorimer followed other rich Americans abroad for a European excursion[4] and, when he did so, whatever pleasure he might have taken in European travel was carefully camouflaged in letters that adopted the style and spirit of Mark Twain's narrator in *The Innocents Abroad*. From Rome he wrote to Beveridge complaining of masterpieces and saints. "If anyone leads me up to another bum old master, or lures me down into a cellar to hold an inquest on the remains of a saint, I shall simply hit him once, but there will be another martyr to venerate. The particular pastime here seems to be kissing St. Peter's Toe and I prospected a little yesterday, but the kissing didn't look good to me, though these people are perfect hogs for it."[5]

Given Lorimer's scorn for war and his unsentimental view of Europe, his response to the outbreak of the war was a foregone conclusion: a thoroughgoing disgust at Old World politics and an intensified pride in a young America, free of sordid entanglements. For two and a half years, Lorimer firmly maintained his stand on neutrality, but the declaration of war in 1917 forced him to abandon his antiwar and isolationist position. With America at war, Lorimer dedicated the power and influence of the *Post* to his country, supporting the war effort without stint or reservation.

The war, however, brought a profound and permanent change in Lorimer's conception of America itself. Before the war, the *Post* had constructed a vision of America as shaped and structured through business. Whatever the philosophical shortcomings of that vision might have been, it had the value of being positive and constructive, with no need to shore itself up with hostility or defensiveness. As a result, a lively good nature characterized the magazine; it was optimistic, liberal, expansive. Broadly speaking, while Lorimer acknowledged and faced opposition, the *Post* and the America it created in its pages were without sinister enemies. Young and strong, they could look with tolerance and cool appraisal at other people's bugaboos; they had nothing to fear from socialism, the Yellow Peril, or any other exaggerated popular menaces.

With the war came the threat of massed enemy forces, not only abroad but at home. At first these were German agents, saboteurs, as well as those who abetted them—a widening population of socialists, radicals, immigrant Americans. After 1917 and the Russian revolution there were Bolshevists, subversives, and again immigrant Americans. The threat was hydra-headed; even jazz undermined Americanism. Against these enemies the *Post* became the champion of what Lorimer determined was truly American. Certainly, Lorimer had always defined the America his magazine represented, but by the end of the war his definition had grown much narrower. What had perhaps always been implicit in the *Post*—a conception of a mainstream, white, middle-class America—now became explicit, and it became exclusive.[6]

As Lorimer's America changed, so did his rhetoric; his tough, racy prose was now larded with venomous language. In 1914 the *Post* stated coolly, "Our most dependable national defenses against war are justice, moderation and good will."[7] By 1918 those virtues had been abandoned; a *Post* editorial that year sought to encourage the war effort at home in a harangue that told readers they must not only suppress German-language papers and the teaching of German in the schools, "those centers of anti-Americanism and German propaganda," but even "take Broadway in hand" in order to "do something to the swine soul of the crowd that leads the jazz life; that swills and guzzles."[8]

It must be kept in mind that at least 10 million people a week read the *Saturday Evening Post* during World War I; the constant repetition of these themes in editorials, articles, fiction, and cartoons worked to create a broad-based acceptance of the terms of Lorimer's Americanism. As Will Irwin, a major *Post* writer during the war years, cynically expressed it, "In pouring the plastic American mind into certain grooves, [Lorimer] had a great social influence."[9]

Whatever Lorimer's own attitude to war in 1914, the opening of hostilities in August represented news, and he immediately made plans for the *Post*'s coverage of the European war. At the same time, he managed a kind of restraint, keeping much of the magazine focused on conventional, prewar subject matter. Nevertheless, his journalistic instincts were aroused. During the first year of the war, his own intention to limit war coverage in the *Post* came into conflict with his editorial desire for first-rate material.

Lorimer's initial action was to send two of his top men abroad, political journalist Sam Blythe and humorist Irvin Cobb. Blythe was to cover England and France from their capital cities; Cobb was assigned to travel to Belgium and from there to try to reach the war zone. Paradoxically, the experienced Blythe sent back mediocre work, while Cobb's war articles proved a sensation.

Blythe sailed August 7 and his first article appeared September 12. As his reports continued through November, they recorded his growing apprehension of horror. From London he wrote with a kind of somber wonder at the scale of the war, talking of a "world . . . being overturned" and warning of "a slaughter unparalleled in history."[10] Two months later he found himself entirely unnerved by the number of dead and wounded, "a toll so terrible that no human intelligence can understand it."[11] For Blythe, with his combination of savvy and cynicism, the war was not a sympathetic subject. Still, he had been affected by a journalist's need to see, to find out, as well as by a kind of restlessness engendered by the war. By the spring of

Irvin S. Cobb

1915 he was sending articles from China and from there he went on to Russia.

Before the war, Irvin Cobb had succeeded at the *Post* with fiction and his own brand of humor, a kind of deadpan confrontation with the absolutely ordinary, subjects like "Hair" or "Teeth," or a satiric view of grander subjects grounded in an apologetic self-mockery. In 1912, for example, he took on the high arts, and his unashamed debunking of elite entertainment was perfectly contrived to win the affection of the *Post*'s middlebrow audience. Here he describes a pianist at a musicale as she reaches the climax of the piece.

All of a sudden the lady operator comes out of her trance. She comes out of it with a violent start, as though she had just been bee-stung. She now cuts loose, regardless of the cost of the piano and its associations to its owner. . . . She grabs the helpless thing by its upper lip and tries to tear all its front teeth out with her bare hands. She fails in this, and then she goes mad from disappointment and in a frenzy resorts to her fists. . . .

As the crashing reverberations die away the lady arises, wan but game, and bows low in response to the applause and backs away, leaving the wreck of the piano pushed back on its haunches and trembling like a leaf in every limb.[12]

Cobb's eye for the ridiculous and the language with which he exploited it might not have seemed the right mix of skills for reporting on war. Even his departure for Europe had its ludicrous aspect. Because of the uncertainty about money orders being honored in countries at war, the *Post* provided for Cobb's expenses with $5,000 in gold. He strapped these coins around his very substantial middle and went off to war "jingling like a milk wagon."[13] As it turned out, his articles were remarkable. Between October 10, 1914, and January 30, 1915, they provided a blend of war reportage and personal experience as Cobb traveled by taxi and dogcart and foot through Belgium and into the German lines. His comic sense served him well in dealing with his own naivete and enthusiasm and in recounting the adventures he shared with fellow journalists Will

Irwin and John T. McCutcheon. But when he arrived at scenes of war, he became acute, sensitive, and penetrating. He had an eye for the symbolic and sentimental detail, like a rag doll on the road, "its head crushed in the wheel tracks" of military vehicles, as well as for the somber spectacle of armies on the march.

> We stayed in Louvain three days, and for three days we watched the streaming past of the biggest army we had ever seen, and the biggest army beleaguered Belgium had ever seen, and of the biggest, most perfect armies the world has ever seen. We watched the gray-clad columns pass until the mind grew numb at the prospect of computing their number. To think of trying to count them was like trying to count the leaves on a tree or the pebbles on a path.
>
> They came and they came, and kept on coming, and their iron-shod feet flailed the earth to powder, and there was no end to them.[14]

Partly because of his aversion to war and partly because he shared the widespread opinion that the war would not last long, Lorimer laid no plans for extensive, long-term coverage. Having sent Blythe and Cobb abroad, he limited any additional overseas war reporting to selected writers he believed especially well equipped for a particular assignment.

But if Lorimer was not searching for war correspondents, American journalists were struggling to find a way to get to the war. A good number of them wanted to get there courtesy of the *Saturday Evening Post*, among them Will Irwin and Ernest Poole. Will Irwin, who ended up junketing through Belgium with Cobb, had graduated from Stanford, where he first came to know Herbert Hoover, and then gone to New York as a reporter on the *Sun* and later as editor of *McClure's*. He had done some work, mostly fiction, for the *Post* since 1909, and early in 1914 Lorimer offered him a chance to leave off reporting in order to concentrate on fiction—for the *Post*: "Why don't you have a sustained go at fiction?" Lorimer suggested to him; "Write me another batch of short stories. I won't guarantee to take them all, but your batting average with us is high."[15] When the war started a few months later, Irwin telephoned Lorimer, asking to cover the war for the *Post*. "Full up!"

Lorimer told him. "Irvin Cobb, Sam Blythe, and Mary Rinehart applied ahead of you." Irwin finally arranged for *Collier's* and *American Magazine* to send him, but in 1917 when the United States entered the war, he became one of Lorimer's principal war correspondents, covering France and Italy.

Ernest Poole had slightly better luck with Lorimer. After graduating from Princeton, where he had studied with Woodrow Wilson, Poole devoted himself to the cause of the poor, moving to the University Settlement House on New York's Lower East Side. In 1905 he went to Russia, and subsequent articles on this subject brought him some recognition. He first appeared in the *Post* in 1906 with short stories about immigrants struggling to gain a foothold in America. These were sympathetic stories, told in the first person, and they represented one of the few ways in which the immigrant's plight was taken up in the *Post*. Both Poole and Irwin were a good deal more radical in their views than Lorimer, but fiction offered one way in which the *Post* could comfortably treat material of this kind. As Irwin noted in his autobiography, "Lorimer did most of his mild muckraking in the form of fiction."[16]

In the fall of 1914, Poole was working on his radical labor novel, *The Harbor,* when he decided to go to Europe. But fall was too late; all the magazine editors Poole knew "had men on British, French and Belgian fronts." He went to Philadelphia and Lorimer agreed to give him Germany. It was, Lorimer said, Poole's "only chance. . . . It isn't yet covered."[17] They arranged for one article, "Berlin," which appeared in April 17, 1915. Like Irwin, Poole's real chance came with America's entry into the war. In 1917 and 1918, when he returned to Russia after the revolution, he contributed important material to the *Post*.

As Lorimer had told Will Irwin, Mary Rinehart was among those who had "already applied" to go to Europe for the *Post* and Lorimer agreed to send her as long as she "really mean[t] business."[18] Rinehart indeed meant business, but her husband was aghast at the idea, and by the end of September the project was scrapped, or so it appeared. But Lorimer apparently liked the idea of a woman correspondent on the war, for on August 3 he had wired Corra Harris, "How would you like to spend a few weeks in London for us doing the woman's side of the war[?]"[19]

The *Post* had anonymously published Corra Harris's enormously popular novel, *A Circuit Rider's Wife,* in 1910.[20] Letters poured in, testifying to the "truth" of the novel and refusing to accept it as fiction. They cheered Harris's conservative attitudes, which reflected those of her audience, "an American middle class reared in an agrarian Protestant society."[21] From Lorimer's point of view, he had just the person to handle the woman's side of the war.

But in Corra Harris's case, Lorimer was wrong. As her biographer, John E. Talmadge, explains, her "anti-British feelings came alive" in London and she was disappointed and puzzled not to find the city festive with martial displays. She ran afoul of members of the Woman's Emergency Corps and Lord Kitchener's staff. From France she made a futile effort to get to the front and, after a second short period in England, returned home. Her articles began late in November and continued into February, but they elicited no enthusiastic response.[22]

Outside of reports from Europe, the *Post*'s war coverage in 1914 was uneven and uncertain, made up essentially of a scattering of articles analyzing the effect of the war on various aspects of American life. Such articles amounted to little more than the work of familiar *Post* writers offering a new slant on their equally familiar beats. The effect of war on business and trade fell to business writer Will Payne, who did a series in October on subjects like "War and Business" and "War and the Home Market." Corinne Lowe, who covered, among other things, various aspects of society life, gently mocked Americans discomfited by the halt in European travel or the sudden unavailability of French couturier clothes. Medical writer Woods Hutchinson turned to war with an article on the upbeat side of wounds from modern weapons. As bad as war might seem, Hutchinson found "considerable ground for encouragement" in antiseptic surgical practices and in "modern high-velocity bullets," which were "absolutely sterile." He offered advice as well: "It is particularly desirable before going into battle to put on a suit of clean underwear." The grim disparity between such wholesome advice and the realities of trench warfare highlights the innocence of the *Post,* and of much of America, in the face of the European war.[23]

The war was almost entirely ignored by *Post* fiction writers in 1914; only lawyer and crime writer Melville Davisson Post wrote a war story, the first Lorimer published, on October 31, 1914. "The Miller of Ostend" is a grisly tale of Belgian vengeance. An old miller loses his son in the German advance, and his granddaughter, who has gone to help the queen at Kursaal, is killed when the Germans shell the town. That night, carrying a scrap of cloth with a red cross on it, the miller collects some wounded German soldiers, and the story reaches its emblematic end:

At sunrise the uhlans advancing along the Brussels road saw a thing that all the multiple horrors of the Great Mad War could never blur nor efface.

In an old timber windmill of the earliest Belgian type, with a tiny muslin red cross tacked on the door, a stooped peasant was grinding wheat; while, lashed to the great arms in place of canvas sails, four human bodies turned in a ghastly circle in the sky.

Among *Post* artists only Leyendecker attempted cover art that reflected the war in Europe. Leyendecker painted the *Post*'s first war cover on October 3, showing Uncle Sam reading a newspaper headlined, "Great Battle Raging." Two weeks later, he drew a much more effective picture: a Belgian peasant woman weeps, her head buried in her arms, while her small daughter looks on; on the floor lies a letter with a red cross. Leyendecker would do some two dozen war covers for the *Post,* including those with his now traditional New Year's baby, who came to serve as an index to America's changing attitudes to the war in Europe.

The paucity of war fiction and war art reflected Lorimer's own diminishing journalistic interest in the war. By the end of 1914, Lorimer prepared to cut down his already rather minimal coverage of the war. He told Will Irwin, "I'm going to play this war hard for six months—in case it lasts as long as that—and drop it. By then the American people will grow sick and tired of reading about it."

THE SATURDAY EVENING POST

An Illus'ra' Weekly
Founded A? D!   Benj. Franklin

JANUARY 2, 1915   5cts. THE COPY

In This Number

Irvin S. Cobb—Frederick Irving Anderson—Samuel G. Blythe
Will Payne—Calvin Johnston—L. B. Yates—Harry Leon Wilson

Leydendecker's New Year baby rejects the European war.

Irwin commented years later that this was "the only time [he] ever knew Lorimer to guess wrong on the psychology of his public."[24]

On January 2, 1915, the Leyendecker baby, like Lorimer, having had enough of war, energetically took a broom to a collection of officers' helmets, sweeping them away. But neither the New Year's baby nor Lorimer could dismiss the war; the six months of coverage Lorimer had allowed for were not going to exhaust America's interest in the subject. War was becoming a fact of journalistic life for the *Post*.

Lorimer did not, however, change his mind about the war, and he flatly refused to print material that glossed the carnage with a veneer of idealism. Beveridge had tried his old friend out several times with ideas for various war pieces and Lorimer had printed a couple of Beveridge's high-minded essays. Then in May 1915 Beveridge sent "Democracy the Conqueror" (June 9, 1915), in which he predicted the postwar world, a kind of universal Progressivist utopia. Wartime laws, such as those protecting the people from exploitation, Beveridge argued, would flower into a "collectivism," a system of "government control of fundamentals for the common good."

In agreeing to print the article, Lorimer insisted on some cuts; he was not going to be swept up in any ecstasies of false piety about anything so brutal and barbarous as war.

This is a mighty good article so long as you stick to the subject which we agreed on, but, personally, I do not feel like printing the religious stuff because this whole war is a negation of religion and I do not care to give the impression in The Saturday Evening Post that either in France or in any other country is there a revival of real religious spirit. I have no doubt that more people are going through the motions of religion because they are scared and turn towards some unseen power in their distress, just as a lot of old reprobates have death bed repentances and timid boys pray through thunder storms, but that hasn't anything to do with real religion.[25]

And Lorimer remained equally level-headed about the romance of heroism. "In the event of war with Germany," he wrote Beveridge, "I am preparing to enlist as Major-General of the artillery. I understand that the big guns are placed about twelve miles in the rear of the firing line, and that the Major-General stands twelve miles behind the big guns."[26]

Through the early months of 1915, the *Post* insistently down-played the war, running only the final installments of Cobb's and Corra Harris's war series and a scattering of pieces that looked at the war from one angle or another—as Lorimer put it, "articles covering America's policy on everything from raising hens to the neutralization of the seas."[27] But when Mary Roberts Rinehart wired Lorimer that she was now prepared to go to Europe, he found the proposition irresistible.

From September 1914, when her husband quashed her plans to travel to Europe to cover the war, Rinehart had been brooding. It was one thing to see Blythe and Cobb reporting the war in the *Post,* quite another to find herself upstaged by Corra Harris. Thus, Lorimer's response to her wire was artful. First he offered solicitous concern for Rinehart's personal well-being; no widow like Corra Harris, Mary Rinehart was a wife and the mother of three sons. "I am only making this proposition to you with the understanding that you are planning to go abroad anyway. Frankly, I do not care to take the responsibility of sending any one over there except old maids, widows and our real rough boys like Cobb and Blythe. Personally, I should urge you not to take the risk, though I under-stand the appeal that it makes to every writer, man or woman, with red blood." Then he managed judiciously to goad Rinehart's pro-fessional competitiveness, particularly acute in relation to other women journalists, closing with a pointed reference to *Post* writer Mary Brush, who had just cabled a report from Russia and had seen "the Cossacks doing business" in Poland.[28] Lorimer offered her $1000 an article, and Rinehart sailed for England early in January 1915.

Rinehart's articles from the war were astonishing. She man-aged to do what could not be done and to write powerfully about all of it. Arriving in England, she learned she could not travel to Belgium or France, that she would have to cool her heels in London waiting with the other foreign correspondents for censored news.

Nonetheless, she crossed to France. There, she learned she could not get to the front; the allied lines were entirely closed to reporters. Regardless, she got to the front and stayed several weeks, even crossing no-man's-land one night. To top it all off, she managed interviews with both the king and the queen of Belgium and, on returning to England, arranged another interview, entirely unprecedented, with Queen Mary of England.[29]

Rinehart's series of war articles began with "A Talk With the King of the Belgians," appearing as the lead article on April 3, and continued through July 31.[30] Their success, like that of Cobb's articles, lay in the narrative of personal adventure and in the clear reporting done in a prose style flexible enough to move from comic or sentimental detail to scenes of horror and pathos. Moreover, Rinehart, again like Cobb, was known and loved by *Post* readers; it was as if a friend were recounting the story of the war. "This is a narrative of personal experience." Rinehart wrote; "It makes no pretensions except to truth."[31] The special quality of personal experience is enhanced throughout; Rinehart quoted directly from the journal she kept, creating an air of immediacy, and she repeatedly measured what she witnessed at the war against what was familiar to her and her readers, evoking a special pathos at the commonplace become terrible. In Calais, for example, she visited her first military hospital; trained as a nurse, Rinehart looked around the ward with the eye of a professional: "I live in a great manufacturing city. Day by day its mills take their toll in crushed bodies. The sight of broken humanity is not new to me." But here was something she had not seen before—"men dying of an ideal. . . . Ward after ward. Rows of quiet men. The occasional thump of a convalescent's crutch. The swish of a nurse's starched dress. The strangled grunt of a man as the dressing is removed from his wound. The hiss of coal in the fireplace at the end of the ward. Perhaps a priest beside a bed, or a nun. Over all, the heavy odour of drugs and disinfectants. Brisk nurses go about, cheery surgeons, but there is no real cheer. The ward is waiting."[32]

Rinehart's final article closed with a denial of that "ideal," washed away in the flood of horror and loss.

Mary Roberts Rinehart

War is not two great armies meeting in the clash and frenzy of battle. War is a boy carried on a stretcher, looking up at God's blue sky with bewildered eyes that are soon to close; war is a woman carrying a child that has been injured by a shell; war is spirited horses tied in burning buildings and waiting for death; war is the flower of a race, battered, hungry, bleeding, up to its knees in filthy water; war is an old woman burning a candle before the Mater Dolorosa for the son she has given.[33]

The war that Mary Roberts Rinehart described was sometimes grand, always terrible, and entirely remote from American experience. That point of view echoed Lorimer's: war was unthinkable for America.

Then, on May 7, German submarines hit and sank the *Lusitania,* unleashing a wave of war fever and, for Lorimer, presenting a new challenge to the *Post*'s staunchly antiwar stand. But Lorimer held fast to neutrality, asserting that in Germany's sinking of the *Lusitania* lay grim evidence of what war does to the mind of a nation. American geography, its two oceans, had preserved it even from "thinking war" and in that fact was "our inestimable advantage. That deep reaction from the bloody and heathen barbarism of war is the finest prize of our culture and our highest justification."[34]

The *Post* could not cover the *Lusitania* as news; it was not equipped to rush articles into print.[35] Its coverage necessarily had to set the *Lusitania* in some context, to construct a meaning out of the event, to turn it to the service of creating public opinion. What Lorimer acquired for the *Post* did all of this and did it with considerable éclat. Owen Wister, Teddy Roosevelt's friend and author of the greatly popular novel *The Virginian,* provided an essay, long and thoughtful, making sense of the *Lusitania* by tying it precisely to the German war mentality. "The Pentecost of Calamity" appeared on July 3.

Wister began his essay by recalling his own former admiration for Germany, for its order and thrift and neatness, an admiration so powerful it had led him to denigrate America. "I thought of our landscape, littered with rubbish and careless fences and stumps of trees, hideous with glaring advertisements; of the rusty junk lying about our farms and towns and wayside stations; and of the disfigured Palisades along the Hudson River. America was ugly and shabby—made so by Americans. Germany was swept and garnished—made so by Germans."[36] Wister continued for pages, evoking and recalling a widespread prewar American admiration for cultured, prosperous, and progressive Germany. Then he suddenly turned to the *Lusitania*. He described a schoolboy festival in Germany celebrating the sinking of the ship with all its loss of lives. The question, wrote Wister, was whether one culture—German *Kultur*—could embrace these two extremes of civilized prosperity and barbarous cruelty. Yes, it was possible, he determined, because "Germany through generations has been carefully trained for this wild spring at the throat of Europe." As Wister developed his argument, he relied more and more heavily on the new rhetoric of the war with its key word *Prussianism*. Thus, the answer to the puzzle lay in the Prussianizing of Germany, resulting in a miasma of "thickening fumes that exhaled from Berlin," out of which "emerged three colossal shapes—the Super-man, the Super-race and the Super-state: the new Trinity of German worship."[37]

So far, Wister and Lorimer were of the same mind, but "The Pentecost of Calamity" struck a new note in the *Saturday Evening Post* as Wister stepped away from the safety of neutrality. His language on this issue may well indicate a compromise struck between isolationist Lorimer and prowar Wister, for his words were never quite explicit and often shifted ambiguously between a call for more American outspokenness against German actions in Europe and a guarded plea for direct, armed involvement. But Wister's conclusion came very close to an outright call to arms. "Perhaps nothing save calamity will teach us what Europe is thankful to have learned again—that some things are worse than war, and that you can pay too high a price for peace; but that you cannot pay too high for finding and keeping your own soul."[38]

Finally, the ideological ends to which the *Lusitania* sinking could be put diverged for Lorimer and Wister. Like Roosevelt, Wister wanted to ride into the war, expressing and defending

American manliness. Lorimer, to the contrary, refused to be goaded into war. Neither the *Lusitania* nor European attacks on America and its war prosperity could shake his stand. Even a year later, an editorial titled "Americanism" (August 12, 1915) insisted on neutrality—not, as some said, because the country had found it profitable, nor "because it lacks spirit or sinews of patriotism, but simply because it has some intelligence." To the opposing point of view, Lorimer replied, "Americans who do not understand this do not understand their country."

Of course, the *Post* had never been precisely neutral; if nothing else, the invasion of Belgium had made that impossible and the German announcement, early in 1915, of unrestricted submarine warfare was a direct provocation to American shipping interests. Still, the *Post* had maintained some evenhandedness, refusing, for example, to credit tales of German atrocities. After the *Lusitania*, that changed, but the change did not bring an end to Lorimer's belief in isolation; instead, it focused his growing anger and frustration on the enemy within.

In part these new attacks simply reflected Lorimer's frustration. The war had not come to a rapid conclusion and, it was now becoming clear, would not soon be over. Moreover, with continuing hostilities abroad came new policies at home; America was shipping munitions to the Allies and in 1915 an Allied war loan was extended. Such policies elicited some vigorous criticism and Lorimer, like many others, was quick to attribute pro-German sympathies to those critics. And rapidly, the distinction between pro-German and anti-American disappeared.

Lorimer heard America and it was not speaking with a single voice. The cause seemed clear enough: there was no real America as yet. Lorimer had dedicated himself to creating precisely such a real America, and clearly he had failed. But the cause of the failure was equally clear: the county was overrun by people who could never be made part of America. German sympathizers, thus, were anti-American in a way that went far beyond a position toward the European war. Anti-Americanism would permanently subvert the making of a nation. And therefore, by the second half of 1915, *Post* editorials began to attack immigrants and first-generation Americans or, in the catchword of the time, "hyphenated" Americans.

An August editorial attacked vocal critics of the United States' policy on shipping war munitions to the Allies. "The activities of our pro-German friends to that end are just so much lost labor," the editorial argued, for the shipping of munitions was entirely consonant with neutrality, and it was "absurd" to "suppose this country will cast aside neutrality in favor of the belligerent that sank the Lusitania."[39] The strained logic of this argument was echoed later in an editorial supporting the Allied war loan. The *Post* warned, "Those who threatened to boycott banks that participated in the loan were not neutral and not American." Since the war loan was simply "A Matter of Business" (October 23, 1915), such persons "were putting the interests of a foreign nation above American finance and commerce." The hyphenated American was proving dangerous, the *Post* concluded: "The case [of the war loan] illustrates again that in citizenship the hyphen is a sign that divides, not one that unites."

Change was manifest in other ways as well, particularly in a shifting attitude toward preparedness, which had now become a matter for public debate. In 1914 the *Post* had asserted that the strongest national defense lay in "justice, moderation and good will,"[40] but now it too was drawn into the debate on preparing for war. Lorimer's position was uncertain; he waffled between a grudging admission that preparedness might be like accident insurance, acceptable if not too costly, and his long held conviction that building up competitive armaments was tantamount to planting the seeds for war.[41]

In 1916 both Will Irwin and Albert Beveridge did articles on preparedness. Upbeat Beveridge glossed over the issue by urging "Preparedness for Peace" (February 19, 1916) and observing that many national endeavors, such as improving the railroads, would be useful in wartime as in peace. Irwin, however, faced the seriousness of the issue, calling it a debate about "a policy which may mean before we are finished a complete change in our national character." It was his contention, nevertheless, that sensible Americans, and especially "those who have seen the European struggle face to face," believed some preparedness "against invasion" was essential. Ner-vousness over possible German activities in Mexico only made this more urgent. Irwin wanted to make *Post* readers aware of their potential danger: "We are very rich, very tempting, and at present almost defenseless." [42]

Perhaps an even more telling omen of America's coming in-volvement in the war could be found in a small number of articles introducing military life to the *Post*'s audience. "Men Wanted for the U.S. Navy," by a former Navy ensign, and "Learning to Fly" by an American recently trained by the French, combined information with exciting first-hand experience. "The Average Man and the Army" took a different tack, pointing out that American men were not generally enthusiastic about an army career and considering what changes might be made so that the army could attract a better class of young men. [43]

Still, by the end of 1916, Lorimer was maintaining his defense of neutrality, citing Wilson's reelection on a peace platform as clear evidence of the American people's unwillingness to intervene in European affairs. The *Post* saw in "this expression of public opin-ion . . . one of the finest incidents in American history." America had refused to be "hurrahed, heckled and taunted into bellig-erency," which was in itself "one of the highest justifications of democracy." [44]

On February 3, 1917, the United States broke off relations with Germany at the renewal of unrestricted submarine warfare. Two months would pass before the declaration of a state of war on April 6, but Lorimer did not wait until then to dedicate the *Post* to the American cause. He had not changed his mind about war; the time had arrived, however, when his personal views necessarily came into conflict with his sense of loyalty as an American citizen and his sense of responsibility as editor of the *Saturday Evening Post*. Without question, the *Post* would unreservedly support Wilson and the war.

The next few weeks were especially difficult; the situation was fluid and uncertain, and Lorimer needed to practice extreme caution. As he told Beveridge in March, "During the present situation, with our three weeks' handicap, we have to take unusual precautions both to seem timely and to be bombproof."[45] Editorials, therefore, while careful to avoid too explicit a definition of Wilson's position at any given moment, offered full support. "Woodrow Wilson deserves the implicit confidence of that great majority of the United States who earnestly desire peace. . . . On his record all those who sincerely wish peace, but would not purchase it by surrender of vital rights, must give him their complete confidence. . . . All attempts to discredit and harass him in the crisis were unworthy and should have no countenance."[46] Lorimer was marking time in print, but as an editor he had undertaken his own preparedness for war. He waited for the outcome while arranging in advance for a special war issue. As a result, the Post's "three week's handicap" was cut to fifteen days. The United States declared war on April 6; the Saturday Evening Post followed suit on April 21.

Charles Livingston Bull painted the cover. Against an intense red-orange wash, the American eagle, its claws extended as it screams its defiance, swoops down on an unseen enemy. And to lead the American people to war, Lorimer had chosen his two most popular war correspondents, Mary Roberts Rinehart and Irvin S. Cobb. Each had prepared an essay and each had found a title with an appropriately religious connotation.

In "The Altar of Freedom," Rinehart spoke to the mothers of America:

We are virtually at war. By the time this is published, perhaps the declaration will have been made.

And even now, all over the country, on this bright spring day, there are mothers who are waiting to know what they must do. Mothers who are facing the day with heads up and shoulders back, ready to stand steady when the blow falls; mothers who shrink and tremble, but ready, too; and other mothers, who cannot find the strength to give up to the service of their country the boys who will always be little boys to them.

Rinehart exhorted and she confessed, revealing her own maternal weakness when her eldest son was about to volunteer. The effect was powerful; Rinehart received thousand of letters from women who had bid farewell to their soldier sons.[47]

In "Thrice is He Armed" (April 21, 1917), Cobb wrote from the vantage point of one who had seen the war and learned first-hand about the Prussian mentality. And he wrote as one who hated war: "It is the most obscene, the most hideous, the most brutal, the most malignant—and sometimes the most necessary— spectacle, I veritably believe, that ever the eye of mortal man has rested on since the world began, and I do hate it." Now, of course, war was necessary but, Cobb explained by way of the rhetoric of Prus-sianism, we must make war not against the Germany of Heine, Goethe and Beethoven, but against "the fanatical, tyrannical, power-mad, blood-and-iron Prussianized Germany of Bismarck." And since "thrice is he armed who has his quarrel just," we must wage war as a holy war, "fighting for the preservation of the prin-ciples of constitutional and representative government against those heads of the few remaining great Powers . . . who believe that man was not created a self-governing creature but a vassal." Cobb's language grew most virulent, however, when he turned his assault on those who opposed the war, attacking them as "weird Americans, some of whom part their Americanism in the middle with a hyphen" or as "professional pacifists . . . little brothers to the worm and the sheep and the guinea pig."

The *Post* had entered World War I with its biggest guns firing and it now set about waging war on every journalistic front. War permeated every aspect of the magazine—articles, editorials, fic-tion, art work, and advertising. With a single-minded war-inspired patriotism that entirely belied his earlier blunt and tough, though equally patriotic, isolationism, Lorimer made the war his cause. Certainly, in this the *Post* continued to express majority opinion in America, but at the same time the weekly installments of a prowar *Post* made a powerful contribution to shaping and sustaining public opinion. Woodrow Wilson recognized and acknowledged that con-tribution in a letter he wrote to Lorimer in the spring of 1918. "My attention has been drawn to the admirable way in which you have

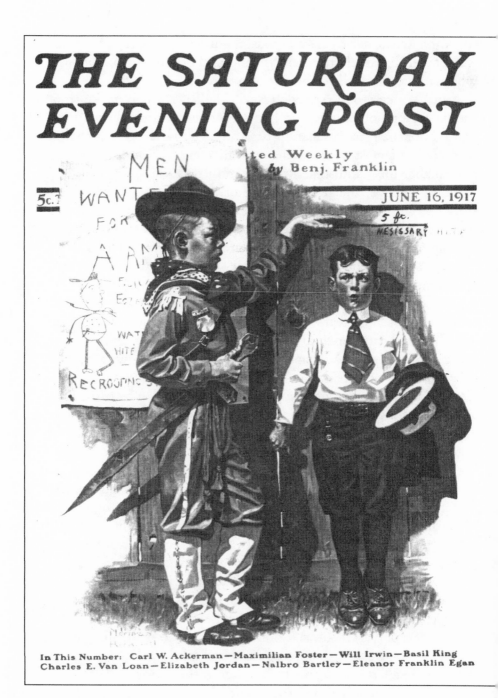

In an early Rockwell cover, boys play at recruitment.

been filling the Saturday Evening Post with matter which inter-
prets and emphasises the objects and meaning of the great struggle
we are engaged in. The method you have adopted is all the more
admirable because it is not carried in headlines but runs like an
essence through the whole contents of the weekly. Will you not
accept my sincere expression of admiration?"[48]

War material in the *Post* came from a wide variety of sources.
Experienced correspondents covered major areas of interest. Cobb
and Will Irwin were sent to France. Eleanor Franklin Egan covered
the Middle East. Elizabeth Frazer contributed nearly weekly articles on the Red Cross. More intimate reporting came from *Post*
story writer George Pattullo, who joined the army and went overseas with the American Expeditionary Force; he sent back both
first-hand reports on army life and war fiction.

Special beats were assigned to writers with appropriate qualifi-
cations. Carl Ackerman, formerly a newsman stationed in Berlin,
analyzed the situation in Germany. Melville Davisson Post and
Arthur Train, both lawyers as well as writers of crime fiction, took
up the subject of spies and saboteurs. Sam Blythe covered Washington and, later, the navy. Mary Rinehart toured military training
camps, essentially continuing her reports to American mothers on
the situation of their sons.

Not surprisingly, the pages of the *Post* were used by numerous
military and government officials. Secretary of War Newton D.
Baker explained "The War and the War Department" (May 26,
1917); David Lawrence, working for George Creel's Committee for
Public Information, dealt with censorship in "Not for Publication"
(December 1, 1917); Admiral Stanford E. Moses made plain "The
True Character of Our Navy"; and Admiral Robert E. Peary talked
about "Air Power for the United States" (both May 12, 1917).

Well-known *Post* writers turned their attention to the home
front, urging readers to show spirit, avoid waste, buy Liberty
Bonds, make sacrifices, avoid becoming slackers. Fiction writers
contributed to the war effort with patriotic stories that idealized
the doughboy or modeled, for those on the home front, the kinds of
commitment and sacrifice necessary for winning the war. And the

Leydendecker's heroic doughboy in France

editorial page featured lectures about solidarity on the home front, setting the example with continuing strong support of Wilson's policies. "The Administration's war program satisfies the nation's conscience. It brings to a consistent climax the patient, forbearing, peace-hoping but not supine course. . . . It must be war with the utmost power of the nation until the enemy is brought to terms. The time for discussion of policies is all past. Until peace is restored there can be but one policy."[49]

Post covers went to war, too, and here the work of Leyendecker was particularly striking since his stylized figure of the youthful, vigorous male, already familiar as the firm-jawed, clear-eyed Arrow Collar man, was easily recast as the cheerful, modest, but entirely manly American doughboy. Leyendecker painted his doughboy kissing his sweetheart farewell, trying out his French-English phrase book or sharing his bread with a little Belgian peasant girl, rushing with bayonet fixed into battle or hurling a grenade over the wall of a trench, writing a letter home by the light of a campfire or jauntily making his preparations for Thanksgiving dinner at the front, with a basket of food slung over his rifle and leading a turkey by a string.[50] At the same time, the Leyendecker baby continued to signal changes in America's attitude toward the war with each new year. For 1917 he observed with distress a globe of the world, a great hole blown out where Europe had been. But by 1918 the New Year baby had joined up, saluting smartly in his helmet.[51]

Post covers generally provided upbeat emblems for the public; only occasionally did a more somber picture allude to the reality of war. Even in those cases, however, images of death were cosmetically sentimentalized, as in a Charles Livingston Bull cover at the end of the war (November 23, 1918) showing a Red Cross dog in front of a barbed wire fence mournfully guarding an abandoned helmet.

A similar avoidance of death marked *Post* fiction. German soldiers, of course, were killed in substantial numbers, but only one American soldier was lost in the *Post*'s short stories during the war years and that soldier was only marginally "American." In "Sweet

Leydendecker's New Year baby joins up.

Honey in All Mouths" (April 13, 1918), Donn Byrne told the story of two Jewish immigrants whose own "Americanization" became complete only when they learned of the death of their soldier grandson and accepted the value of his sacrifice.

A good many stories in the *Post* contrived similar experiences, employing the change of heart as a way of emphasizing the theme of Americanization. Americanization, with its celebration of single-minded support for the war and its focus on a loyal home front, was the most popular theme for *Post* war fiction. Booth Tarkington's first story for the *Post* told of an old German-American in Cincinnati who found his love for the fatherland rekindled by the war. It is his thoroughly Americanized granddaughter who brings about his change of heart, setting him straight on the path to Americanization.[52]

This theme, however, was not always restricted to hyphenated Americans. In some cases, even apparently bona fide Anglo-Saxon Americans were discovered letting their country down until some shock brought about a change of heart. Rich fathers and protective mothers were special targets, usually contrasted with their noble, self-sacrificing sons. Grace Ellery Channing admonished the selfish woman in "The Years of a Man" (August 31, 1918), and Frederick Orin Bartlett set out to reform the parvenu father in "Chateau-Thierry" (November 2, 1918).

The protagonist of Barlett's story, a kind of Old Gorgon Graham who had forgotten his roots, grew rich and with his new money took his son out of trade school and sent him to Harvard. In a shifting of generational values encouraged by the war, this story located virtue in the son. Unlike Graham's son Pierrepont, he was not spoiled or selfish; he remained humble, sensitive, courageous, leaving Harvard to enlist in the army and eventually being sent to France with the AEF and seriously wounded at Chateau-Thierry. Hearing the terrible news, the father learned his lesson: he sold his fancy new house and pledged $10,000 to the Liberty Loan. To make sure the readers learned their lesson as well, Bartlett ended the story with a ponderous moral: "The time had come for the Huns to take seriously the entry of the United States into the war."

In change-of-heart stories the line between didactic fiction and fiction presented as if it were authenticated memoir or confession grew blurred during 1917 and 1918, and at times was entirely eradicated. Frequently, material presented as an anonymous first-hand account of an authentic change-of-heart experience reads suspiciously like fiction. "From Conscience to Khaki: Being the Confessions of a Man Who Objected to War" (October 27, 1918) purported to be the record of a New York broker who objected to war on religious grounds. His antiwar resolve nearly wavered when he considered where Christianity might be today had men not fought for it, but he rejected such thoughts only to be brought to his senses at last by the sight of a military parade: "I saw the nobility of all those men marching by thousands to do God's will upon the earth; to reaffirm all the Christ had taught." Two hours later he enlisted.

Another kind of fiction presented as authenticated fact provided *Post* readers with a close-up view of the enemy. "The Submarine Conscience" (September 15, 1917), again anonymous, gave the story of a captured German U-boat sailor. He told of his training and the subsequent onset of doubts and even treasonous thoughts as he learned of the destruction and death the submarine war was causing. When he heard about the United States' declaration of war, he grew more confused and deeply troubled to find himself the enemy of "the great country that Uncle Frederick had written of to us." Captured and interned by the British, he at last discovered the true nature of the German character: his fellow captives ostracized him because of his lowly birth.

Blurring the lines between fact and fiction or, more bluntly, passing off fictional accounts as authentic experience was a remarkable breach of journalistic ethics for the *Post*. No doubt, the urgency of wartime seemed adequate justification, but a dangerous precedent was being established. The propaganda power of such pieces was formidable, especially when backed by the prestige of the *Post,* and when Lorimer's sights were turned away from the enemy abroad and trained on the enemy at home, he had a potent ideological weapon in hand, one he would continue to use well after the Armistice was signed.[53]

In mid-1917, when the fear of spies and subversion had created a national panic, *Post* fiction masquerading as fact attacked the savage enemy who undermined morale with German propaganda and thwarted the war effort with acts of sabotage. A two-part article on spies, for example, buttressed its argument with photographs of captured letters, purportedly written by German spies in the United States. Captions translated these preposterous documents. "Four weeks ago I was released from prison after spending eleven weeks under arrest. So many powder mills have been blown up over here that the scoundrels, the swine locked me up. Ha! Ha! Evil seeds flourish. . . . The people are stupid."[54]

Post articles and editorials fanned national fears of spies and saboteurs. An editorial, "The War in Your Town" (December 8, 1917), warned of America's "most dangerous" enemies. "Some spy out and report our military preparations; others foment strikes, set class against class, preach pacifism and pessimism and poison the springs of public thought." Some did this for "the Kaiser's dirty dollar" but others were "merely half-baked perverts." It was, in the final analysis, an easy matter to spot the enemy, to discern the difference between "Prussianism and Americanism." The editorial urged a vigilante stance, seeking out and reporting the enemy at home. And if it was not possible to have him jailed, then "shun him as if he had the smallpox." Show him he is "unfit for the company of loyal Americans."

As the rhetoric of war and subversion heated up, the coolest minds seemed to lose objectivity and equilibrium. There was no cooler or more objective mind on the *Post* than Sam Blythe's; yet the war affected even his viewpoint and consequently his prose style. In 1916, reporting on the Mexican situation, he had trained his ironic lens on Pancho Villa and on United States policy. This was Blythe at his best. "Very few nations maintain pet bandits, but the United States had a very nice one for two or three years. Always in the van in these little idealisms, we picked a perfect specimen and coddled him admiringly and fondly. To be sure, as I write this, some eight or nine thousand American soldiers are chasing him through the cactus in Mexico, with orders to disperse him, disperse being a euphemism for kill or capture, such as it is polite to apply to instructions concerning old and formerly valued friends."[55]

By contrast, in 1917 when Blythe lent his pen to the war effort, he did so with a piece that was chilling in its ferocity. "Der Tag for Us" (December 22, 1917) exploits the strange blurring of fact and fiction that had become characteristic of many *Post* war pieces, and it opens as if it were straight reporting. The German army marches into Topeka and in the very first paragraph bayonets a little child. Atrocities follow, mounting until the final page. Only then does Blythe turn to explanation and warning: such atrocities are typical of Germans and, yes, it could happen here.

In the spring of 1918, Blythe turned to the hyphenated American. "Our Imported Trouble and Trouble Makers" (May 11, 1918) was illustrated by *Post* political cartoonist, Herbert Johnson. Uncle Sam was shown ladling scum marked "Pro-Germans" and "Treason" out of the "Melting Pot" as it hung over a fire; the caption read "The Scum Always Rises to the Top." But as Blythe's article showed, by 1918 the German spy had been joined and even upstaged by a new menace, the Bolshevik subversive. For the *Post*, America was now not so much a nation at war in foreign lands, as a country beleaguered by enemies within.

The Russian revolution had at first been greeted with delight in the *Post*. As early as 1915, editorials were insisting on the innate greatness of the Russian people: "We like to think the Slav has up his sleeve a finer civilization than any yet seen." Only the "bad and powerful" czarist government stood in the way of great progress and the only possible solution lay "in a successful revolution." When the revolution came in the spring of 1917 and failed to bring with it an immediate fulfillment of democratic expectations, the *Post* counseled patience. The peasants might not be living up to our high principles, but, after all, even the American Revolution led at first to expressions of confusion and discontent, as in the Whiskey Rebellion.[56]

By October, the *Post* saw real problems ahead unless the revolutionary leadership under Kerensky could "develop the ability to govern." In that case, though, the failure of the revolution would be a "calamity," especially because this revolution alone had been thoroughly democratic. Unlike other similar movements, the Russian revolution had not arisen out of one of the established classes in society, explained an editorial that sounded curiously like a Marxist primer, but out of the "people at the social base." This was, therefore, "the only revolution which was thoroughly democratic from the beginning."[57]

It took three or four months for the *Post* to discover that the October Revolution and the Bolshevik government it brought to power were the antithesis of democracy. In April 1918, an editorial called Russia a "huge experiment in anarchy," offering "a bogus democracy and a bogus liberty."[58] Russia was, of course, free to deal with its internal situation as it chose; the real danger lay in Bolshevik sympathizers in America and they were the problem Sam Blythe set out to deal with when he wrote "Our Imported Trouble and Trouble Makers."

Blythe had taken one of his frequent trips across America, conducting his own brand of public opinion poll, not this time about a presidential election but about the question of whether America would turn Bolshevik. Despite pockets of the "disorderly spirit of defiance," Blythe concluded that democracy was safe, given vigilance and a tough line with agitators. The significant point, however, is how pro-German sentiment, bolshevism, and the subversion of the war effort became mingled and confused in Blythe's article as he listed the sources of internal danger: "the advocates of force, sabotage, revolution, the incendiaries . . . the I.W.W., some sections of the foreign-born population, some types of socialists, radical opponents of the war, and all of the various elements of disorder that exist in this country because of the heterogeneous nature of our population." The enemy was legion, but from mid-1918 on, the radical began to displace the pacifist, and the Bolshevik the Prussian, in the *Post*'s nightmare of subversion and revolution in America.

Direct reporting on Russia was not so entirely single-minded as were editorials and articles about bolshevism at home, principally because some of the articles were being written by Ernest Poole, who had returned to Russia in order to guide public opinion at home.[59] Having arranged with Lorimer for *Post* articles, Poole traveled to Russia and sent back reports on the chaos following the October Revolution as well as pleas for American friendship. Although Poole, too, had supported the Kerensky government and lamented the death of the liberal movement in Russia and the victory of the Bolsheviks, he believed the United States had to remain on good terms with Russia under whatever government. Such a posture was necessary as part of the effort to keep Russia in the war and also as a way to avoid having her set up close commercial ties with certain other nations, particularly Germany, after the war.[60] "I come from doubt and confusion into a deepening belief that, in spite of present disorders, when the storm has cleared away there is to arise slowly through the years such a prodigious democracy there as, in cooperation with France, England and America, will make the dreams of Berlin utterly hopeless."[61] His articles continued into March 1918, with particular focus on the apolitical Russian peasant, his material needs, and the political and commercial advantage to the United States in supplying those needs.[62]

At the same time, newsman William T. Ellis was also traveling in Russia and sending back *Post* articles with a very different message. In February 1918, he reported that Bolshevik Russia was under the control of "Russian Jews who returned from America after the revolution." These Jews were fattening on prostrate Russia, living well while real Russians starved. Ellis's anti-Semitism discovered the hyphenated American in a new locale, now sowing chaos abroad. Unlike their doubly estranged leaders, however, the Russian peasants were true patriots, and Ellis saw a bloodbath ahead, when the peasants rose up to loot the rich in a society that "represents the limits of classism."[63]

Given Ellis's political philosophy, it is not surprising to find that he turned his attention to hyphenated Americans back home. He presented his views early in 1918 in a virulent article called "The Overflowing Melting Pot" (March 2, 1918). "This is a fire-alarm article," he announced. America was already endangered by aliens who, along with native-born "unconventional" thinkers, were trying to change our country. Such people admired the I.W.W. and denounced the Puritans as bigots; they gave "an erotic cast to much contemporary literature"; they mocked Victorian morals. Ellis's foreshadowing of the Jazz Age filled him with horror. America's only hope lay in closing the door to future immigrants, particularly those for whom Russia was growing "too formidable." "Our most sacred duty," he declared, "is to conserve the American type for the American mission" of democracy. From his confused vision of political, moral, and aesthetic degeneracy, Ellis found enemies everywhere. Against them he rallied his fellow Americans with a closing sentence intended to evoke the furthest borders of horror: "Shall men with an alien lisp to their tongue be permitted to stand at our doors and cry that our fathers were rogues and our mothers unchaste?"

Ellis's views were echoed in *Post* editorials that similarly exploited the melting pot metaphor in order to concentrate, as in Herbert Johnson's cartoon, on the scum that had "risen to the top." Every "dirty cur" was taking advantage of American civil liberties to subvert American democracy, said a May editorial. But underneath the scum, "Americanism is coming to the boiling point," ready to turn the tide against those immigrants who were lazy or weak or vicious and against those native-born Americans who were "nut-sundae Socialists" or "lemon-pop Bolsheviks." The work must begin by cleaning the "rats" out of "the schools, the press and the government." To save democracy it was apparently necessary to jettison democratic principles: "It is better to keep ten men out of office on suspicion than to let one traitor in."[64]

For the *Post*, America's entry into the war had been undertaken along simple enough lines: America was going to defeat the Hun. But by the summer of 1918, as the tide of war finally turned decisively in favor of the Allies, the *Post* was in arms against a host of new enemies. Lorimer had originally called for national solidarity against Germany, then against Prussianism at home, now against bolshevism. Back in mid-1917 it had seemed entirely adequate to

Lorimer to define one's patriotic duty during war in moderate, restrained language. It was not necessary, an editorial had explained, "to like" the war, but it was required, as "a matter of self-respect" and "decorum," to keep such views to oneself.[65] A year later moderation had given way entirely to a shrill hysteria. It would turn out, moreover, that the end of the war would not mean a return to a cooler, more judicious rhetoric; hysteria did not easily abate.

Therefore, when the war at last came to an end, only Leyendecker's New Year's baby celebrated the new year as one of peace, releasing a caged dove. On the editorial page, Lorimer remained at war. For the last issue of 1918, in the place of the customary half-dozen editorials, was a single essay, "Only the Stump of Dagon was Left" (December 28, 1918). Autocracy had been defeated, Lorimer wrote, but the Allies were now fighting a second war against bolshevism. Lorimer had been adamantly neutral in 1914. Now he asserted that America could not "remain an innocent bystander," for the enemy were among us, "agents . . . everywhere among the ignorant, the sapheaded and the vicious." They were only a few thousand; nevertheless, they were a menace. The solution lay implicit in the definition of the problem, for the enemy was "largely foreign born." And if more were on their way to our shores, we must be ready to turn them back. "So in planning our list of imports let us include only desirables. Under our laws we send rotten food to the dump because it is a menace to our health. Rotten men who are poisoning America with rotten propaganda belong there too. Why do they linger here when in Russia they can live the idea that they preach? Utopia yawns for them. Make them go to it. We do not want them. America for Americans and men who want to be Americans."

This editorial announced the *Post's* agenda for the years ahead. Lorimer had discovered a new mission, to define America anew by delineating the true American. The first step was to eliminate all that was not truly American, and to that end the journalistic tactics of war would be employed in a new offensive.

"The Foolish Ideas We Have Imported"

Lorimer brought the *Post* out of the war with patriotism unfurled and nativism unleashed. Facing the dislocations of postwar America—unemployed veterans, labor unrest, business recession—he brought old values into play, urging hard work, common sense, and a belief in American progress through business. But old values were no longer adequate in themselves; it was necessary as well to discover and attack the sources of disruptive change. At the root of what Lorimer saw as the dangers to the United States lay radical ideas imported from abroad. The work ethic was undermined by Bolshevik propaganda. Labor was corrupted by red infiltrators. America itself was polluted by immigrants.

Lorimer took on the challenge of saving his country. He had been taught two powerful lessons by the war, and he applied them both in these years. First, he had learned how to deploy his army of writers so as best to exploit the talents of each against a common enemy, and second, he had discovered who this enemy was. The specter of the Hun, along with Prussianism, had begun to fade in 1918. That menace had stalked Europe but the Allies, once the AEF arrived, had vanquished it. The new and more dangerous threat had also emerged in Europe, but it imperiled America at home, attacking the foundations of the American way. It had a variety of names, including bolshevism, communism, socialism, radicalism—and the melting pot.

The *Post* had exploited and mocked the metaphor of the melting pot during the war years; in the years immediately following the war it became an obsession. Survival seemed to hang in the balance between the radical ideas imported from abroad and symbolized by the now sinister melting pot and the wholesome, but threatened, values of Americanism. Lorimer threw the *Post* into the struggle, for the *Post was* American.

Everywhere Lorimer saw the poisoning of American institutions and culture by the noxious influence of aliens, subversives, and hyphenated Americans. An editorial called "Melting-Pot Literature" (May 13, 1922) attacked recent novels and plays as salacious and found that "this polluted stream" had its source "between the Baltic and the Aegean." Privately, Lorimer lamented the passing of an old America in a letter to fiction writer Julian Street. "There was so much that was good and simple and American in that life, as contrasted with the stuff that we have imported during the past twenty years. . . . Sometimes, I think that we have ruined everything from our cooking to our social life with the foolish ideas that we have imported from European capitals,—good enough there, perhaps, but not for America."[1] Lorimer dedicated himself to resuscitating that old America. For him, Americanism remained best represented by business, and the businessman remained the most positive type of the American. But as an economy based on production shifted to one based on consumption, the *Post* accommodated with its own adjustments. The American Everyman was now frequently presented as the consumer, especially insofar as the consumer found his interests threatened by the excessive demands of labor.

But in the creation and popularization of the consumer, the *Post* was laying out a minefield of contradictions. In the 1920s the *Post* consumer turned profligate, as if seduced from hard work and thrift by the glamor of the very advertisements that were enriching the Curtis Company and promising the *Post* reader a world of luxurious material goods. The full realization of this paradox lay a few years ahead, but in the decision to combat radicalism by constructing the figure of the American as consumer, Lorimer unwittingly contributed to the subversion of his own vision of America.

Lormer's conservative ideology, the celebration of traditional values along with the violent repudiation of radical ideas, made the *Post* an American institution in these years. Moreover, Lorimer, editor and master spirit of the weekly, was now presented to the public as an avatar of Americanism himself. In 1918, Irvin S. Cobb wrote a piece on Lorimer for *Bookman,* stating, "Lorimer more nearly approximates the popular conception . . . of the typical American than any man I have ever known."[2] Rugged features, plain-spokenness, down-home humor, clean-mindedness, patriotism—these are some of the attributes Cobb may have had in mind. A man's man. But there were other qualities as well: power, influence, wealth. Did the first set of attributes, those American features along with an absolute addiction to work, automatically promise and unfailingly lead to the second set—to power and influence and wealth?

Certainly Lorimer's own story was the American ideal—or, to put it another way, the sheer trajectory of the *Post*'s success was itself Lorimer's story. That was how Isaac Marcosson put it in 1919, calling Lorimer's "own story . . . the larger wonder story of The Saturday Evening Post." The *Post,* Marcosson said, "is in reality the expression of [Lorimer's] own personality; . . . he has incarnated himself into a magazine that attracts vital things and people like a magnate." "Incarnated himself into a magazine" is a bizarre and richly contradictory phrase: the living man creating himself as alive through and within the agency of an inorganic medium; the powerful ego effacing itself into an anonymity finally more ego-fulfilling than mere personality. And for Marcosson, as for Cobb, what Lorimer expressed was "a frank Americanism."[3]

That "frank Americanism," however, was on the defensive as Lorimer moved from patriotism to nativism. Of course, the *Saturday Evening Post* did not invent nativism. Just as it had reflected and helped solidify and affirm a widespread Republican liberalism in its early years, and as it mirrored and helped direct America's changing responses to the war, it now both expressed and cooperated in shaping a broad consensus of conservatism and reaction. The difference between the early years of the *Post* and those immediately following the war was that it was no longer in the van-guard. A new and vocal generation challenged authority and the status quo, and Lorimer, born in Victorian America and inculcated with nineteenth-century American values, could not accede to these ideas. He was now, in his early fifties, moving inexorably toward the rearguard, and if his *Post* continued to hold a vast audience of Americans, that fact reveals only too clearly how des-perately the mainstream, like Lorimer, sought the assurances of the past.

In Lorimer's first years with the *Post*, the editorial page had frequently featured lists of the sayings of Poor Richard. The sayings provided a useful evocation of Ben Franklin and generally ran to blunt wit encouraging the cardinal American virtues. Poor Richard had long been abandoned when suddenly he reappeared early in 1922. A full editorial page was devoted to his sayings, each care-fully explicated and each bitterly politicized. The point of the whole page was to pit the conservative wisdom of Poor Richard against the new theories of politics and economics. Lorimer intro-duced the page ironically, but it was an irony that revealed a deep insecurity.

Poor Richard Says

Poor Richard, with his homely philosophy of life and his simple economic theories, must seem hopelessly old-fashioned, almost doddering, to our generation of intelligentsia. Yet his philosophy has one quality that theirs lacks—it works.

Attacking "communism, socialism, government ownership of rail-roads, Non-Partisan Leagues, and the like," the editorial prescribed "steady work, self-help and self-denial," and recommended in op-position to all economic "panaceas" and "cure-alls," "the middle of a long, hot road as the shortest safe way between two points."[4]

Work had always been a prime value for the *Post*, always the safe and efficacious road to success, or at least to self-reliant respect-ability. As Lorimer understood the situation, or as he chose to present it rhetorically, various radical programs offered the lazy and the credulous the promise of success without hard work. The war was responsible for the "loss of the habit of work," argued a 1920 editorial. It was, under the circumstances, malicious "to preach the millennium of fewer hours and less individual toil just now when the whole world is on the verge of a nervous breakdown in that direction." Even more baldly, another editorial reminded *Post* readers that Eden would not return and played with biblical language to warn that "in sweat is salvation from all economic ills. There is no other."[5]

Returning soldiers presented another face to the problem of work. Some were not ready to work just yet, as an anonymous 1919 account explained. Currently unemployed, this returned soldier wanted a better position than the one he had left, and he needed time to readjust. But he was no Bolshevik, he explained; nor were his comrades: "We know what we have got to do. Be sure that it will be done."[6] But such promises were not adequately reassuring. Late in 1919 Herbert Quick took another tack. In "Where Do We Go From Hoboken?" (October 11, 1919) he acknowledged the need for readjustment but then turned to the real issue: where do the ex-soldiers go now? "Back of course; that's where you go. Back to the soap work, the foundry, the warehouse, the rags and old iron business, the cracker factory, the drug store, the street-cleaning gang, the roundhouse, the meat wagon, the sample case, the typewriter, the ledger, the school, the pulpit, the stage, the trombone, the anvil, the steamhammer, the cattle ranch, the orchard, the plow—the job, in short; or the hunt for the job." Quick's vision of life, his torrential catalogue of petty jobs and grinding labor established the ground against which the demobilized protagonists of Hemingway and Dos Passos would make their fictional protests.

As the Poor Richard editorial implies, work was at the center of a cluster of conservative values currently under attack. Lorimer continually turned his editorial attention to the support of these values, insisting they were not outworn. Geniuses, he argued, were not needed; "common sense," "the old and the obvious" would see us through. Unlike the theories of the genius, the old and obvious were based on "natural law"; obviously, natural law cannot be evaded.[7]

It is hard to discern the line between natural law and American mythology, between the need to work (certainly the principal law) and the promise of success (the guiding myth), as a February 26, 1921, editorial entitled "Class Consciousness" makes clear. According to the *Post*, America had always been a classless society; the poison of class consciousness, "an Old World product," was spread by Bolshevik sympathizers. Indeed, if most American men were asked their class, they'd simply be puzzled. "A keen, ambitious youngster of old American stock" might say he can't tell. His mother is a "poor washerwoman," but he might study, work, and succeed, becoming "a great banker or manufacturer, scientist, president." "Such changes of fortune and estate are the reason we have no class consciousness."

The putative keen youngster of the editorial was the young man the *Post* had celebrated and instructed for twenty years, and he was summoned up with familiar affection. Nevertheless, Lorimer had had a glimpse of modern youth and he was alarmed. Too many young men expected to get rich quick; "Rosy dreams and rosier promises" had wooed them away "from the plow and the shovel." Moreover, youth was becoming assertive, demanding; they "shout down their elders in a daily mounting chorus of derision and scorn." Irresponsible economic theories and perversities in the arts could largely be blamed on the young: "Art, literature, education and economics—all these are being dominated more and more by the reckless, half-formed judgments of youth." And with regard to modern girls, there was simply bewilderment. A striking instance appeared in a 1920 editorial, published some six months after F. Scott Fitzgerald's famous flapper story, "Bernice Bobs Her Hair," advising the "old-fashioned parents of new-fangled girls" to enlist their daughters in the Girl Scouts![8]

Throughout the postwar years, editorials harangued *Post* readers on the old values and the old virtues, intending that these messages serve as needed counterweights to the preachments of various shades of radicals. It was pretty much an article of belief with Lorimer that Americans would not have needed any added stiffening to resist radicalism had not the war had the pernicious effect of softening national character. Having discovered how much could, in an emergency, be left to the federal government, Americans had abandoned the rigors of self-reliance. A rare two-page editorial explained and attacked this problem.

We have really been living in a semi-socialist state, and it has half ruined us. To finish the job we have only to perfect our socialistic system of confiscatory taxation; to further increase our governmental activities in restraint of trade and liberty, so that nobody can do anything without a license and a passport and a permit; to continue our policy of regarding destructive alien reds as wronged innocents, and constructive American businessmen as suspicious characters. . . . If the United States is going to remain a going concern it must discard this soft, lie-abed, sugar-teat socialism, this asking-papa-for-anything-you-want theory of life, and begin to practice self-denial and self-help.[9]

So central and salient did this analysis seem to Lorimer that he turned to important *Post* writers to supply similar material. Corra Harris responded with a polemic set in the bucolic "Wilsonville" of her *Circuit Rider's Wife* and even echoed one of Lorimer's images. She argued that we had come to accept as permanent and natural the emergency intrusion of government into our lives. One effect had been to "place a crown on the head of labor" with an ongoing commission "to raise its wages and keep a sugar teat in its mouth." It was time now to resume our burdens and conduct our lives as adults.[10]

Self-reliance sapped by the paternalist wartime role of government, Americans had become prey to the blandishments of Bolsheviks. It was urgent that the *Post* alert Americans to their danger by educating them about bolshevism. At one level this meant no more than puerile attacks on radicals as failures—that is, as men who shunned hard work. Thus, a "Bolshevist . . . means a quitter . . . a self-confessed and avowed quitter who has thrown up the game." Ashamed of his own failure and envious of the industrious, the Bolshevist calls them by "his supreme epithet of loathing . . . bourgeois."[11]

At quite another intellectual level, *Post* regular Will Payne provided a long article explicating *Das Kapital*. Payne's piece is curious, part propaganda by innuendo and part economic history and analysis. The title, "The Socialists' Koran," establishes Payne's stance toward his material, as the opening sentence establishes the tone; the character we are introduced to is not one to be admired: "During our Civil War a stout, swarthy, heavily whiskered Ger-man Jew was living with his wife and four children, in very strait-ened circumstances, and industriously working on a bulky book." *Post* readers would not have been deceived by the apparently sym-pathetic "industriously"; had industry been applied appropriately, the wife and children would have been maintained in other than "very straitened circumstances."

Payne's article is representative of much that Lorimer's *Post* prided itself on. It tackles a difficult subject in such a way as to make it accessible to the general reader, and it provides information in a form that is not only intelligible but pleasurable. At the same time, Payne's work is typical of much that the *Post* was beginning to be criticized for. He takes liberties in interpreting *Kapital* that end up by trivializing Marx's work. Moreover, the whole piece is shot through with snide irony, providing laughs by demeaning its subject. But most significantly, in terms of both its strengths and its weaknesses, the article does precisely what a *Post* article was in-tended to do: inform readers in such a way as to create in those readers a feeling of control over their world, even when that meant creating an entirely spurious sense of mastery over, even superiority to, the matter at hand.

Payne blends a biography of Marx and a mini-history of socialism/communism with his reading of *Kapital*. Marx's life be-comes a lens for the reading; his failures, an index to his book. And his failures are those that haunt a *Post* reader. He had "no practical ability" and "was unable to deal successfully with the hard facts of life that touched him nearest—the support of his wife and chil-dren." He could not "apply himself to the situation." With such a man as writer, one should not be surprised, Payne implies, that his "bulky" books are dense, unreadable, and pretty much unread.

Nevertheless, Payne sets about his reading and, up to a point, works through the difficult argument of *Kapital* while simultaneously commenting, debating, and undercutting through irony. A striking example comes in his discussion of the theory of surplus value, "commonly regarded by Marx's followers as one of his greatest achievements—probably his greatest achievement as an economist. [Marx] is struck by the familiar fact that capital increases. A man throws a given value into production and exchange, and presently takes out a greater value. He wants to construct an elaborate, scientific explanation for that phenomenon." A brief explanation follows, along with examples both of simple surplus value and of its effect when applied to labor. Payne then sets about exploding the theory first by mocking the "bulky" book and then by turning it into the plain language of "the man in the street."

The theme thus baldly indicated is elaborated to a prodigious extent. Part three of the book, comprising a hundred and forty-five pages, is devoted to absolute surplus value. Part four, comprising two hundred and fifteen pages, is taken up with relative surplus value. Part five, comprising twenty-nine pages, deals with absolute and relative surplus value. Nominally, nearly the whole book is about surplus value.

Of course the man in the street would dispose of the whole matter by saying: "A capitalist hires workmen, puts them at work, and sells the product of their labor at a profit, getting back more than he paid out." What Marx is really talking about all this while is what common folk call profit.

Once surplus value has been tamed, turned into what "the man in the street" understands perfectly well, and admires, as profit, then Marxism—along with bolshevism, communism, socialism, radicalism—is no longer intellectually daunting.

Moving toward his conclusion, Payne summarizes Marx's theory of revolution and the coming of the classless state, where "there is no more private capital, no more wages, no more profit, and consequently none of those evils of overwork and poverty which Marx says are an inevitable result of the system of private owner- ship of productive property." Payne's response is Lorimer's: this is no more than the pipe dream of the "quitter." "He might have simplified it, leaving out the long, dry discussion of abstract eco- nomic theory and the algebraic formulas he is so fond of using— putting it this way: 'If you are ill off and your neighbor is well off, his good fortune is the cause of your ill fortune; therefore, oust him. . . . ' An ill-off, discontented man can readily grasp that prop- osition. Probably, in the main, that is just what discontent does grasp in Socialism."[12]

Discontent was much on Lorimer's mind, particularly discon- tented men who were not settling down as they should to a post- war world of hard work and self-restraint. The readjustment period claimed by returning soldiers and the continued high wages de- manded by labor were ominous signs, as editorials on work and articles by Corra Harris and Herbert Quick made clear. In address- ing labor questions directly, however, the *Post* was at first cautious, offering nineteenth-century visions of abundant opportunity and urging cooperation and compromise. But as strikes spread, that view gave way. Lorimer now saw in the labor unrest of these years the ubiquitous hand of bolshevism.

Until the Boston police strike in the summer of 1919, the keynote in labor articles remained cooperation. In at least one in- stance, the *Post* went further, backing labor against unfair manage- ment. But the article that took this position was essentially historic, looking back to life in the western mine fields through lenses blurred and unfocused with nostalgia. The anonymous article, in the form of a letter, reminisced about life in Leadville in 1879, a time when there was no radical talk, when fortunes were quickly made and just as quickly lost, and when labor and management lived in happy harmony. Great opportunities still remain, the writer promised, and the answer to the present strife lay simply in manage- ment listening to labor. "If miners to-day are talking class war and proletariat the main cause, we believe, is simply bad management."

"The answer to the soap-box class war and proletariat stuff is fair and just treatment of labor." [13]

Like the old Leadville miner, the *Post* was confused in its response to modern labor. Immediately after the war, a middle-of-the-road position seemed wisest as well as truest to American fair-mindedness. A 1919 editorial urged an avoidance of extremist views toward labor even though that often meant "rest[ing] under the imputation of really having no policy at all." Even so, "the walking is a whole lot better in the middle of the road." And that same year business writer Forrest Crissey, in a preview of what would come to be called the "American Plan," did a series of articles arguing for new relations between labor and management as the best means for avoiding strikes. The most advanced employers, he pointed out, had invited labor to join in policymaking. There are "a heap of new feet under the council table at which the working policies of the companies are decided, and most of them are shod with the heavy brogans of the shop type." [14]

But the Boston police strike ended the *Post*'s equable position on labor. Strikes were becoming epidemic, and strikes, as the *Post* maintained, were the work of radicals. Lorimer now worked out his analysis and his political position: strikes were the work of radicals; labor unrest was the product of aliens. "For its own selfish good labor should not try to unionize men who cannot under any circumstances be unionized with propriety, unless our government ceases to be democratic and American and becomes autocratic and Russian." Once the police strike was settled, the *Post* summed it all up as "a show-down between the radical elements of organized labor and the American public." As George Pattullo, home from the war, explained, this was not a "black eye for labor" but for the radical elements in the labor movement. Samuel Gompers, "who proved himself 100%" in his handling of radicals during the war, never sanctioned this strike, which, it is clear to Pattullo, had been caused by "elements which formerly were identified with I.W.W. thought and aims." [15]

By late in 1919, with the Pittsburgh steel strike, Lorimer printed a particularly virulent piece; set in "Donassen," a portmanteau name for steel towns Donora and Monessen, it pictured native Americans as "helplessly afraid," finding themselves outnumbered by foreign-born steel workers, "imbued with a new kind of class hatred." Only a "puny fifteen hundreds" of Americans with "a dozen state police" stood between "thirteen thousand five hundred . . . Magyar, and Slovak, and Austrian, and Croatian, and Servian, and Bulgarian, and Italian, and Greek, and Polish, and Lithuanian, and Russian, and Rumanian" strikers bent on "owner-ship—actual ownership!—of the Pennsylvania mills."[16]

The association of strikes with radicalism was, like the *Post*'s nativist outlook itself, far from eccentric; again, Lorimer was at once reflecting mainstream ideas and shaping popular opinion, giv-ing form and substance to the more inchoate fears and prejudices of his less articulate and powerful countrymen. The editorial page served him well here, but when Lorimer identified an issue as critical, he turned to his stable of familiar *Post* writers for support-ing articles. When the steel strike broke out in Gary, Indiana, in 1920, he turned to Emerson Hough.

During the war, Lorimer had demonstrated his genius at find-ing the right man or woman for a particular assignment. This did not always, or even most often, mean a writer experienced at cover-ing a particular area. What Lorimer learned was that the writer the *Post* audience had taken to its hearts through fiction, like Mary Roberts Rinehart, or humor, like Irvin Cobb, would be the writer that audience would trust to tell the story of the war. With Emer-son Hough, Lorimer worked the same vein.

Hough had been writing for the *Post* since 1902 when his western story, "Dinner at Heart's Desire," appeared. Its popularity spawned a series of "Heart's Desire" stories, and in 1905 he ac-cepted Lorimer's offer to write the "Out-of-Doors" feature, dealing with "sports of the field."[17] In 1906 and again in 1907 he did a series of pieces on cattle, and early in the war another on the national parks. Then in 1919 he returned to western subjects in "Traveling the Old Trails."[18] To the *Post* reader, Hough was inti-mately connected with the American West and with all the West conveyed.

Lorimer got good work out of Emerson Hough and he encouraged him, most spectacularly in the early 1920s when Hough was working on his best-selling western novel, *The Covered Wagon*, serialized in the *Post* in 1922. But Hough was an unpleasant man, and, according to his biographer, Delbert E. Wylder, Lorimer "was one of the few editors who could get along with him." The problem was Hough's vicious bigotry. In the early 1920s, of course, nativist attitudes made him a comrade of all patriotic anti-Bolsheviks, but he had come to this position a good deal earlier. In 1908 he had written to the editor of *Success Magazine*. "Three things no sane editor will touch—and they are the only three things which ought to be touched—immigration, Jews, and labor. These, with the Negro problem, cover pretty much all the big in's and out's of Americanism today. If we could wipe out all the Jews, Negroes, Immigrants, and Labor Unions in the world, we would have a fairly decent country to live in; otherwise not, I fear." [19] Among the sane editors in 1908, Hough certainly could have counted George Horace Lorimer; furthermore, at no time, whatever the provocations of patriotism, would Lorimer have subscribed to these extreme views.

But to the readers of the *Post* Emerson Hough was not a fanatical bigot, but rather a bard of the West, an evocation of old American values. It was in this guise that Lorimer sent him to cover the Gary steel strike in a two-part article called benignly, "Round Our Town" (February 14 and 21, 1920).

Hough, like a parodic Walt Whitman, lounges and invites; he and the reader are one. "It must often have occurred to you, as it has to me, that one or two of the rings of the planet Saturn are a trifle bent and ought to be adjusted. How would it do for you and me to take our little hammer and saw and go out into the stilly night and fix up those rings as they ought to be?" These opening sentences provide an analogy to the project of socialism: "Let us prove that all men, being equal, must always be alike, and never may grow or advance." And Gary was the place to take a look at this proposition, a look made particularly significant because "you and I have been paying for all these strikes, though you and I have not struck at all, have not asked for any more money, have only asked to be allowed to live our own lives and do our own work."

The American consumer, Hough and his chummy "you," is the goat. Because the consumer is going to pay for this strike and all the others, labor has "made life in America of late almost unbear-able. The old American happiness and content are gone." So, says Hough, "I went to Gary." And he returned with his articles, illus-trated with photographs of workers' houses and gardens, with boardinghouses, with the YMCA.

A brief history of Gary follows, with emphasis on its immi-grant population of laborers and its proximity to the quintessential American city, Chicago. Hough went there an innocent. "I was just like you—a plain, decent, hard-working American who paid his bills and let someone else run the country. . . . I voted sometimes. I read a little. I did not know anything about Gary. And while you and I dreamed and drifted along Gary happened."

Hough recounts his experiences meeting and talking with people along the way, trying to keep his balance in a wash of immigrants and socialists, finally arriving at a labor council hall where he attempts to argue the virtues of the American way. Thus, as he put it, "I passed most of my first day or so among the oppressed, who could hardly make more than twenty or thirty dollars a day and who were ground under the heel of a military and industrial despotism." His ironic judgment is supported by "a young bank president," who tells him " 'There never has been a time when labor was paid so well as it has been right here.' " Furthermore, " 'It is entirely correct to say that bad leading of the unions here made this trouble. . . . This town is red right now. It's I.W.W. right now inside.' "

At the very heart of this analysis, of course, lies the issue of the immigrant. There are Americans to be found, most visibly the federal troops, "splendid young chaps . . . unmistakably Ameri-can." But as the bank president explains, " 'The great majority of the population . . . is foreign.' " Some might see the problem as one of Americanization, but Hough is savage toward this idea—so sav-age, indeed, that he takes Thomas Jefferson to task. "Mr. Thomas

Jefferson handed out a nice juicy mental peach to the world when he suggested that all men were free and equal."

When the *Saturday Evening Post* attacks Thomas Jefferson and by an obvious extension the Declaration of Independence, we have a measure of the editor's frustration and desperation. On Jefferson's shoulders are laid as well those "mentally subjective theories about altruism and democracy, which in [Hough's] belief have pretty much brought America to ruin." The only answer is deportation and, in its absence, the law of the vigilante. A member of the Loyal Legion described for Hough how they handled a "bunch of these foreigners," even though they were outnumbered six or eight to one. "'Our method of work was to grab a man's right arm with the operator's own left hand, then bring down the black-jack across the hand bones or wrist of the man thus caught. One rap was enough.'"

Backed by his interviews with workers, labor leaders, soldiers, bankers, and most authoritatively with "a gentleman whose iden-tity must remain unknown," Hough calls for action, action against the "political cowardice" in Washington that refuses to halt immi-gration and to increase deportation. His visit to Gary has taught him that American laborers are straight, but that radicals, immi-grant radicals, have infiltrated their ranks, bankrolled by "European money," for, as his high-level anonymous source explains: "'A deliberate and systematic process of infiltration is going on, through which America is being penetrated by the Red doctrines and the poison of Soviet propaganda.'"

Labor problems hit home for Lorimer in the spring of 1921 as the business recession affected the *Saturday Evening Post* and some Curtis workers went out on strike. This was a particularly damag-ing blow to the Curtis Company, which prided itself on the model facilities the Curtis Building had offered employees since its com-pletion in 1912. As if in answer to Lorimer's fears of the worst, the strike came over hours; Curtis employees, like the rest of over-indulged America, wanted a shorter work week. A dignified edi-torial, under the guise of asking subscribers' indulgence should their copies arrive late, pleaded the *Post*'s case. "A number of our employees are at present on strike . . . not over wages, which are higher than ever before in the history of the printing trades—from sixty-five to more than one hundred percent up from prewar fig-ures—but over a demand for a reduction from forty-eight to forty-four hours. . . . Coming at a time of general business depression, when the whole economic trend is toward lowered costs, this demand cannot be complied with."[20] This high-minded editorial took its stand on the premises of economic law, the necessity to meet recession with reductions in costs. Whatever chagrin the strike cost the *Post,* the belief in economic law was sincere; for Lorimer it had the same status as natural law.

With the bituminous coal miners' strike in 1921, Lorimer took a similar approach, assigning the story to business writer Floyd Parsons who analyzed the strike in terms of economic law. While Parsons's stand was essentially antilabor, and although he was writing about "what may be the greatest labor struggle in history," his tone was restrained, reflecting the idea that the issues behind the strike were amenable to reason. Parsons, therefore, explained the issues. "We are paying a heavy price to-day because of the failure of certain classes to pay careful attention to simple but irrevocable economic laws." These simple laws mandate the lower-ing of costs in "all basic industries." Labor has failed to recognize this because "the various unions of mine workers are under the control of some of the country's most radical labor leaders."

Despite its antilabor stance, the Parsons article did not set about castigating the miner himself. Instead, an upbeat note was attempted in a preposterous section that laid out the advantages of work in the coal mines. In comparison to farming, for example, mining is "less arduous" and offers shorter hours. Moreover, "the idea of working in a cool place in the summertime and a warm place in the winter months appeals to many men." As if that were not sufficiently appealing, there were also economic advantages due to the "lower cost of living which exists in most coal-mining communities."

At the close of his article, Parsons returned to the radical threat and to a dystopian vision of the future: "The dream of the United

Mine Workers and several of our famous United States senators—
government control of the mines." But the major point did not lie
there; it lay in the rights of the consumer, the public who paid for
these strikes, the public who needed coal at a reasonable price.[21]

A few weeks after the Parsons article appeared, the *Post*
opened its pages to Ellis Searles, editor of the *United Mine Workers'
Journal,* who wanted to plead the miners' case. It is worth noting
that he turned to the *Post,* anticipating there the widest circulation
of his argument. He understood, of course, just where the *Post*
stood and he took care to distance himself, and the United Mine
Workers, from any taint of radicalism.

UMW members, insisted Searles, were "amazed" that the
bituminous coal operators refused to negotiate. More significantly,
the UMW had not been clearly represented to the public; it needed
an "editor"—or as we would now say, a PR man. Searles assumed
the role, and he carefully explained the miners' demands. The six-
hour day and five-day week were not a demand for more pay for less
work (here Searles showed how well he understood Lorimer's position), but for a "reasonable assurance that they would have the
opportunity to work steadily six hours a day and five days a week
throughout the year, instead of eight hours a day, six days a week
only a part of the time."

After laying out the facts and the arguments, Searles turned to
the real issue. The miners are "good American citizens," with the
same "patriotism and loyalty in their hearts that exists among other
Americans." Eighty thousand of them fought in the war "with the
same fervor as other men"; they bought Liberty Bonds and "volun-
tarily they suspended many of their most cherished rules of employment in order that they might do their full bit." What the miners
want is "steady employment under proper working conditions and
at a decent rate of wages, so that they may earn enough to maintain
their families on a real American standard of living." "It is not fair,"
Searles insisted, "to raise the cry of radicalism against such men."[22]

Searles hit the issue precisely, if plaintively, with his protest
against the unfairness of "raising the cry of radicalism." Radi-

calism had become the antonym of Americanism. If this had begun during the war as rhetoric, it now carried the weight of fact. To save America it would be necessary to purge it of non-Americans, of aliens, of immigrants. Immigrants were fouling the clear stream of Americanism; they were importing the noxious theories of bolshevism. If immigration could be stopped, America had a chance.

The first step was deportation, and the *Post* began a campaign to rally the public to full support of the deportation laws. An editorial wove the sailing of the first shipload of deported aliens into the fabric of American history: "Two ships, the Mayflower and the Buford, mark epochs in the history of America. The Mayflower brought the first builders to this country; the Buford has taken away the first destroyers."[23] But, as another editorial on the same page made clear, deportation was only half the solution; "drastic action" regarding immigration was also urgent. From Lorimer's point of view, his task was to rid the public of sentimental ideas about America as a haven; the Emma Lazarus poem on the Statue of Liberty had gone out of date. "We must rid our minds of the notion that America is some kind of institution for the care of nuts . . . that men who cannot speak our language have a God-given right to tell us where to get off." And assimiliation, Americanization, at least as it was generally understood—i.e., as learning "not to keep the coal in the bathtub"—was not the answer. Real Americanization took generations. Thus, "the rank and file of these unassimilated aliens still live mentally in the ghetto or as peasants of the great estates. In thought they are still stoned by the gentiles; still ground down by the master—yoked in mind to the ox of the field."[24]

As Congress debated the immigration issue, the *Post* kept up its barrage. When the Johnson bill was passed, late in 1920, shutting off immigration for one year, Lorimer had breathing space to plan his own campaign. Meanwhile, he lectured his readers again on the fatuity of outdated and sentimental American credos: "It used to be one of our proudest boasts that we welcomed the down-trodden, the oppressed, the poverty-stricken, the fit and the unfit to a land of freedom, of plenty, of boundless opportunity. Our hindsight tells us that this boast was fatuous."25

Typically, Lorimer now set out to find himself a writer, one who could do a special series on immigration for the *Post*. For this assignment he found Kenneth Roberts. Roberts had written a couple of stories in 1917 that the *Post* bought. The next year, as a captain in the AEF posted to Siberia, he wired Lorimer suggesting that he write a report for the *Post*. Lorimer wired back that he was very interested and in 1919 published Roberts's "The Random Notes of an Amerikansky" as the lead article on May 17. The two finally met that spring and Lorimer asked Roberts, "Got anything on the way Bolshevik ideas work out in actual practice?" Roberts responded, "Communism is an aristocracy of superboobs, determined to impose their own murderous and destructive beliefs on the whole world."26 Lorimer had his man.

The next month the *Post* published Roberts's "The Super-Boobs" (June 7, 1919), a depiction of Boston as captured by a Bolshevik leader who appoints his ignorant chums to head Harvard, the Boston and Maine Railroad, and the public schools, while he moves into Mrs. Jack Gardner's house (now the Isabella Stewart Gardner Museum). All the notable Boston Brahmins are forced to wash dishes in the Parker House, dig graves, clean floors, and make beds at the Charles Street Jail, their wives and children held hostage. If this sounds like a wild send up of anti-Bolshevik propaganda, it assuredly was not. "Boston was a city of filth, of disease, of incompetency, of ignorance, of squalor, of vice—a typical Bolshevik city."

Then in August appeared a play script Roberts had written while with the AEF, in collaboration with Robert Garland. This work dramatizes the last days of the Romanoffs, as they are finally murdered by being dropped into a well into which explosives were "lavishly" thrown. In an author's note, Roberts pointed out that "in all salient features" the play followed facts discovered by U.S. Intelligence and other observers. The murder in the well and the "liberal use of explosives" explained why no bodies were ever discovered.27

By the summer, Lorimer was ready to pop the question: "You

know anything about immigration?" and on learning Roberts did not, concluded, "Well, find out all you can about it, because that's one of the things I want you to cover."[28] Lorimer was sending Roberts to Europe. In one of his rare long letters he laid out Roberts's assignment: "The prime object of your trip is to secure a series of articles on immigration." Lorimer was particularly interested in the fact that some immigrants were no longer coming to America in search of freedom or even for opportunity in the old sense. Opportunity now meant merely making "a stake" and then returning to Europe. Such aliens were not candidates for Americanization. His instructions to Roberts emphasized this.

First, you should get in touch with as many aliens recently returned from America as possible and get their reactions on the situation they find at home and their intentions as to settling down in Europe or returning to America. Secondly, we want to find out to just what extent aliens are planning or hoping to emigrate to America: the causes behind their decision; whether they are going to make a stake with the idea of returning to Europe and settling down there or whether it is their plan to become citizens of the United States.[29]

Roberts's articles from Europe appeared frequently through the first half of 1920. The first, "The Rising Irish Tide," appeared as the lead article on February 14. The article opened with Roberts pointing out that there were 14 million foreign-born in the United States. Such a number suggested "hordes," and "hordes," in turn, "Vandals." On that inspiration, he did some research, discovering that the Vandal horde that overran Europe was only one-fifteenth of the number of those who immigrated to America between June 30, 1913, and June 30, 1914. "It is partly for the purpose of delving into this hazy problem that I am wandering through the highways and byways of Europe."

The articles charted Roberts's progress through Europe and consistently attacked sentimental beliefs about America as a haven and America as a melting pot. Lorimer was delighted and decided to send Roberts back for a second trip. "We've got to hammer at immigration," he told Roberts, "until Washington and the country at large wake up to what's happening." This time, Lorimer wanted him "to start with the emigrants at their homes and go right down to the ships with them. . . . And when you're done with the ports of embarkation, give us an article or two on what's happening to the Russian refugees kicked out of Russia by the Bolsheviks."[30] The work Roberts did for Lorimer was extremely effective: the commissioner-general of immigration attributed the passage of the Immigration Act of 1924 to these articles in the *Post*.[31]

Meanwhile, Lorimer continued to wage war from the GHQ of the editorial page, and in 1921 he had found a new weapon in "race theory." In April of that year, with entirely unconscious irony, he cited the scientific work of Luther Burbank in support of the need to restrict immigration: an ignorant Congress, unwilling to curb immigration, was itself becoming "the propagators, almost the vicarious ancestors, of whole populations of future Americans, for theirs is the say as to their racial parenthood."[32]

In May the issue was more carefully delineated, for now Lorimer could bring to bear Mendelian biology and the genetic race theories of Lothrop Stoddard and Madison Grant. From Mendel, an editorial lectured, comes "the data that have enabled scientists to study intelligently the beginnings of our racial degeneration." For a while we deceived ourselves about this; industrial necessity and the consequent need for cheap labor led us to invent "the rose-colored myth of the all-powerful melting pot." But we can no longer afford this view. Fortunately, two books have been published which "every American should read if he wishes to understand the full gravity of our immigration problems."

Unprecedentedly, the *Saturday Evening Post* took the editorial page to promote these books: Madison Grant's *The Passing of the Great Race* and Lothrop Stoddard's *The Rising Tide of Color*, both of which predicted the defeat of the white race at the hands of people of color. Bolstered by "science," Lorimer could once again urge his readers to surrender their sentimental view of immigration. "Many a good soul taught from childhood in the Pollyanna school of immigration literature is genuinely puzzled by the newer view of its problems, and is inclined to think that all this hue and cry about the alien peril is the outgrowth of a passing hysteria or the lurid fiction of sensation mongers." "There is," Lorimer added with melancholy wisdom, "no process more disagreeable than the repudiation of an ancient and boasted policy," but now, with scientific evidence before us, there is no choice.[33]

Lorimer did not let up in the battle against immigration, but neither that cause nor the continuing attacks on radicalism exhausted his editorial energy. He came more and more to see the *Post* as a political force committed to a particular position and with the responsibility to turn public opinion toward that position. Lorimer had a clear vision of America, and the *Post* became the medium for that vision. As he wrote to Julian Street, "I have a dozen running fights on my hands, growing out of crusades in which we are engaged."[34]

Because Lorimer now saw America as endangered by new forces and ideas, much of what he wrote was negative, taking the form of an attack on a system or an idea. But at the same time, older *Post* causes were supported, and supported with whatever shreds of optimism Lorimer and familiar *Post* writers could wrap themselves in. Most promising were the old themes of business and politics and particularly an idealized fusion of the two—both a businesslike running of the government and a businesslike man in the White House. The 1920 presidential election seemed to provide the occasion.

Lorimer had no question about who should be president: Herbert Hoover was his man. The *Saturday Evening Post* began campaigning for him at the beginning of the election year with a long editorial called "Business is Business." After exposing the poor reasons for which we generally vote for a candidate, essentially a question of "sentiment," Lorimer turned to the problem of the public misunderstanding of the term "business man." The great majority of businessmen were not creatures of "ledgers, syndicate profits and special privilege," nor were they "self-advertised multimillionaires resident on Manhattan Island." Neither type was "representative of the big, broad, constructive business of the country."

Returning to the rhetoric of the *Post*'s first decade, Lorimer declared, "The genius of America is business; the real leaders in America are business men"; moreover, "the real business of states-manship is business."

Of course, Hoover was not precisely a businessman, but the editorial folded the work of the engineer into the capacious defini-tion of business. "We need men in office with the constructive-engineer type of mind—for rebuilding the world is a job of con-struction, a business job." It was a question of a quality of mind and of the kind of training business provided. The final paragraph at last provided the generic businessman with a specific name: "Yet Her-bert Hoover is just a plain American business man."[35]

The editorial page continued to press this argument and at the same time to rehearse the old theme of the shame of machine poli-tics, party loyalty, and the nominating conventions. It was urgent to try to undermine the old political system, one the *Post* had been heartily sick of since the Bull Moose election of 1912. Moreover, Hoover's own party position was unclear, since he was nominally a Republican but had worked for the Wilson administration. The *Post* dreamed of the possibility of bipartisan endorsement of Hoover and the formation of a coalition government, but such a proposition remained in the realm of fantasy given the realities of the political process: "That dreary old show, Presidential Party Politics, is now in rehearsal, preparatory to going on the road. It looks like a revival of The Black Crook or Haverly's Minstrels. There isn't a new idea, a new dance or a new gag in the piece."[36]

Eager to offer Hoover the *Post*'s multimillion audience, Lori-mer solicited a piece from him and published it as the lead article on April 10, 1920. "Some Notes on Agricultural Readjustment and the High Cost of Living" is just as learned and quite as dull as the title suggests. *Post* writers knew how to instruct while delighting; Hoover knew only how to instruct. He laid out eight propositions regarding inflation, speculation, and the shortage of world agri-cultural production, buttressed them with many figures and a good deal of complex analysis, and warned that "there are no easy for-mulas" for a solution to these problems.

Two weeks later, a pro-Hoover editorial argued, "A new world is upon us"; nineteenth-century "ideals and methods" would no longer work. From that stance, it referred to the Hoover piece: "Nothing that has been written so clearly outlines the situation as the article published in THE SATURDAY EVENING POST of April tenth, and coming from the pen of Herbert Hoover, who may well be called the world's best-informed man and keenest thinker regarding the industrial situation that now confronts society, and the bases on which a solution must rest."[37] A month later, arguing that business readjustment would be "almost the sole concern of the coming administration," Lorimer told his readers "that the country must choose a man of wide experience, with broad knowledge of agriculture and industry" for the next president.[38]

The *Post*'s appeals to the power of the people were entirely unavailing against the entrenched power of the politicos. After the Republicans nominated Harding, Lorimer noted that the convention was the same old circus, controlled by politicians. Although the people wanted "the right sort of business man," they failed to organize. Commenting wearily that Harding might be the best man, the *Post* added a sour note on Hoover himself: he might have outflanked the party politicians who defeated him; both sides feared him and he should have kept them afraid by declaring for neither party.[39]

In the summer and fall, Sam Blythe toured the country and wrote articles about the candidates. Although the *Post* was committed to Harding as the Republican candidate, it was hard to whip up any enthusiasm. Blythe dutifully catalogued his virtues: he was cautious, methodical, serious, responsible, modest, deliberate, dignified, easy, cordial, neighborly, and regular in his habits. It was a wearisome and overblown list. Summing up, he told *Post* readers that if Harding were elected, "He will do his job, both as a candidate and as a President . . . sincerely, simply and solemnly as a regular American. He is just that—a regular fellow."[40]

Turning to the Democratic candidate, Blythe analyzed Cox in an article marked by an uncharacteristic ambivalence. Of course, Blythe's presidential candidate pieces were still supposed to maintain evenhandedness, which meant that the anti-Cox—or more precisely, anti-Democratic—position had to come out through asides or irony or merely tone. But Blythe seemed to prefer Cox the man to Harding the man, and the more he emphasized Cox as a fighter and even an unfair fighter, the more energy his writing assumed. Fighting becomes Blythe's principal theme and metaphor. "There are no amenities in the fighting tactics of Cox—not an amenity. He is not an amenable person. As I have said, he is of serious mind, not at all imaginative or visionary. He may be classed as an unkind fighter. It is his creed that the object of a fight is to win it." The fact was that Cox, even in his role as an "unkind fighter" seemed to incorporate more stereotypically American qualities than the "real American fellow," Harding. Born poor, Cox was now "a millionaire and his best friends are the coal miners." He read a good deal, particularly serious books and especially biography. He hunted and fished, and as a golfer, "he could give Harding seven or eight strokes and beat him handily."[41]

Through October the *Post* supported Harding on the editorial page. Turning Harding's banality into his strength, Lorimer insisted that this was no time for dreamers, geniuses, or experimenters, but for "common sense." "[Harding] is accused of being an old-fashioned rather obvious American, who keeps his feet on the ground as well as his ear to it, who has a practical, businesslike view of men and of government. No one has charged him with being an experimental idealist. If this sketch of Harding is accurate . . . that is the kind of leadership [the country] needs right now."[42] At the same time, *Post* political cartoonist Herbert Johnson mounted direct attacks on Cox and the Democrats, culminating in the pre-election issue of October 30. Sam Blythe's lead article on the presidential contest was illustrated with a pair of Johnson cartoons. One shows a dignified Harding on his Ohio front porch, tormented by neighborhood brats under the Fagin-like control of Cox; the children mouth the Democrats' accusations against Harding, specifically that he and his rich cronies were buying the presidency. In the second cartoon Cox appears as a frantic newsboy hawking papers with more phony charges.[43]

Cox responded with outrage to this Herbert Johnson view of his campaign
against Harding.

Cox was sent a prepublication copy of the October 30 *Post* and
he responded like the fighter Blythe described, attacking Lorimer on
the grounds that the *Saturday Evening Post* had no right to endorse
a candidate. The argument from Cox's point of view was that the
Post had engaged in "disloyal propaganda" by "throw[ing] off the
cloak of nonpartisanship . . . [and] imposing on the confidence of
the American people."

Lorimer was furious. Cox had violated a confidence, disclosing
the contents of a magazine before it was distributed to the public; as
a journalist, Cox knew and understood this unwritten rule. Such an
"unethical" act showed Cox's "unfitness for his office." Even more
to the point, Lorimer had no question about where his rights lay;
the *Post* was his magazine and it would express his opinions. "The
cartoons to which Governor Cox takes exception were ordered by
the editor from the cartoonist of The Saturday Evening Post." And
let there be no question: "The policy of The Saturday Evening Post
is now, and has always been formulated by its editor."[44]

Despite the urgency of immigration bills and presidential politics, Lorimer could not devote himself entirely to his crusades;

business matters demanded his time as well. The recession of 1921 took its toll on the *Saturday Evening Post,* as advertising fell off sharply. The "whole economic trend" was discouraging their advertisers, and as a result the *Post* began to print fewer and fewer pages each week, maintaining its advertising percentage but severely reducing the number of stories and articles. Two-hundred-page books had not been uncommon during the war years, and one was printed as late as mid-April 1921, but by July issues had fallen below a hundred pages, partly as the result of the typical summer slump in circulation. That year, however, no typical autumn recovery occurred and the issue for December 24 was a meager sixty-four pages.

Increased circulation seemed the best route to increased advertising, so in July the editorial page announced a new subscription rate. Reminding readers that the *Post* had remained at five cents a copy throughout the war, despite huge cost increases, the editorial noted that the magazine had indeed raised its subscription rates at that time to $2.50 a year. Now, although "wages are still at the peak of wartime heights," the *Saturday Evening Post* would reduce that cost to $2.00, acting on the belief "that every move that tends to put business back on a normal basis is of the greatest possible value at this time." [45]

Circulation did increase by just over 4 percent, but not until the business recovery of 1922. The *Post* soon regained some of its girth as well, though not to the extent of 200 pages. In the better months of 1922, the magazine carried issues of over 100 pages, occasionally as many as 180, but no extravagant 200-page issues. Even though prosperity had returned, the Curtis Company was exercising a degree of prudence.

Prudence, in fact, had always lain at the root of the *Post*'s belief in business, at least for the country at large. Lorimer had always preached saving over speculation, and the columns of investment advice the magazine had provided from its earliest days had consistently warned against get-rich-quick schemes. Early in 1922, as business improved, a *Post* editorial reminded its readers of the need for thrift, for budgeting, for bank accounts, adding that investments should be made in the interests of safety rather than for large or quick returns.[46]

Speculation was accompanied by another danger, a new extravagance the *Post* worried over. Extravagance was, after all, intimately tied to the desire for easy money, quick success, and hence speculation; it was the enemy of thrift. The *Post* tried to suggest a middle road; an editorial talked about "Making the Best of Luxury" (July 30, 1921), noting, "We are not yet wise enough as a people or race to know how to have enough luxury and not too much of it." And Albert Atwood wondered, "Are We Extrava-gant?" (January 3, 1920). Examining this "grave charge," Atwood determined that there was some truth to it, but surmised that the problem was only temporary; at least he hoped that was the case, for extravagance was "one of the forerunners of national decay."

During these years when the *Post* began to characterize the great body of Americans as "consumers," the term was employed without any sense of conspicuous, or extravagant, consumption. The *Post*'s "consumer" was the ordinary man who had to supply himself and his family with housing, heat, and food. It was this consumer the *Post* conjured up in defense of conservative values, the average American as the "ultimate consumer," his patience wearing thin over strikes on the one hand and high prices on the other.[47]

But by the end of 1922 the American consumer was emerging in another guise, the consumer of new and expensive nonessentials, the consumer on the installment plan, the consumer who depended on speculation to maintain his habit. With that consumer, the 1920s were born. The *Post,* committed to business and American prosperity, found its old value system more and more of an anomaly in the new era. It maintained its caution and periodically warned of the dangers ahead, but cautionary articles and editorials were embedded in the slick and seductive pages of advertising. Those advertisements and the consumption they encouraged were in one way the realization of Curtis's career in magazine publication. His magazines were intended from the start as vehicles for adver-tisers, and as the marketing sophistication of the Curtis Company increased, the relationship between consumer and advertiser was itself promoted as an economic nexus *created* by the *Post*. Still, as the Curtis Company conceived it, advertising, while it fueled consumption, did so as an impetus to ever increasing production.

Back in 1915 the Curtis Company had staged a major advertising campaign of its own in the interest of gaining new advertisers for the *Post*. The literature for the campaign analyzed the way *Post* advertising worked in the interests of business. "The whole influence of the Post upon manufacturers, merchants and other businessmen goes back to its tremendous appeal to the individual *consumer* in the individual home. Its first success as an advertising medium was built upon its appeal to the family including not only the woman but the man. Then, as it demonstrated its ability to sell goods and become a more and more widely used medium, it added to its original strength a constant importance to all business men." The *Post,* therefore, was sold less as a magazine than "as a commodity," and potential advertisers should see its vast circulation as a "Commercial Opportunity." In short, the campaign rhetoric argued, with a curious borrowing from Karl Marx, the *Post* "delivers to advertisers a surplus value."[48]

Thus, advertising was part of the great American enterprise of business, and a uniquely modern aspect of that enterprise. Through the advertising it carried, the *Post* contributed to business productivity and beyond that, as the campaign material put it, became itself a commodity. So intimately were advertising, consumption, and production tied to one another for Curtis and Lorimer that neither could have envisioned the new and independent role that consumption would play in fueling the economy of the twenties. And although the *Post* had led the way toward a consumer-oriented America, neither publisher nor editor could have anticipated this paradox: the advertising that so enriched the Curtis Company also fired the new consumerism that threatened to corrupt the very virtues Lorimer's *Post* most solemnly celebrated.

In the issue of the *Saturday Evening Post* for November 11, 1922, precisely four years after the Armistice, appeared two articles and an advertisement that foretold the *Post*'s story for the 1920s in microcosm. A pair of anonymous moral tales was printed on facing pages. "Please Remit" recounted the experiences of a man who had succumbed to the lures of the charge account; a course of wild overspending on credit had led him deeply into debt. "The Sucker" told of a man's going broke; even safe investments had bankrupted him. For twenty years he worked and invested prudently, never taking any plunges; now, with his money gone, he noted ruefully that he should have put his money in a bank. Anonymous moral tales in the *Post* are always a little suspect; it is a reasonable guess that Lorimer commissioned them from reliable writers.

But what effect could these cautionary tales have had against the full-page advertisement for Oneida silver plate? Across the top half of the page an elegant drawing in silhouette presents two young women drinking tea; at the bottom is a detailed picture of a teaspoon in the Adam pattern. The text supplies the remarks of the hostess.

It's just *melting* our bank roll, you know. But ever since we came back from abroad I have been *revelling* in buying things ✓ ✓ A *gorgeous* Persian rug for the library that I'm *crazy* about. And the *loveliest* old Chippendale dining set. Then I simply *had* to have COMMUNITY in the ADAM design ✓ ✓ Tom says we'll land in the poor house, but he's really proud as he can be—'specially of the COMMUNITY.

Eventually, as the *Post* came more and more to fear, the whole country did land in the poorhouse, but until then, despite Lorimer's increasing disapprobation, America revelled in buying things. Unfortunately, this was not another of those foolish ideas from abroad.

"This Niagara of Print"

"**W**ho reads The *Post?*" asked Leon Whipple in a 1928 article in *Survey* magazine. And he answered: "Everybody."[1] It might well have appeared so. *Post* circulation had reached two million early in 1919 and through the 1920s it increased annually, rising to a weekly average of 2,865,996 in 1929. In the 1920s, the millions who subscribed to the *Saturday Evening Post* or who bought it for a nickel at the newsstand got their money's worth. In 1922, for example, the *Post* offered its public 20 serialized novels, 7 two-part novelettes, 272 short stories, and 269 articles.[2] On the average, each issue brought into American homes just under eleven different pieces of reading matter each week, in addition to regular weekly features like the editorial page, the two rather weak attempts at humor, "Short Turns and Encores" and "Cartoon and Comedy," and regular departments like "Who's Who and Why" or "Getting On in the World."

Like the circulation, the number of stories and articles increased annually throughout the 1920s. By 1926 the yearly contents had grown to 20 serialized novels and 16 novelettes, as well as 437 short stories and 421 articles.[3] The average number of pieces per issue had risen to 16.5, and a really large issue of over two hundred pages carried as many as 22 or 23 stories, articles, and serial installments.

The massive editorial side of the *Saturday Evening Post* floated on a sea of advertising. Advertising now made up between 56 and

61 percent of each issue, the great majority in full-page display ads. In 1919, advertising rates had been set at $5,000 for a full-page ad in black and white, and for two-color ads, which grew more and more common, $7,000 a page.[4] In 1924, the Curtis Company board voted to use four-color advertising, and by 1926, as both circulation and advertising continued to rise, they increased the *Post*'s advertising rates.[5] Now a full-page advertisement in black and white rose to $8,000, a two-color page cost $9,500, and four-colors went for $11,500. The price for the back cover was $15,000,[6] a great deal of money to be sure, but it bought an ad that was certain to be seen by at least 10 million people.[7] By 1927 advertising revenues for the *Post* exceeded $50 million.[8]

Certainly, the 1920s were the great heyday of the *Post;* circulation, advertising, profits—all rose like the stock market. The magazine itself seems to stand as a material representation of that buoyant time, with its Rockwell and Leyendecker covers, its F. Scott Fitzgerald stories and Charlie Chan serials, and articles that appeared to cover all of the prosperous and frivolous American scene, from politics and land booms to antique hunting and sports celebrities.

Each big glossy issue presented a portrait of American success, lavish, powerful, abundant. And in our first era of mass media celebrities, the *Post* and its editor achieved celebrity status themselves. The "national weekly," the magazine was called, a "Mirror of These States,"[9] and Lorimer, "one of the great arbiters of public opinion."[10] Newspaper and magazine stories measured the success of the *Post,* calculated in numbers that continued to rise: the number of pages per issue, the number of stories and articles printed each year, circulation, advertising rates and revenue, net profits, even personal income. By 1929, the Curtis Company net earnings were reported as $21,534,265.[11] Lorimer's salary was $225,000.

As the temple to this prodigious journalistic empire, the Curtis Building became an icon, a sign announcing its roots in the freedom and democracy imported from classical Greece and the grandeur and power borrowed from imperial England. As the Curtis Company explained in an in-house history, the entrance "with its paired

Rockwell paints the absent-minded professor.

marble columns . . . was inspired by one of the porticoes of Hampton Court" and the lobby was "faced with marble from the ancient quarry of Mount Pentelicus which . . . supplied the stone for the Parthenon in Athens." But Curtis stood for America and the present, as the building also demonstrated. On one side it overlooked Independence Square; on another, "the Old State House in which the Declaration of Independence was adopted and in which the Liberty Bell is still housed." To the east was the final requisite authenticating landmark: "the old building of the American Philosophical Society, founded by Benjamin Franklin." From this lookout on America, came the *Saturday Evening Post,* with the self-imposed mission to "interpret America to itself." [12]

The *Saturday Evening Post* was not alone in taking itself so seriously. Its celebrity status made it newsworthy to other magazines. Occasionally a magazine article attempted a sober analysis and evaluation of the effect of the *Post* on the America it claimed to interpret. But more often these articles were merely puff pieces, personality profiles, the work of journalists who, seduced by *Post* numerology, paid homage to Lorimer's genius.

In 1926, for example, *Collier's* interviewed Lorimer, under the title "Nothing Succeeds Like Common Sense." Some biographical information and a brief history of the Curtis *Post* preceded salient Lorimer quotes on success, popular magazines, and hard work. Hard work lay behind all success: "'Without effort, without struggle, I have seen nothing worth while achieved even by those heavily endowed with talent.'" But even more basic was common sense: "'Nothing,'" we learn, "'succeeds like common sense and common sense is an expression of sound morals.'" The interviewer concluded by analyzing the chemistry of Lorimer's own remarkable success: "a robust native endowment of talent and character, a rare combination of creative genius and business acumen, ruled by unwavering will, enacted by aggressive industry." [13]

In 1928 *World's Work* published another interview, again celebrating Lorimer's genius and his success. There was unreserved praise for the policies and positions of the *Post,* an "enormous engine of publicity [employed] consistently as a power for good, espousing causes for the public weal." At one point the interviewer tried to discover how Lorimer kept his finger on the public pulse, how he learned whether the magazine pleased or displeased its audience. In replying, Lorimer discovered and named "the silent majority." "People who are satisfied with a periodical are not in the habit of writing many letters to the editor. They have to be greatly moved before they will go to the trouble of writing. I am not too greatly influenced, anyway, by the people who send in their opinions; the silent majority are the ones to wonder about."14

Certainly, the silent majority were the ones Lorimer set out to entertain, to inform, and to influence, and it was precisely this point that Leon Whipple wished to examine in "SatEvePost: Mirror of These States," published in *Outlook* in 1928. The salient point for Whipple was the impact of the *Post* on the national consciousness, for by his figuring, multiplying the estimated weekly readership by the number of issues a year, there were annually nearly "half a billion impacts on the minds and hearts of the American people."15 What does "this Niagara of print" do to us, he asked; "What channels is it wearing in our society?" And he determined astutely that the *Post* was a "magic mirror: it not only reflects us, it creates us." It raises our desire for material things, it "molds our ideas" on the major issues of the day, and "it does queer things to our psychology by printing tales that deceive us with a surface realism, but are too often tissues of illusion." Given those powerful effects, it is important to try to understand, argued Whipple, what the *Post* does "wittingly . . . and what unwittingly."16

Whipple saw no conspiracy between the *Post* and the interests of big business; the *Post* was itself big business. With Curtis net earnings in 1925 of over $15 million, "The *Post* has the business point-of-view—what else could it have?" And if the magazine favored "the status quo, the kind of America that made it, [that] is behaviorism, not malefaction." Even more to the point, "their readers and their advertisers both at bottom hold the same faith." Whipple recognized that although America was "slowly changing in morals and political ideals, the basic principles of the Curtis creed are so deep struck into the national character that they remain fresh and workable."[17]

For Whipple, the central issue was what "economic and political environment the *Post* seeks to reserve and foster." Lorimer's own response to this question was simple: "We try to make a better America and better Americans." But as Whipple assessed it, the "half a billion impacts" amounted to a "campaign of education (to use a gentler word than propaganda) [that] is conscious and studied."[18] Because that "campaign" pervaded both fiction and nonfiction, and might be overt sometimes in no more than a single paragraph within a long article, it was necessary, said Whipple, "to learn how to read this paper." And careful reading showed both positive and negative effects. "No one will deny that this skilled direction of popular thought is often used for fine purposes. But it is, I think, dangerous. It replaces debate with a kind of Machiavellian paternalism; it molds popular thinking without popular knowledge; it blurs the picture by calculated emphasis and unsuspected omissions." Omissions, like serious consideration of the race problem, and one-sidedness, as in the *Post*'s handling of the immigration question, were two shortcomings. Another came with issues that were carried only so far, never far enough to reveal the painful contradictions that might inhere in them. For example, the *Post* resisted foreign entanglements, "yet it wants raw materials and world markets. The vast surplus of this incessant mass-produced machine The Post has helped to create must be sold somewhere! How can we secure materials and sell goods, yet not get entangled, it does not reveal, unless its publication of Rear-admiral Magruder's plea for naval efficiency, and Colonel William Mitchell's for air efficiency, tells of The Post's anticipation that one day we must fight it through."[19]

Personally, Whipple missed the spiritual side, something beyond the everyday and the material. As for other, more typical criticism of Lorimer's *Post*, criticism of its political and economic views, he countered this criticism in closing with the same thesis he stated in his opening: "The critics who declare that in politics The Post caters to a group; that its economics is self-interest practiced as an art; that its international views are competitive, have missed the nub of the matter. The Post will answer—'That is the kind of world we live in.' There is the heart of the quarrel, age-old and non-arbitrable."20

Another thoughtful appraisal of the *Saturday Evening Post* appeared two years later in *Outlook*, which considered that "*Mr. Lorimer justly belongs in the Outlook's gallery of moulders [sic] of opinion.*" In "Merchant in Letters" Benjamin Stolberg took the position that there were remarkable similarities between Benjamin Franklin, who "founded" the *Post* and George Horace Lorimer, who made it great. Both "love the common virtues"; both "worship at the shrine of plain American horse sense"; and both are "arch-Americans in their profound belief that the meaning of life is not hidden but wrinkled on its surface." Both are pragmatists and materialists, believing in "success as the best possible measure of personal and social adjustment."21

Stolberg's analogy to Franklin is not to be taken as an encomium. Franklin's image had come out a bit tarnished from the revisionist interpretations of twenties intellectuals and to Stolberg's mind it was that unvarnished Franklin Lorimer most closely resembled. As a "Merchant in Letters" he is seen as negotiating America's vision of itself and the position from which he does so is essentially manipulative. As Stolberg put it, Lorimer "protests his common sense too much." It is a markedly different faculty that keeps him in control of American Babbitry, "whose granddaddy was good old Ben Franklin and whose outstanding philosopher, guide, and friend today is Mr. Lorimer, who does their thinking and is therefore *not* one of them. The Franklins and Lorimers themselves, of course, do not lead by virtue of their common sense, which they have and apply in those petty affairs for which it is serviceable. They lead by virtue of an uncommon sensitiveness to the ordinary mind of their day, by a sort of calculus of horse sense, which is something quite different." What this meant for Lorimer personally was a great "disparity between his intellectual perspicacity and his bromidic philosophy."22

Stolberg acknowledged the greatness of Lorimer's work as an

editor, but he argued, and correctly, that his role as one of "the main official spokesmen" of his culture coexisted with the period of America's growth into a great world power. Thus, "Mr. Lorimer was the great editor of the national weekly—from 1900 to 1920." Since the war, he had only grown "stronger as a conformist," "irrationally contemptuous of everything 'intellectual' and insolently irritated with all dissent from the dominant standards."[23]

Still, Stolberg conceded, "Mr. Lorimer is a great editor." "He got himself a timely philosophy when he and Big Business were young and adventurous together" and the combination of his philosophy and his strategy gave him "a vast control of public opinion." The success of the *Post* was no more or less than an expression, rounded and complete, of "the character of George Horace Lorimer," and this, despite the fact that "personally, he is above the stuff he prints in exactly the same sense that he is above a literal belief in the fabular promises of advertising." Thus, through power and skill, "it is really the mentality of the American people that [Lorimer] had been editing."[24]

Stolberg concluded moralistically. Lorimer had sold his intellect for a mess of circulation. "He trimmed his philosophy to the pragmatism of one brief generation, and he identified it with a long destiny of a great people." As a result, he had lost his place in history: "And that is the reason why Mr. Lorimer is so very important in and to his own day, and not at all significant in the making of American history."[25]

Lorimer may or may not have found himself a place in history, but his impact on the shaping of the American present could not be ignored by his contemporaries. Even the radicals, the "intelligentsia" Lorimer scorned, had to attend to him if only to attack him and the *Post* as the fortress and fountainhead of reaction.

Upton Sinclair, from the standpoint of his extreme and voluble radicalism, found in the *Saturday Evening Post* all that made America vile, most especially the power and money that seduced writers away from their true art, true politics, and true nature, turning them by what he liked to figure as "tropism" into robots for the celebration of materialism. In *Money Writes,* 1927, Sinclair named names.

Some were simply materialists from the outset, like Peter B. Kyne who once told Sinclair the *Post* had paid him $25,000 for a new story. Others were fallen angels. Emerson Hough, as Sinclair naively believed, was once "an amiable teller of outdoor tales and frontier histories"; then he turned on radicals and immigrants. "I don't think," wrote Sinclair, "I have ever read anything more vicious than the articles he contributed to the 'Saturday Evening Post' glorying in the raids upon 'reds.'" And his "old friend Isaac Marcosson," who had once promoted Sinclair's *The Jungle,* now "promotes whatever his boss has to sell . . . having Lorimer as boss, Ike has promoted the wholesale murder of those same poor devils whom in the 'jungle' days he professionally pitied." For Sinclair, Marcosson's current articles on the international economic situa-tion provided "the standardized doctrine that the masters of world capitalism are benevolent supermen engaged in conferring the bless-ings of civilization upon the inferior races, but having their efforts imperiled by evil-minded intriguers called 'reds.'"[26]

And so he continued, through Harry Leon Wilson, whose "charm and humor are wasted upon the empty sugar and water themes required by Lorimer," and Nina Wilcox Putnam, who "possesses real brains, and wit, and radical sympathy [but] no social conscience," to Booth Tarkington who "interpret[s] the well-to-do classes of the middle west, and make[s] them gracious and charming for Colonel Lorimer." Wallace Irwin, Will Irwin's brother and comic poet and writer, "makes pitiful efforts to be funny while kowtowing before an idol of Cal Coolidge." Other targets were Joseph Hergesheimer, whose "Old House" articles were the culmination of a career that brought him an estate "only an hour's motor ride from the estate of Colonel Lorimer" and marriage to "a daughter of one of the reigning families," and Ernest Poole and Herbert Quick and Brand Whitlock, all of them recanting in their later works the radical visions of their youth.[27]

To Upton Sinclair all this revealed the weakness of the writers against the potency of fascism, for in this despairing and savage vision the Curtis publications became "the great central power-plant of Fascism in America," and Lorimer, the "great literary Fas-cist." But he was more clearly on the mark when he addressed the siren call of *Post* publication for America's writers.

From the point of view of the literary business man, these Curtis publica-tions are perfection. They read your manuscripts promptly, and pay the very highest price upon acceptance. So they are the goal of every young writer's ambition, and the most corrupting force in American letters. Their stuff is as standardized as soda crackers; originality is a taboo, new ideas are treason, social sympathy is a crime, and the one virtue of man is to produce larger and larger quantities of material things. They have raised up a school of writers, panoplied in prejudice, a lynching squad to deal with every sign of protest against the ideas of plutocracy.[28]

Sinclair knew, though he did not acknowledge it, that the *Post* had not always been the citadel of "fascism." And he knew, and more or less acknowledged, that what he found in the *Post* was what could be found in most of America. Both are implied in his comment on David Graham Phillips, "one of the great moral forces of our literature. . . . I do not know how I can better sum up the change which has come over America in twenty years, than to mention that those novels of David Graham Phillips were pub-lished one after another in the 'Saturday Evening Post.' If their author were to come back to the gorgeous show-palace in which his publishers now dwell, he would not get by the detectives in the lobby."[29]

The fact was that the change that had come over America and the change that had come over the *Saturday Evening Post* were one and the same.

As the icon of American prosperity, and for all the success represented in each glossy, overstuffed issue, the *Post* of the 1920s had about it something flabby, even fatigued. Perhaps the compla-cency that came not only with success, but with an America that, in most ways, lived up to Lorimer's expectations, sapped the energy level of the editor. He still had his "crusades," as we shall see, but with the exception of immigration policy, they did not elicit the old fire, and the editorial page was rarely fiesty with Lorimer's racy prose. In fact, much of the editorial writing at the time was left to Albert Atwood, a competent and serious contributor without much dash. In his autobiography Atwood recalled advice he received from associate editor F. S. Bigelow, who felt his "articles were too long-winded and too dependent on clippings, books, notes and the like. . . . I should be locked in a room, he said, without food, water and notes, with only a typewriter and paper, writing fewer series and more short articles on more different subjects. 'Put more jazz in your stuff,' said Big. 'Make it more readable.'" The next day Atwood lunched with Lorimer and told him about Bigelow's suggestions. "'Pay no attention to him,' said Lorimer, 'I don't want jazz from you.'"[30] But is was to Atwood that much editorial writing was relegated in the twenties, and as a result the editorial page for much of the decade lacked rhetorical flourish or the salty, pugnacious language that marked Lorimer's own editorial style.

There were other costs, as well, for the privilege of a comfortable, conservative berth in the era of prosperity, business, and Republican presidents. A serious cost came with the loss of Will Irwin, whose fiction and especially war reporting had brought considerable vitality to the *Post*. Irwin had had an arrangement with the *Post* since 1915; he gave Lorimer "first choice" on his fiction and agreed "not to contribute articles to any other American magazine without Lorimer's special permission." But seven years later the arrangement came to an end. In his autobiography Irwin devoted a single paragraph to the severing of relations.

I was beginning to find the exclusive arrangement with The Saturday Evening Post unsatisfactory. For one thing, Lorimer was a set opponent of the League of Nations, I was a hot partisan. Temporarily in New York during the national election of 1920, I supported Cox; but when as a labor of love I turned out some of the Democratic campaign literature dealing with the League, decency compelled me to send it forth anonymously. By 1923, I was writing mainly for *Collier's*.[31]

Political lines had hardened and political differences were no longer tolerated.

Lorimer's way of handling heretics was to keep their serious nonfiction out of the magazine. In those cases where more or less exclusive arrangements existed, the result was more far-reaching, for these writers could not publish elsewhere without Lorimer's agreement. Thus, in 1921, when *Collier's* had asked Irwin for two pieces on disarmament, Irwin wrote to Lorimer to see whether there would be any objections to this. Lorimer's reply managed somehow to disavow any exclusive arrangement while at the same time denying Irwin permission to publish elsewhere.

As you know, we have made it a rule not to tie up authors by contract, or to have any list of Thou Shalt Not's for them among the magazines. At the same time, there are, as you know, several of our competitors who make a speciality of picking off Post writers whenever and wherever they can, and this naturally lessens the value of these men for us. There is so much duplication in the list of contributors to the popular magazines that they have practically lost any individuality that they might once have had.[32]

Early in 1923 Irwin was sending in the last parts of an entirely noncontroversial series about the West, the results of a trip he made in the summer of 1922. With the final installment he sent Lorimer a long letter, terminating their exclusive arrangement. "I wouldn't feel honest," he wrote, "did I not tell you . . . that this is the last manuscript that I shall be submitting to the POST under our old arrangement." But he had more to say than that, a need to air a grievance perhaps or even to attempt a reestablishment of old relations under new conditions. "Because I want, in justice to an agreement which has lasted so many years and has been at no time tarnished by misunderstanding, to make everything clear, I am going to tell you the reasons for this step." Irwin then pointed out, "During the war, everything I wrote was instantly accepted by you." But in 1920, "things changed. I suddenly found that there seemed to be little or no article work that you wanted me to do." He did contribute some material, like the pieces on the West. However, he said, "On most subjects which really interested me I was forced to keep silent owing to the gradual divergence of my views on things from yours."

The exclusive arrangement, Irwin reminded Lorimer, had forced him to turn down offers by other editors, including Hearst, for articles on important issues. Now *Collier's* had made another offer; "[it] will permit me to express exactly what I think on national and international affairs," and "pay me as much in a year as ever I made from the POST." 33

Hamstrung by the *Post,* forced into silence on "matters [on] which [he] didn't want to remain silent" and losing potential income from his article writing, Irwin broke with Lorimer. Still, he hoped the break would not be complete: "I hope—perhaps vainly— that you may still want my fiction and an occasional article in the range that does not touch on political belief." In any case, he felt "bound" to give Lorimer first refusal on a historic novel of the West. And then, "I cannot close this letter without saying how pleasant my connection with the POST has been; I am breaking it with genuine personal regret. I have never had such agreeable busi⁄ ness relations with any man." 34

Lorimer replied by return mail, clearly relieved to end the arrangement. "I have never wanted anyone to continue with the *Post* when he felt that financially, or in any other way, he would be happier with another periodical. The men in this office are all your warm friends and have a great liking for you personally, but we do not expect you either to make a financial sacrifice or to change your point of view in any respect on that account." As for the future, Lorimer wrote, "We shall be delighted to consider any suggestions for articles or for stories that you may, at any time, care to make and at any price you may suggest, though we may not feel able to follow you into very high altitudes." On the specific subject of Irwin's western novel, Lorimer would like to see it, "but you must not feel that you are bound to submit it to us on account of any talk over it that we may have had." 35

Writers who had been personally much closer to Lorimer than Will Irwin were also drifting away from the *Post.* In 1921 Sam Blythe had announced his retirement, and Lorimer sent Kenneth

Roberts to Washington to cover the political and the social scene in his place. But Roberts, for all his ability, was no Blythe, and it was the *Post*'s good fortune that retirement did not turn out to be Blythe's métier. He had planned, as Lorimer put it to Roberts, to retreat "to California to play golf and philosophize," [36] but the 1924 election found him back on his familiar cross-country tours and his equally familiar place in the *Saturday Evening Post*. Later he traveled around the world, writing articles about Australia, Java, Indonesia. And while he no longer covered Washington for Lorimer, he did contribute occasional personal and humorous pieces, one on golf, another on turning sixty.

But if Blythe remained at least a part-time presence on the *Post*, even "in retirement," Irvin Cobb did not. In 1923 Ray Long took over *Cosmopolitan* and set out to raid the *Saturday Evening Post*. Offering high prices, he bagged not only Cobb but also Peter B. Kyne, long a writer of *Post* stories about Cappy Ricks. Both men had been close friends of Lorimer's as well as frequent contributors, and something of Lorimer's dismay may be seen in a 1923 memo from the *Post* editorial offices to the circulation and advertising departments. After pointing out that "a group of magazines" was currently engaged in a raid, the memo reasserted the *Post* editorial credo: "The Saturday Evening Post never makes contracts with authors, never buys stories that have not been read by its editors before acceptance, and never buys stories on 'name' only." And then—some sour grapes and the promise that certain authors would come to regret their apostasy: "With very few exceptions, every writer who has left The Saturday Evening Post to sell his output under the contract system to another magazine, has given us the first opportunity at his work before tying up elsewhere, and almost invariably at the conclusion of his contract, he wants to come back to the Post again. But an author who was slipping a little when he left us has usually slipped a long way at the end of three years of contract work." At the termination of his three-year contract with *Cosmopolitan,* Cobb did try his luck with Lorimer again, but to no avail. [37]

The Peter Kyne defection rankled for both business and personal reasons. Lorimer heard that Ray Long was outbidding him not from Kyne himself but from Charles Van Loan, at that time working as a contact man for the *Post*. Van Loan learned that Kyne had signed a contract for *Cosmopolitan* at a much higher price than Lorimer was paying and, as Lorimer put it, "There was nothing more I could do about it." He resented both the fait accompli and the whole business of competitive bidding. "I had hoped that, in view of our long relations with Pete and my friendship with him, he would come over to Philadelphia and talk with me personally before leaving the Post. If he had I don't think that he would have left us. Within a short time he would have had a raise, but not a raise based on Cosmopolitan competition." Later, Kyne did submit a few stories to the *Post,* but Lorimer turned them down: "I did not feel that they were up to the standards of his old work and they were returned on that basis, not because I had . . . any personal grouch on Pete."38

Along with high-bidding competition, age, too, was beginning to tell on the *Post*. In 1923 Emerson Hough died. The editorial page celebrated him as a patriot who fought for conservation and against unrestricted immigration. A year later, George Randolph Chester died, the creator of Get-Rich-Quick Wallingford, a favorite *Post* comic character for twenty years. Then in 1925 Eleanor Franklin Egan died after a long illness, having survived the rigors of reporting from some of the most politically unsettled and dangerous places in the world: the Philippines, Baghdad, India, Turkey, China. That same year, Guernsey Moore died; an illustrator and cover artist from the beginning of the Curtis *Post*, Moore had designed the distinctive type face of the *Post* logo. Herbert Quick, lawyer and mayor and longtime contributor, died shortly after delivering to the *Post* the manuscript of his autobiography, *One Man's Life,* which began serialization in June 1925. Then in 1927, Albert Beveridge died. Lorimer wrote an editorial obituary, praising Beveridge's life and work, his "spirit of courage, honesty, self-reliance, and fine Americanism." There was only a subdued personal note: "For friendship Senator Beveridge had peculiar gifts."39

Some familiar writers remained, notably Albert Atwood and

Isaac Marcosson. Along with Garet Garrett and Kenneth Roberts, these men carried the principal serious work of the *Post,* writing on business and the economy, on Europe and recovery, on American prosperity and international trade. All were able writers and Marcosson had a special talent for the interview, but they lacked the verve and range of Blythe or Cobb, the intellectual gifts of Will Irwin, the statesmanlike posture of Beveridge.

To fill the gap, Lorimer found Richard Washburn Child—found and essentially adopted him. Child had been a novelist and lawyer who went to work for Frank Vanderlip, chairman of the War Savings Committee, during the war. Like Lorimer, he was anti-immigration and pro-deportation, and as editor of *Collier's* after the war he carried on those campaigns. Having worked for Harding's election, he was rewarded with the ambassadorship to Italy, from which post he watched Mussolini's rise to power. The story of Lorimer, Mussolini, Kenneth Roberts, and Richard Washburn Child is a tangled one, but entirely exemplary of the 1920s *Saturday Evening Post.*

The *Post* had first greeted Il Duce early in 1923 with a long article by Sam Blythe. Blythe started off by commenting on the absence of earlier reliable information about the Facisti. We had heard of them, he wrote, as "some sort of Bolshevist, or Communist, or Molly Maguire, or banditti [who] should be put in jail." But now he could trace Mussolini's switch from socialism to fascism, to his attack on the "Reds [who] swarmed in Italy," to his victorious rallying cry to exterminate all red ism's. And now he could explain that Mussolini's victory was "the story of youth—triumphant, impassioned, eager, ardent, reckless youth." Yet if Mussolini was certainly "the most interesting of all the new forces cast up to the surface of politics by the vast convulsions of the peace," Blythe was still not sure of the final verdict: "Mussolini may be the statesman to found a new Italy or he may merely be a political adventurer who completed the wreck of the old." [40] Blythe's measured assessment was the *Post's* last. From that point on, the *Post* repressed any criticism of Mussolini; at the very least, his rise to power could be exploited as an example of the backlash against radicalism.

In March an Englishman provided a fervid endorsement, taking particular satisfaction in examples of the Black Shirts' crude
persuasive techniques. To avert a threatened general strike in
Milan, teams of two Fascisti, "in their black-shirt uniforms, but
without masks, holding in their left hands a bottle and in their right
a pistol," were sent to find each Communist leader. "They wasted
no words and said quite simply . . . 'You may take your choice.'"
The Communists to a man, readers were told, chose the bottle of
purgative and the next day there were no speeches and no general
strike. The article went on to celebrate Italian Fascism as a middle-
class revolt that had spread to all classes, so that "it now embraces
all the brains, the energy, the money, and the love of law and order
that are to be found in every class." To underscore the potency of
the movement, the article featured "photographs of bodies of Fascisti . . . physically and intellectually the cream of the Italian
people."[41]

By summer Kenneth Roberts was ready to report that Fascism
was the logical and inevitable result of liberal and left-wing politics,
the reaction that occurred after radicalism had sapped a nation's strength. The message he wished to deliver was a warning to
Americans.

Anything that is written about the Italian Fascisti movement should have
a dedication. It should be dedicated to all the reds and pinks; to parlor,
bedroom, bath and gutter Bolsheviks; to communists, anarchists, syn-
dicalists and Socialists; to government-ownership cranks and to fanatics
on the subject of state-assisted cooperative societies; to organized minor-
ities and legislative blocs and advocates of class legislation; to legislators
who impose fool taxation on the people and who waste the nation's
income on paternalistic schemes and reckless appropriations for vote-
getting; to men and women who scream for the elimination of the army
and navy with no thought of the nation's security; to all strikers who
would imperil the nation's interest for their own selfish and immediate
ends; and to all radicals, subverts, aliens and morons who work for themselves first, last and all the time, and for their country never.

Lorimer could not have said it better himself, for Roberts's furious catalogue provided a comprehensive list of the public issues the *Post* addressed and its position on each of them.

Roberts went on to praise Mussolini and Fascism, though what he admired was rather the Fascists' success in having destroyed the Italian left than the Fascist movement itself. Fascism, he told *Post* readers, using a familiar Lorimer phrase, "is merely common sense applied to the problems of a fool-ridden nation." [42] But in a second article he expressed a more comprehensive approval of Fascism, a program that "represented square dealing, patriotism and common sense." [43]

By the fall of 1924 Richard Washburn Child had taken over the burgeoning Mussolini industry at the *Post* with three articles praising the achievement of Fascism. In the next two years stalwarts Garet Garrett and Isaac Marcosson took their turn. Marcosson, who had been indefatigably covering the economic situation in Western European countries, found much to admire in Mussolini's business instinct. The major point, as far as Marcosson was concerned, was to determine the danger of the rise of dictatorships since the war, but with the exception of Russia, he determined that they had all been "life-savers." The real contrast with Mussolini was Lenin, "the evangelist of the terror that destroyed"; Mussolini, conversely, had "created a force that [was] commercially constructive." Both men had "resorted to force and autocracy. But it is by results that we must measure." The piece was decorated with a photograph of an intensely sensitive looking Mussolini, and the message, "inscribed for The Saturday Evening Post." [44]

But all this was merely the warmup for 1928 and Mussolini's serialized "autobiography." It began in the May 5 issue with "Youth" and continued at two- or three-week intervals into November. Unprecedentedly, six of the eight installments were given the privileged lead position. The story of the autobiography turns back to Kenneth Roberts and Richard Washburn Child. They had run into one another as early as 1923 when Lorimer sent Roberts to Europe on another of his anti-immigration tours. Roberts went to Italy hoping to interview Mussolini "about his offensive

insistence that all Italian emigrants to the United States must permanently retain their Italian citizenship, sympathies and manner of
life while living in New York, Chicago and other American centers." Roberts asked Child, at that time still ambassador, to help set
up such an interview, but, according to Roberts, Child stalled long
enough to prevent it, since he planned to do his own Mussolini
book and wanted no rivals on the spot.[45]

By the winter of 1924 Child had left Italy and become a foreign
correspondent for the *Post,* as Roberts complained in a letter to Sam
Blythe. Blythe counseled patience.

For me lad, you must recognize that your esteemed Boss is suffering from
an aggravated attack of Mr-and-Mrs-Richard-Washburn-Child-itis, not
made any less febrile by the fact they was once ambassador-and-ess. He'll
recover in time. He always does. I've sat for twenty years and watched
them come and go. They only last so long. Presently you will get a chance
at the expense account joys, but not now. At present, the S.E.P. traveling
representative is the Hon. Child, and you might just as well reconcile
yourself to that fact and devote yourself to such good liquor as you
can find.[46]

Blythe was right, though the time was long and both Richard
Washburn and Maud Parker Child (later, simply Maud Parker)
were *Post* regulars throughout the twenties.

Still Roberts did get his chance to travel for the *Post* again
fairly soon, on the occasion of the Mussolini autobiography. Kenneth Roberts recounted the episode in his life story by way of a long
passage quoted from John Tebbel's *George Horace Lorimer and
"The Saturday Evening Post."* Tebbel told a combination cloak-and-
dagger and Keystone-Cops story that appropriately reflected the
nonsense afoot.[47]

S. S. McClure and been in touch with Margharita Sarfatti,
Mussolini's former mistress, who was interested in acting as go-
between in a ghost-written autobiography. McClure came to
Lorimer with the proposition: $40,000 for Mussolini—his fee for
collaborating on the serial—and another $5,000 for McClure as
agent.[48] Lorimer called Roberts to Philadelphia and applied a good

deal of strong-arm persuasion before Roberts agreed to go to New York to talk to McClure. What he found there was a one-page agreement that "if McClure would furnish a book Mussolini would sign it if he found it satisfactory." Roberts was extremely skeptical; moreover, Lorimer wanted the serial only if Mussolini would give time to it, which looked doubtful. Still, Roberts was sent to Rome to pursue the matter.

There he met with Sarfatti. He told her he needed a number of interviews with Mussolini, at least forty, but Sarfatti insisted that was out of the question. "The book . . . must be compiled from a volume which she herself had written on Mussolini, from a collection of speeches and newspaper articles for which Mussolini was supposedly responsible, and from hitherto unpublished material written by Mussolini's brother Arnaldo." Such a proposal was far from what Roberts wanted or what Lorimer had sent him to get. McClure made a last-ditch effort, even offering Roberts his own agent's fee. Roberts declined, wiring an outline of the situation to Lorimer and sailing for home.

Back at the *Post,* Roberts discovered that Lorimer now wanted him to brief Child on the McClure-Sarfatti situation. Ex-Ambassador Child was to take on the autobiography in the cynical, or perhaps fatuous, belief that "his own personal knowledge of Italy and the Italians might prevail on Mussolini to write his real 'inside story.'" Lorimer bought it, Child sailed for Italy, and in short order the eight-part Mussolini story was in print.

The autobiography was heralded on March 24, 1928, with a piece by Child called "Mussolini Now," which warned, "One of the commonest faults in our thinking is to measure greatness by our personal approval or admiration of a man." In fact, he explained, that was an error, for both Lenin and Wilson were great men—a bizarre coupling even for the ever more loyally Republican *Post.* According to Child, true greatness was justly measured by a man's effect, "profound and lasting . . . upon the largest number of human beings." And he prophesied: "In our time . . . it may be shrewdly forecast that no man will exhibit dimensions of permanent greatness equal to those of Mussolini." After that fanfare came the warmed-over and translated materials, presented to the *Post* audience under mawkish titles like "Ashes and Embers" and "The Garden of Fascism," and made up of prose so overwrought as to become unintelligible: "It is absurd to suppose that I and my life can be separated from that which I have been doing and am doing. The creation of the Fascist State and the passing of the hungry moment from sunrise to the deep profundity of night, with its promise of a new dawn avaricious for new labors, cannot be picked apart."[49]

The Child-Mussolini axis is representative not only of *Post* politics in the twenties but of *Post* journalistic practice as well. The publication of a spurious autobiography, cooked up out of the work of friends and family and stirred together by a ghostwriter was not entirely anomalous. Throughout the decade, Lorimer grew more and more to rely on both ghostwriters and collaborators, and for two quite distinct reasons. For one, he had no other way to bring most celebrities to the pages of the *Post,* since most were unable or unwilling to do their own writing. And for another, anonymous and pseudonymous pieces actually written by trusted old hands were a powerful device for propaganda. Lorimer had learned this lesson in the war, and he turned it to advantage in the twenties when the situation seemed to him to warrant it, for such pieces allowed him to publish nonfiction every bit as free of the criterion of factuality as any of the short stories and novels in the *Post.*

But ghostwritten articles had their primary function in bringing celebrities to the millions of *Post* readers. In the 1920s the *Saturday Evening Post* helped America discover celebrity worship as a new and vital form of popular culture. Although the word *celebrity* in the meaning of a person of fame or notoriety had developed in the mid-nineteenth century, it was not until the twenties and the advent of fully developed mass media, especially the movies, that celebrity watching became a national pastime. The *Post* fed the taste for celebrity, and in doing so the magazine underwent a major change.

When Lorimer had first taken over as editor of the *Post,* he had turned to experts, men with experience in a field and a name or a title that proved it. Experts helped to make the *Post* informative, to give it the seal of significance in its early years. But before circulation reached one million in 1908, experts had given way to professional writers, men like Sam Blythe and Isaac Marcosson. Certainly, Blythe knew his field; no one knew the American political scene better. But Blythe was not a participant, not an actor. Like all the great *Post* writers, he was an observer and analyst, and he could write. During the war the *Post* had demonstrated how successfully such observers could report.

Of course, experts never entirely disappeared. Richard Washburn Child, by virtue of his ambassadorship, qualified. Experts were also useful for Lorimer's major campaigns; to battle open immigration, for example, he turned to Lothrop Stoddard, expert on "race theory," or to James Davis, secretary of labor. *Post* readers could learn about the criminal mind from George S. Dougherty, former deputy commissioner and chief of detectives of the New York City Police. Technology, too, came wrapped in expertise: President S. W. Stratton of MIT unveiled the new "robot"—or computer—and Major General J. G. Harbord, now president of the Radio Corporation of America, explained America's future in the field of radio.[50]

But did they? With the exception of President Stratton, all these men had their names signed to articles in the *Post*. In Stratton's case, the article was identified as written "In Collaboration with Frank Parker Stockbridge," and it is easy to understand an academic's discomfort with falsely identifying himself as author of a piece he had not written. It is also easy to understand that no such discomfort would necessarily trouble busy men of affairs—the secretary of labor or the president of RCA.[51]

Experts were often indispensable to Lorimer's mission to inform—and to influence—his public. But celebrities were important as well for their entertainment value, and if it is possible to pick a starting date for the parade of celebrities, it would be 1924 when boxing great Jim Corbett published his memoirs. The next year Fannie Brice appeared, and John Philip Sousa. In 1926 Luther

Burbank's autobiography began, and Paul Whiteman wrote about his life in jazz; 1928 brought Eddie Cantor, Harold Lloyd, and Sir Harry Lauder, the life stories of these popular entertainers sharing the pages of the *Post* with that of Mussolini.[52]

Not all these serialized memoirs, nor all the shorter single articles on one or another celebrity in sports or film or music or vaudeville, were passed off as the work of the celebrity. By the mid-twenties, the *Post* was testing a variety of ways to identify collaborators—where collaborators were identified at all. In 1925 Barney Oldfield's story was "Reported by" William F. Sturm. And Samuel C. Hildreth's series on racehorses was signed by him "and" journalist James R. Crowell. The following year provided a spate of articles with various means of identifying collaborators. Burbank's story was done "With" Wilbur Hall. Henry Ford lectured on prosperity and on technology, "As Told to" William A. McGarry. Amos Alonzo Stagg "Told" his football story to Wesley Stout, and David Sarnoff "Told" about radio to Mary Margaret McBride, who also signed on with Paul Whiteman.[53]

By 1928 the *Post* was studded with both experts and celebrities, some signing their own names and others helped into print by collaborators. By virtue of these middlemen in writing, *Post* audiences were entertained, informed, and improved in a dizzying variety of ways. Prince Christopher of Greece, courtesy of Mary Margaret McBride, explained "This King Business." Dr. George G. Kunz, who had introduced women to the mystery of jewels back in 1908 when the *Post* was courting a female audience, reappeared on the same subject, but now "Told" it to Marie Beynon Rey. Geraldine Farrar "Told" about opera, and J. C. Penney, about the Bible and business. Eddie Cantor, too, "Told" his story, while Harold Lloyd, more whimsically, was "Directed by" Wesley Stout. Even anonymous persons were granted voices, on subjects as varied as trotting races and the business opportunities in scrap metal and junk.[54]

One side effect of the celebrity business was that collaborators were coming to see themselves as professionals, ghostwriting was becoming a business. Wesley Stout, who took over as *Post* editor himself in 1937, did a considerable amount of this work, and other names reappear, like Frank Parker Stockbridge, Marie Beynon Rey, Courtney Riley Cooper, Mary Margaret McBride.[55]

Celebrity pieces, whatever the author attribution, were meant to entertain. As the *Post* swelled to ever greater size in the middle and late twenties, it came to offer increased quantities of frivolous reading in the interest of entertainment. Informative material was fairly swamped in the glut of lighter stuff—including, of course, the fiction Lorimer was printing in ever greater amounts. And without question he was printing the stories of most of America's popular and successful writers. F. Scott Fitzgerald, J. P. Marquand, Ben Ames Williams, Joseph Hergesheimer, P. G. Wodehouse, Don Marquis, Earl Derr Biggers, Sophie Kerr, Nunnally Johnson—all were frequent contributors.

Post fiction continued to be particularly strong in stories created around a familiar character. Mary Roberts Rinehart's spinster Tish remained a *Post* exclusive, her popularity demonstrated by the stories' appearance in the lead place in an issue and by the rising sums Lorimer paid for them. "Tish Plays the Game" was worth $2,200 in 1922; in 1929, "The Dipper" brought Rinehart $4,000.[56] Octavus Roy Cohen still pleased *Post* audiences with his grossly racist comedies about Florian Slappey, but if Lorimer's audience found these stories funny, others called them "caricatures" that were "obtuse and offensive travesties."[57] Humor without denigration was provided by Arthur Train's shrewd lawyer, Mr. Tutt, and in 1927 William Hazlett Upson created the quintessential *Post* comic character, the bumptious, striving, undismayable Alexander W. Botts, salesman for Earthworm Tractors, probably the funniest businessman in American fiction.

The stories in the 1920s *Post* offered humor and romance and adventure, and they entertained. But the fiction Lorimer published was for the most part not distinguished; it did not, even at its best, measure up to the *Post*'s earlier achievement in fiction when Lorimer had brought his readers Robert Herrick and Frank Norris and Harold Frederic. Even the business fiction Lorimer had earlier promoted was now largely absent, its place taken by historic romance, western romance, and comic romance. By no means is this to say that *Post* fiction was poor; as popular literature a good deal of it was very good indeed, but it was safe, it was conventional, and it shunned abso- lutely situations, characters, or ideas that undermined nineteenth- century American values and sensibilities. These were decisions Lorimer consciously made and staunchly defended as part of his edi- torial responsibility. Everybody knew that *Post* stories were "clean, wholesome stories, fit reading for a clean and wholesome people."[58]

Wholesome stories, like celebrity pieces, were sought in ever greater numbers to fill the pages of the *Post,* for it had become necessary to come up week after week with increasing amounts of editorial material for the swollen issues of the magazine. With advertising growing throughout the decade and with the percent- age of advertising in each issue held fairly constant at about 60 percent, the number of pages per issue and the amount of editorial content necessarily grew as well. By 1929 the average issue con- tained 180 pages, and one-third of the issues exceeded 200, at least 40 percent of which had to be filled with fiction and nonfiction. As a result, there were typically twenty or more pieces of material in a single issue and occasionally as many as twenty-eight pieces, exclusive of weekly features.

These issues were crammed with diverse material. The April 27, 1929, book, with 232 pages, led off with a new serial by Chester T. Crowell. There was another serialized novel by Hal G. Evarts running, as well as a series of stories by E. Phillips Oppenheim. In addition, there were nine short stories, by Charles Francis Coe, J. P. Marquand, Bernard De Voto, F. Scott Fitzgerald, Courtney Riley Cooper, Lucian Cary, Octavus Roy Cohen, Edith Fitzgerald, and Ben Ames Williams. Nonfiction included Albert Atwood on investment and speculation, George Allan England on a small Mayan island, John E. Hazzard "and" Robert Gordon Anderson on magic tricks and magicians, Isaac F. Marcosson on the history of American banking, Thomas Beer in a series on Mark Hanna, Rear Admiral T. P. Magruder on the role of the navy in the war, an anonymous piece "As Told to" Mara Evans on raising hares, and a humorous essay by Kenneth Roberts.

This potpourri is representative. Its primary end, both in fiction and in nonfiction, was entertainment. The fiction is forgettable and—with the possible exception of Fitzgerald's minor story "Basil and Cleopatra" and Marquand's war tale, "Oh, Major, Major"—has been forgotten. For the *Post* reader, articles on Mayan islands, the magic business, and raising hares were merely ways of passing time. Information was certainly provided in the articles by Atwood and Marcosson, and in Atwood's case there was the further intention of persuading, of pointing out the dangers of speculative gambling. Magruder's work on the navy was part of a series of antidisarmament articles. Beer's work on Hanna was one of a number of historical series focusing on America's past and its emerging greatness.

The April 27, 1929, *Post* was a glossy showcase of entertainment, but it was a decidedly second-rate effort. As Lorimer had come to recognize, it was no mean task to find enough first-rate work to fill the monster issues of the magazine. And Lorimer knew as well that he was filling those weekly issues with second-rate material. He called it "#2 stuff."

A long letter that survives from the summer of 1929 documents Lorimer's concern over the *Post*'s contents. Ready to leave for vacation, Lorimer was turning affairs over to associate editor Thomas Costain, promising him that he would be "in full charge of everything and everybody on the *Post* floor" during Lorimer's absence: "Use your best judgment and I will, of course, back you up in whatever you may do." But four pages of instruction and information followed, making clear to Costain, and to us, what was on Lorimer's mind regarding his magazine.

He began with a list of materials he had recently turned down, apparently to bring Costain, just returned from his own vacation, up to date. The tough-minded editor intent on high quality is evident here. Although Ben Ames Williams published enormous amounts of fiction in the *Post* during the twenties, Lorimer had returned his serial. And the tough-minded editor hewing to his own political line is equally evident. Although Clarence Darrow was both expert and celebrity, Lorimer had rejected his article on crime, because it was "thoroughly one-sided and [gave] a false picture of the criminal classes as a whole." A hard-liner on crime, Lorimer could not accept Darrow's sociological explanation: "We could agree with what he says about one class of criminals, but he took the position that practically all crime was entirely due to early environment and poverty." Al Jennings, who had collaborated with Will Irwin in 1913 on a very successful series about the rehabilitation of a former convict, also had his new work rejected, for the "first article was thoroughly false and sentimental in tone; . . . the net result was a glorification of the criminal."

Then Lorimer found it prudent to inform Costain about the expectations of two other *Post* contributors, George Allan England and Courtney Riley Cooper, both of whom hoped to develop a series of articles out of single pieces Lorimer had accepted. These writers, he told Costain, were "good for an occasional piece, but not for too many."

With writers like England and Cooper on his mind, Lorimer turned to the larger issue. While he was content with the material in the summer numbers coming up, "there are more #2s in it than I like to see. While I am away I wish that you would read very closely, accepting nothing but #1 stuff." In particular, the *Post* needed "some light, one-part special articles [and] a couple of crackerjack serials." Current serials were, he judged, good, but "they are none of them really world-beaters. . . . We have several men writing for us in the Earl Chapin May class, who present subjects that look good and that almost always turn out to be #2s. I think it would be wise to get rid of these men and try to add more special writers who can do first shop articles for us. As a matter of fact there is no reason why we should ever use either #2 stuff or stuff that is on the line in the Post."

Given the stature and the circulation of the *Saturday Evening Post*, Lorimer believed that "first shop articles" were all he should accept. Then why all those #2s? Thinking it over, Lorimer decided, "We get landed with it either through asking people to revise stories and articles that do not get over in the first place or by letting some of these special writers come to us with ideas which we say are possibilities." After all the work in writing or revising, "we do not quite feel that we can turn them down." Better "not to start with them at all."

Aware of "increasing competition," Lorimer insisted that the *Post* needed to improve all the time. As part of that program, they needed to look for new names, for "the public seems to tire of too much stuff by the same writers." Searching for examples, he turned to his chief defectors, the men who had jumped to *Cosmopolitan* six years earlier: "A lot of the old-timers, the Cobbs, the Kynes and so on, are really living on the past."[59]

The problem of #2s, however, was not altogether a result of well-intentioned but misguided editorial encouragement, nor even entirely due to the continual need for ever more pieces of material to fill the magazine. In great part, mediocrity was the price Lorimer was paying for his policies, his politics, and his prejudices. If the *Post,* like the majority of America, was solidly conservative in its values, increasingly reactionary in its politics and, as we shall see, in its aesthetics, and if it set out to defend those values and politics against opposing positions and newer aesthetic expressions, the result had to be a pervasive second-rateness.

In the early years, the *Post* had taken on debate, used its pages for forums, fought to bring new values and ideas into play and prominence. Certainly, it had never been radical, never muckrak-ing, but it had been filled with the excitement of a new America in a new century. It had spoken for Teddy Roosevelt, for the Pro-gressives, provided a pulpit for Beveridge, published the fiction of Frank Norris, Robert Herrick, Harold Frederic, and David Graham Phillips. Upton Sinclair was right about Phillips; had he lived, he would have had to defect, not like Cobb—for money, but like Will Irwin—for principle.

As the major expression of mainstream, middle-class American opinion and values, the *Post* was ever more resolutely conservative. This was as true for the arts as for politics; in Lorimer's view, modern art, modern literature, and modern drama were pervaded and degraded by radicalism and sex. As he made clear in an interview, he had "little patience" with modern art. The "invasion" of the newer art forms he attributed to "certain magazines, bizarre and Bolshevist," and "he [would] not have it in the Post."[60] Occasional *Post* cartoons pilloried movements in modern art, and a 1923 editorial mocked the artist who lamented his poor sales. What did he expect when his work had been poisoned by "the flood of insanity that brought to the fore in successive waves Cubism, Futurism, Vorticism, and all the other schools and isms?" These isms's were not only insane; they were un-American: "May we point out that neither the war nor the New Art originated in America?"[61]

But avant-garde movements in the visual arts were less troubling to Lorimer than were fiction and the theater, no doubt because abstract art provided no obvious vehicle for doctrine. The theater particularly distressed Lorimer, who saw it sinking into a mire of sex. Editorials warned that salacious plays would call censorship into being, and the *Post* remained a foe of censorship. Theater managers should police their own area. Nor should the "quick buck" lure managers away from "the ordinary, well-understood rules of good taste and good sense." "The line between realism and dirt, pandering and art, is not hard to find."[62] Lorimer also sought theater articles and theater memoirs by old-timers, continually preaching the soundness of taste and standards in the good old, prewar days. The theater, moreover, was not only straining standards of decency; it was sometimes flatly unpatriotic. When Maxwell Anderson's and Lawrence Stalling's *What Price Glory?* opened in 1925, Lorimer heard from frequent *Post* contributor F. Britten Austin that "it was an unwarranted insult to the American Army." Repeating this information in a letter to Kenneth Roberts, Lorimer added: "It has, of course, been very extensively touted by our pacifists and young intelligentzia [*sic*]."[63]

For the intelligentsia, Lorimer had nothing but scorn, and when a former, and frequent, *Post* contributor jumped ship to join them, the battle lines were drawn. With the publication in 1922 of Sinclair Lewis's *Babbitt,* the war received its code name. Babbitt enraged Lorimer. He found in Babbitt a mockery of conventional values, a denigration of much that he prized in Americanism and especially in the American businessman.

During the last weeks of the 1924 presidential campaign, Lewis did a series for the *Nation* called "Be Brisk With Babbitt," in which he continued his satire of middle and middle-class America. The cheerfully ignorant Babbitt was firmly for Coolidge. Babbitt remained a booster for America and for prosperity, and he cited as the source of his information about both the *Saturday Evening Post*.

There was a cartoon in The Saturday Evening Post that showed where, unlike Europe, every American laborer owns a nice automobile and a dandy little detached cottage, and you don't find that in Europe, do you!

So that's why I'm going to vote for Coolidge, and I hope I have made my line of reasoning clear to you.[64]

Lorimer responded. He decided it was time to say something about Babbitt and the businessman and rather more about the role he played as editor of the *Saturday Evening Post* in the production and distribution of literature. In December, *Bookman* printed his "The Unpopular Editor of the Popular Magazine." Commenting on the characterization of the American businessman as Babbitt, Lorimer conceded that *Babbitt* might show us one kind of businessman, "but there are quite as many Babbitts among the critics, the writers, the lawyers, and the professors as there are among the Rotarians." Having linked the hated name to several classes of the intelligentsia, Lorimer turned to the larger matter of his role as *Post* editor.

Lorimer took the position that "the editor of a popular magazine is unpopular with all critics except those who contribute or hope to contribute to his magazine." Among the failed contributors were those who attacked the *Post* by warning that America was being "debauched by lowbrow editors [who] are wilfully barring genius from the public." Lorimer countered, insisting that as *Post* editor his role was that of guardian; since the *Post* was read by millions of "all classes, ages, and conditions," he must necessarily act as "their reviewer." Moreover, his quarter century with the *Post* had taught him "to have confidence in the good sense, good

judgment, and good taste of our popular audience." And if that audience was revealed to be "lowbrow" because it "does not care for
pornographic writing, nor the novel of perversion," then Lorimer
would have to accept the "lowbrow" label himself as well.[65]

In polar opposition to the lowbrow stood the intelligentsia
whom Lorimer despised. These writers, artists, and intellectuals
were responsible, in the *Post's* view, for poisoning the pure stream
of Americanism. Their toxic influence was both aesthetic and political; in fact, the two were deeply interconnected. In the years
immediately following the war, when Lorimer had mounted his
attack on alien radicals and subversives, he had charged them not
only with economic and political subversion, but with subversion
of the arts as well. Now Lorimer found the same aggregation of
vicious ideas in the intelligentsia. Thus, in his continuing attacks on
immigration, Lorimer identified the real enemy as the intellectual,
and he used the *Post* to expose and attack the liberal policies of the
intellectual left. Lorimer was arguing his case before the great body
of the American middle class and arguing it against the intellectuals
who supported and promulgated the liberal and radical ideas he
saw threatening America.

Lorimer continued to hammer away at immigration with the
same arguments he had developed in the immediate postwar
years,[66] but now, as if to counter the liberal intelligentsia, he reinforced his anti-immigration stance with the authority of science. He
turned once again to "race theory" and in 1924 hired its principal
exponent, Lothrop Stoddard, to do a series of articles on European
"races." Stoddard explicated the strengths and weaknesses of the
several European races, complete with a map of the "Present Distribution of European Races," supplied by Madison Grant, the
other reigning race theorist of the day. Prose and maps were supported by photographs, full-face and profile, of Nordic, Alpine, and
Mediterranean types. Under its pseudo-scientific veneer, Stoddard's work was pure scare tactics. Arguing that race is of "fundamental importance . . . in human affairs" and that "the racial factor
lies behind most of the world's problems," he finally revealed that

the superior "Nordic Type [had] diminished racially in Europe during the past 1000 years." In America, however, the Nordic was still in the majority—at least, so far.[67]

With material like this, Lorimer hectored the *Post* reader. His audience remained "the silent majority," and he left the rest, the radicals and intelligentsia, to their own media. And despite the growing influence of newer ideas and newer art forms, the majority, silent or not, remained *Post* subscribers. Although much of the magazine in the 1920s was no more than entertainment, often weak editorial material to tail through the pages bloated with advertisements, there always remained some amount of material in each issue that had the purpose of informing, educating, and persuading that majority. Leon Whipple was correct in his judgment that there was a kind of "machiavellian paternalism" in Lorimer's *Post,* and Stolberg was keen enough to see that the typical *Post* reader was not intellectually Lorimer's peer. But the paternalistic relationship between Lorimer and his audience was a fairly recent development that had grown out of the war to become consolidated in the twenties.

Early on, Lorimer had seen himself and his audience as essentially one; or perhaps more precisely, he had conceived of his "ideal" reader as someone very much like himself, as essentially a businessman, in the *Post*'s broad application of that term. Certainly, not all readers were "ideal," and many had to be educated into the role of businessman. This was especially clear in the case of young men, whom the *Post* lectured and encouraged in the early years in the expectation that they would one day become businessmen. But in the 1920s a new distance between Lorimer and his audience appeared.

One sign of this change was the appearance of editorials lecturing readers on the virtue of certain kinds of behavior that Lorimer himself in no way followed, particularly in regard to prohibition and speculation. Many of these were the work of other contributors, and a significant number were written by Albert Atwood; nevertheless, Lorimer approved them all. The style might not have been his, but the message assuredly was.

In the cases of prohibition and speculation there is something of a *Post* history; in other words, it is not a question of a sudden change in point of view. From the outset, Curtis had refused to carry ads for liquor or for speculative ventures. Given the *Post*'s general adherence to the old American virtues of hard work, thrift, and sobriety, this is not surprising. What changes in the 1920s, however, is the distance between the world Lorimer personally inhabited, a world where both drinking and speculating were accepted and important activities, and the world he created for his readers. It was, in a way, as if the audience he now imagined were all youths in need of moral guidance. Youth, of course, was not a condition related to one's age.

Thus, while Lorimer no more respected the Volstead Act than did most other men of his age and class, *Post* editorials continued to lecture on prohibition. The editorials did not, however, make drinking itself the issue. What was at stake was a law-abiding society, the compelling need to obey the law regardless of one's personal attitude toward liquor and prohibition. A 1925 editorial insisted on the relationship between breaking the prohibition law and abetting crime. "The backbone of the crime wave that has followed in the wake of this law is not the bootleggers and their associated crooks, but that large and thoughtless body of respectable citizens whose agents and servants they really are." So important was the necessity to stem the crime wave that, in the *Post*'s view, it was worth surrendering one's individual freedom: "The time has come when the importance of 'personal liberty' must be weighed against the value of personal safety."[68]

The paternalistic distance between the *Post* and its readers appeared as well with regard to speculation. In this instance, language itself carried moral judgments, for stock transactions were referred to by three terms in descending order of virtue: *investment, speculation,* and *gambling.* With speculation, as with drinking, Lorimer preached what he did not practice, for he certainly put money in the market. Even the 1929 crash did nothing to temper his enthusiasm, for he wrote to Mary Roberts Rinehart on October 31 of that year, "[I] got in at the bottom of the break, low, wide, and handsome, and at the opening this morning the stuff I bought shows from ten to thirty points profit." To be sure, like many others Lorimer believed the collapse was no more than "a temporary set-back"; the real point, however, was that, along with millions of other Americans, he saw the market as a way to make big money.[69]

Investment, unlike speculation, was a privileged term, connot-ing financial stability and foresight. Moreover, investment was not only good for the wealthy, according to an Atwood article in 1926, but also an agent for class mobility by spreading prosperity. By means of stocks, here understood as "investments," ownership was passing from the wealthy classes to those of "small but moderate" means.[70] Gambling, however, was pernicious, and buying on mar-gin (or speculation) was gambling. Buying on margin not only put one's own money at risk, but harmed others by inflating stock prices. That kind of speculation was "viewed with disapproval," wrote Will Payne, by all who don't profit directly from it. It was "gambling," and it was "immoral." Speculators, he pointed out with a number of examples, never prosper.[71]

But the deepest evil in stock gambling lay in its effects on character, for gambling, like intemperance, was a negation of the basic nineteenth-century virtues. The profits of speculation, unlike the money earned by hard work, provided cash that cried to be spent. Consequently, American habits of thrift were endangered. But at this point, the Post grew confused. The new economics argued for continued prosperity through continued consumption. Where did that leave thrift?

A 1924 editorial addressed the conflict between the old value of thrift and the new economics of liberal spending. Attempting to determine whether such spending was reckless, especially for the workingman, the editorial writer floundered. What had been American gospel became a matter of personal decision: "Thrift, of course, is a question of individual judgment. What is good or bad judgment varies in every case." "There are natures which flourish best under a reasonable indulgence; others gain the most from self-denial." [72]

Ten days before the stock market crash, another editorial

treated the debate as a generational problem. "The human animal must possess remarkable adaptability, or perhaps resistance, to live through the changes of opinion and theory which mark the progress of thought. In the youth of those now middle-aged, and indeed, of those still in their thirties, thrift was the most prized of virtues. . . . But the emphasis is changing. Now it is the virtue of spending which is extolled." The decidedly middle-aged *Post,* however, wished to show itself as able to cope with change and even with this "seeming paradox." All that was required was "a little common sense." But then the writer found himself in the same mire of confusion that muddied the 1924 editorial; some are better off saving, others spending, and yet others turning their energies to earning more. But even that "moderate statement cannot be erected into a general principle." And again, as if the only comforting refuge lay there: "It is all a question of common sense."[73]

The question of speculation and the associated dilemma surrounding saving or spending were of course tied in the *Post* to the larger issue of business. Business had been Lorimer's theme from the outset and now, in the twenties, business was triumphant—despite attacks from Sinclair Lewis and others of the "intelligentsia." Curiously, though, there now seemed less to say about American business than there had been in the prewar years. The occasional articles that did appear sounded like boosterism, appropriate for meetings of the Rotary Club. Thus in 1924 Floyd Parsons announced, "America's business today is the most powerful force affecting and determining world civilization."[74] Three years later Garet Garrett celebrated U.S. world supremacy, based on the cooperation of free men aided by machine power. He noted as well the significance of finding in the same person the producer and the consumer. Doing some shadow boxing with Marxist theory, he asserted that a new division of labor had been created: the producer and the consumer were now one.[75]

The American as consumer was an idea that had appeared in the Post during the war years. The notion provided a counterargument to radicalism and the idea of class warfare by arguing that

Americans were not essentially either capitalists or laborers but were joined in the single class of consumer. But by the 1920s, the definition of the American as consumer had become less rhetorical and more functional: consumption underlay the optimistic economics of the period. As long as wage earners continued to consume, business would continue to improve, and upbeat economic theory now predicted the end of business cycles. With some misgivings, Lorimer and the *Post* concurred: the world had changed with the new possibility of producing *for* a consuming market. Therefore, insofar as it directed attention to business on the grand scale, the *Post* embraced the theory of the consumer. At the same time, as a number of ambivalent editorials reveal, the *Post* was decidedly uncomfortable at urging the individual wage earner to abandon the old values of saving and thrift in favor of consumption.

In 1926 the editorial page faced the competing claims of thrift and consumption in a full-page editorial on "Installment Buying" (May 29, 1926). In this instance the *Post* supported consumption—"the balance wheel that maintains the even operations of production and distribution." Installment buying, although it had been "contumaciously denounced as a species of speculation, the perversion of cheap money, like plunging on the stock exchange," required cooler consideration. Such consideration, however, turned out to be practical rather than theoretical. Did the installment purchase "represent a reasonable program of expenditures, judiciously interpreted in the light of the probable prospect of maintenance of prosperity?" Were the objects so purchased useful? It was "the purpose of purchase and the quality of the article, not the form of payment, that is decisive." Taking the automobile as an example, the editorial approved the purchase and determined that by and large installment buying "is a development and not a perversion of modern business."

Although Lorimer never found it an entirely comfortable doctrine, the *Post* pretty much went along with this newfangled economics.[76] But occasionally, a more cautious note was sounded, for the old beliefs died hard. Floyd Parsons, whose business articles had been appearing in the *Post* for three decades, had a word to say in

"Old Yardsticks" (February 11, 1928). He supplied his share of boosterism, writing of America as "an amazing industrial romance" and "a story of success unequaled." On the other hand, he cautioned against turning away from "the lessons of experience." But his article bogged down in the rut of antiradicalism, confusing the lessons of his "old yardsticks" with the warnings of radical voices. In other words, to question perpetual prosperity was to fall into the enemy camp. The best Parsons could come up with was a final sober note: "One may well doubt that prosperity has become perpetual. The worst thing that could happen to the United States today would be for Americans to let go the hand of caution."

A sober and ambivalent article like Parsons's could have had little impact measured against the euphoria of spending. Extravagance was always more glamourous, even when it led to temporary insolvency. F. Scott Fitzgerald wrote "How to Live on $36,000 a Year" (April 5, 1924), revealing that his and Zelda's spendthrift ways had consumed all his earnings—earnings that amounted to the substantial sum of $36,000. Merrily, Fitzgerald embraced a new budget; even though it would allow them only three-quarters of a servant, he was prepared to hire a one-legged one. And as for recouping some of their losses, he had followed Zelda's suggestion: writing and selling a piece on how to live on $36,000 a year.

If ever increasing consumption was to be the road to perpetual prosperity, the *Post,* editorial misgivings aside, did its part to encourage it. But such encouragement did not come principally through occasional pieces on business and economic values but through advertising and through the constant, subtle, and pervasive appearance of lighthearted articles that offered readers a window on high living. In advertising and entertainment, in the lighter articles that appeared continually, two or three a week, the *Saturday Evening Post* was a temple to consumerism.

A weekly issue of the *Post* often contained over a hundred pages of advertisements. Many in two or four colors, nearly all beautifully drawn and designed, the ads could not be ignored, and as stories and articles tailed through the back of the book, a reader was drawn into the great merchandise mart of American things. As

"HOW SHOULD CANDY BE USED AT A DINNER PARTY?"

EMILY POST says: there should be at least four dishes of candy on every well-appointed table, formally set for twelve or fewer. For a dinner of from fourteen to eighteen places there should be from six to eight dishes of candy. Still more for a larger table.

On an average sized table, at least four dishes should be large enough to be decoratively important. (From 2″ to 2-½″ high, by 8″ to 8-½″ in diameter is ideal.) Small saucer-sized compotiers—whether flat or on stems—are foolishly under scale except on a very little table in an equally little room.

Candy suitable to a formal dinner table is rather limited to bonbons, caramels, almond paste, chocolates—most especially chocolates—and, in a

dish by themselves, chocolate peppermints. Except the peppermints, each of these candies should be in its individual paper frill.

Candy dishes must be arranged so that each dish on one side of the table is balanced by a similar one on the other. Brown chocolates balanced by chocolate caramels, pink bonbons balanced by other bonbons equally pink, etc.

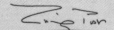

EMILY POST is the Author of
Etiquette: The Blue Book of Social Usage and
The Personality of a House, etc.

FOR THANKSGIVING

ON this occasion you are apt to be more than particular about the candy you serve. Which is to say, you will surely select Schrafft's! For we are as fussy about its flavor and freshness as *you!*

SCHRAFFT'S *selected candies and chocolates are packed in many styles, from one to five pounds to the package—at $1.00, $1.25, $1.50 and $2.00 the pound.*

SCHRAFFT'S
Selected Candies and Chocolates

W. F. SCHRAFFT & SONS CORPORATION · *New York and Boston* · OWNED AND OPERATED BY FRANK G. SHATTUCK COMPANY

Middle-income products promise upper-class prestige.

P E E R L E S S

W H O O P E E !

The new Six-61! Sit behind the wheel.
You will know you are driving a *real* car.
Power · Pep · Looks · Everything!

$1195

Wire wheels at slight extra cost

The Six-81 · · · · · · · · $1595 and up. The Straight Eight-125 · · $2195 and up.
(All prices at factory)

PEERLESS MOTOR CAR CORPORATION · Cleveland, Ohio

Before the Crash—the heyday of the Post's automobile ads

Leon Whipple put it, "The text is like a teller of tales hired by the merchants in a bazaar; you come for the tales but en route you listen to the vendors."[77]

It is worth taking a moment to listen to the vendors and discover what they were selling. The April 13, 1929, issue of the *Post* had 196 pages, including the covers. Just over 60 percent, or 118.25 pages, contained advertising, with 95 of those pages used for full-page or double-spread advertisements by 82 different advertisers.

The *Post* had begun as a man's magazine, and in the 1920s automotive products were added to business and industrial goods and services to appeal to the male consumer or investor. Some 27 percent of the advertising in the April 13 issue promoted products and services for industry and business; the range was very wide, from business stationery suppliers to Anaconda Copper and Union Pacific. Automotive ads, making up 24 percent, offered not only cars—seven different cars and four trucks in this issue—but also tires, batteries, and motor oils.

But it was household products that made up the largest single category of ads in this issue, fully 43 percent. Clearly, advertisers in the late 1920s continued to see the *Post* as a medium through which to reach the woman consumer. The Curtis Company had succeeded again, profiting from the trend that had begun in 1908 when the *Post* discovered the rise in consumer products for the home and set out to attract women readers.

Like the industrial-business ads, those for the home were quite varied. Roof tiling, flooring materials, paints, and varnishes suggested large-scale home improvements. Electric appliances appeared as well: refrigerators and dishwashers, electric mixers and vacuum cleaners, clocks and radios. Some food companies advertised, most notably Campbell's with its weekly ad following the editorial page, but also Dole Pineapple, Quaker Oats, and Planter's Peanuts. There were cleansers and toothpastes, candy and soap, new wonders like Cellophane and, for the upwardly mobile, Community Plate silver. From the useful to the ornamental and even glamorous, the *Post* was a display window for heavy consumption and high living.

That new car of yours

The first time you need a quart of oil—drain the crankcase. Fill with Texaco Golden Motor Oil and never use any other kind in the engine. See that the oil gauge is always at the proper level. Keep plenty of water in the radiator at all times.

With these few precautions your engine will deliver the full mileage and years of service its manufacturer intended.

Any automobile dealer will tell you that Texaco is the safe "year-round" oil. It has the body to stand the strain of summer driving and the ability to flow instantly on winter's coldest day.

Clean as it looks, full-bodied as it feels, Texaco Golden Motor Oil is the finest of lubricants— and a year's supply averages less than the cost of a car license.

THE TEXAS COMPANY
TEXACO PETROLEUM PRODUCTS

Texaco Golden Motor Oil and the *new* and *better* Texaco Gasoline—high test at no extra price—are sold in every State.

TEXACO

TEXACO
GOLDEN MOTOR OIL

FULL BODY

CLEAN-CLEAR-PURE

Motor oil—with the allure of youth and privilege

"It came in this beautiful wrapping"

"I always choose the things wrapped in Cellophane—you can see what's under it."

Du Pont Cellophane is the modern, scientific wrapping material used by manufacturers on a great many different products for your home. It enables you to judge your purchase with your own eyes and assures you of getting it undamaged—sanitary—clean—just as it left the factory.

At grocery, drug and department stores—in fact, at all good shops, the Cellophane-wrapped packages are more and more numerous. You can always buy them with confidence.

Du Pont Cellophane Co., Inc., 2 Park Avenue, New York City. Canadian Agents: Wm. B. Stewart & Sons, Limited, Toronto, Canada.

Cellophane

Cellophane is the registered trade mark of Du Pont Cellophane Company, Inc., to designate its transparent cellulose sheets and films, developed from pure wood pulp (not a by-product).

Technology woos the woman consumer with aesthetics.

Many of the articles that made up the lighter side of the *Post* provided a gloss on the advertisements. In them, readers could learn about new cosmetics, escort systems, Paris fashions, the mores of high society, fancy pets and flowers, jewels, entertaining, travel. Running as a not very silent undercurrent through these pieces on consumption was the idea of money. Scores of items were presented for consumption—flowers, pets, jewels, antiques, paintings—and all carried a price tag; often it was the tag that created the interest.[78]

Collecting was something of a mania in the *Post,* with special attention given to the collecting of antiques.[79] Readers could learn a great deal about the financial and social advantages of collect- ing almost anything expensive. In a series of articles in 1927 Dr. A. S. W. Rosenbach "Told" Avery Strokosch about collecting old books; titles like "A Million Dollar Bookshelf" made the point. Art collecting was good business, too. In 1928 Esther Singleton wrote "Old Masters Enter High Finance" and Boyden Sparkes contribu- ted "The Bulls of the Art Market." The business metaphor was infinitely applicable as the title for a piece on birds illustrates: "Polly Talks Her Price Up!" Amid all this consumption, the *Post* finally published a guide to the perplexed with Edward A. Betts's "What to Collect—and Why."[80]

From the point of view of the *Saturday Evening Post,* con- sumption, and the continuing prosperity it promised to fuel, depended on conservative, which is to say Republican, govern- ment. Herbert Hoover had long been Lorimer's candidate, but when political realities threw the 1920 nomination to Harding, the *Post* had gone along, if not with great enthusiasm. Blythe's private reports from Washington on the Harding presidency were fiercely cynical, even by Blythe standards. As he told Lorimer, the "interporcine war" was under way. But when the Teapot Dome scandal was revealed, there was virtually no discussion in the maga- zine. One editorial tried to blunt the problem by linking it with conservation, one issue on which the *Post* had remained entirely consistent. "Teapot Dome is more than a scandal," announced an editorial that set out to prove it was in fact much less. "Teapot

Dome and all that it symbolizes are the logical outgrowth of our old attitude toward our national resources." The whole question of "conditions in Washington" was much exaggerated, for "of actual corruption we do not believe there is a great deal."[81]

Driving the editorial, and the general silence about Teapot Dome, was party loyalty; once anathema to the *Post,* in the days of Beveridge and Progressivism, party loyalty now became a patriotic virtue. The 1924 election seemed to demand particularly firm adherence to party; therefore, Lorimer was prepared to back Coolidge solidly although he had no great admiration for him. Neither he nor Blythe saw much of a threat in Democratic nominee Davis, but they were worried about the effect of LaFollette in the West, especially if he was abetted by liberal Democrats. Blythe wrote to Lorimer in September that William Jennings Bryan was "out on a double-crossing campaign that urges all Bryan men to vote for LaFollette" in the hope of throwing the election into Congress. Thus, Blythe planned his election articles as "a bit more partisan than usual . . . notwithstanding the deficiencies of Coolidge." He repeated, "this LaFollette stuff makes me panicky at times."[82]

Shortly before the election, the *Post* printed a lead article by Joseph Cannon on "Party Discipline" (September 27, 1924). For years both Lorimer and Blythe had excoriated party politics and their expression in the futile circuses of political conventions dominated by party regulars, crushing the expression of a free people. Now former Speaker Cannon had a message for America. "Government by party appears to me to be the only means by which a free and self-governing people can secure, in a practical and dependable way, the enforcement of the will of the majority." Without naming LaFollette, Cannon made his point: "It is recorded that the first great insurgent of the universe declared that it were better to rule in hell than serve in heaven. That seems to me to be the real inspiration for insurgency now as in all times since history began." It is worth recalling that one great Insurgent, of somewhat more recent date than Lucifer, had been Alfred Beveridge.

Eventually, patience—if not party loyalty—was rewarded as Hoover became a leading candidate for the Republican nomination in 1928. Lorimer had kept Hoover in front of the *Post* audience throughout the previous two administrations, with articles on his work as secretary of commerce. By 1927 *Post* regulars were keeping Lorimer informed about Hoover's chances for the nomination as well as the extent of Hoover's eagerness to pursue it. Marcosson wrote to Lorimer in September with the melancholy news that the high-minded and politically naive Hoover "would make no effort to get the nomination," finding "the scramble for delegates . . . 'a degradation of the office.'"[83]

Even when persuaded to run, Hoover exhibited so little political savvy that Lorimer sent Garet Garrett to advise him. *Post* writer Hugh Wiley was also keeping an eye out for Hoover; he wrote in April to let Lorimer know that "this country needs an inspiring bulletin" about the candidate; "I think you are the only man who could write it."[84] But Lorimer needed no encouragement; editorials on Hoover were becoming commonplace: "Hoover—a National Asset," "Mr. Hoover's Savings Account," "Herbert Hoover—Candidate," and "Hoover's Speech of Acceptance."[85]

After Hoover was nominated, the *Post* took no chances with his election. Lorimer believed Hoover would be a first-rate president despite the fact that he was far from a first-rate electioneer. Al Smith, conversely, knew how to run for office. With all that in mind, Blythe was back on his own campaign trail sending back articles and strategy-planning letters. In late July, Blythe went to California to discuss with Hoover the most effective campaign article the *Post* might run.[86] He wrote to Lorimer from San Francisco in late July, reporting on the meeting. Blythe had come to certain conclusions after "after talking with our peerless but somewhat gun-shy candidate."

I think the first and best thing to be done . . . is to write a calm and detached article contrasting Hoover and Smith in the light of the necessities of the country; the theme being that the United States is the motor of all the world, that our greatest necessities and advantages are economic—business—that the two platforms, being almost identical, are political and hokum, and the thing the voter must decide is whether Smith or Hoover, judged dispassionately from the angles of experiences, educations, abilities, and adaptabilities for this particular job of President at this particular time, and in this particular situation is best fitted for the office. Of course, the showing will be all in Hoover's favor.[87]

Lorimer approved and Blythe wrote "The Fundamentals of This Campaign" for the September 15, 1928, issue. Dismissing the Catholic issue as ballyhoo, he told the "average American" to ignore it and all other campaign rhetoric, and look for the "great issue at stake." In case the average American had trouble locating the "great issue at stake," Blythe identified it: "the United States of America and [the reader's] own stake in it as a citizen, or business man, an employer or employee, and as the head of a family." Economics, not politics, was the issue; therefore, one must judge the man and not the party. Admitting that no man would set out to "wreck business," he alerted readers to the dangers that could come from an inexperienced president.

Blythe seemed to keep on the dispassionate straight and narrow, but (as he had promised in the July letter) it was all in Hoover's favor, despite the apparent evenhandedness. He reviewed the experiences of each candidate with emphasis on education, work experience, and by extension, class difference. Smith attended parochial school; Hoover, Stanford. Smith's "two years in the trucking business comprise [his] entire business experience . . . except that attained in his casual jobs as a boy and young man before he went into politics."

In fact, it was not necessary to read the article in order to get the point. On facing pages the *Post* displayed photographs of the two candidates. Al Smith, whose Catholicism readers were told was not an issue, was pictured with a large family group, including three grandchildren. They are photographed straight on, staring into the camera, in front of the family Christmas tree. Hoover, too, is photographed *en famille,* with his wife, two sons, and a daughter-in-law. Husband and wife are seated decorously, with the younger Hoovers behind, and they are photographed in what appears to be an elegant garden, against a wooded setting. The picture, taken at a slight angle, is at once more graceful, more intimate, and somehow more respectful.[88]

The issues of the campaign, at least as the *Post* witnessed it, were prosperity, prohibition, agriculture, and immigration. Continued prosperity demanded a businessman, as Blythe had argued. On prohibition, Lorimer was very cautious. Smith was strongly in favor of ending prohibition. Hoover's position was more complex; he took the stand that any change in the prohibition law had to come about constitutionally, insisting that enacting a new law would in effect nullify the Constitution and set a dangerous precedent. Generally, the *Post* stayed out of the argument, except for an occasional piece, like one by Salvation Army Commander Booth's daughter Evangeline, tying prohibition to good business, or more specifically to the increased productivity of the sober laborer.[89]

Agriculture was more problematic. Farmers had not shared in the prosperity of the 1920s, and a number of federal proposals for support and subsidies throughout the decade had met with nothing but scorn from the *Saturday Evening Post*. As far back as 1923, editorials had argued that agriculture was a business and not a "social function." As a business, farming needed "neither government control nor charity," nor did farmers want it; they had a right to "a square deal," but that did not mean "false economic precepts or maudlin sympathy."[90]

The agriculture situation threatened government intervention, and the *Post* would not accept that. In 1924 Garet Garrett set out to do a piece on agriculture, demonstrating that federal subvention was unnecessary. When he wrote to Lorimer outlining the farm piece he observed, "There is no farm problem, save the one we have created in the minds of the farmer." And some ten days later, mailing the article in, he added a note: "Here is the farm article. God help us! It will make everybody mad." Lorimer responded, "There will probably be some screams back in the bushes when we print your article but it is great stuff and what's more it tells the truth about the farmer."[91]

On November 8, 1924, "Exposing the Farm Problem" appeared. Although, wrote Garrett, the undervaluation of the farmer was a millennia-old problem, the American farmer was "the most prosperous, the most assisted, the most entertained, the most exhorted in his own behalf, the best informed, the best housed, the best dressed, the most extravagant, and the least bent farmer in the whole world." The farmer's complaints, then, had no relation to his situation. While there are many and complex economic problems, there was "no farm problem." In fact, the farmer was doing very well, for "coincidentally with the rise of industry, the condition of agriculture has enormously, magically improved."[92]

It was all well and good to tell farmers that there was no farm problem on the unlikely expectation that they would believe it; it was another thing altogether to expect farmers to vote Republican if their economic situation did not improve. In 1928 the *Post* met this problem with a series of articles on agriculture, all more or less dedicated to proving that modern technology was the answer to the farm economy. Technology was a very attractive answer because Hoover was an engineer. Thus, in October Garrett did another piece, now acknowledging that farm prices had fallen, but in "Farming With Security and Independence" (October 13, 1928) he promised again that technology would change everything. An editorial a week later took on the question of the farm vote directly. Farmers, the writer asserted confidently, were learning that market prices were an unreliable index to prosperity and were beginning to pay more attention to long-term trends than to "short-term price fluctuations." With equal confidence he promised Hoover the farm vote; farmers could not be so small minded as to desert the Republicans: "We take it that farmers will vote on the basis of long-standing political convictions, and opinions on candidates, rather than on the basis of seasonal prices of particular farm products."[93]

Having done its part to assure readers that the farm vote would remain Republican, the *Post* now turned to the even more difficult issue of the labor vote. The entire question of labor was deeply problematic, given Lorimer's ideology. At the root of the problem was the specter of class, and in Lorimer's economic philosophy generational upward mobility was the best defense against charges that America was a society of economic classes. The logic of upward mobility, however, eliminated—albeit only in theory—an American-born labor force.

As early as 1923, business conditions had challenged the contradictions in Lorimer's positions on labor, class, and immigration. The upturn in business after the 1921 recession had created a labor shortage, and that led proimmigration forces to argue for new immigration to supply needed laborers, particularly laborers who would do the jobs Americans no longer wanted. Lorimer responded with various counterarguments. He insisted that there was no labor shortage. He asserted that adequate labor would appear if a little more money were offered. He castigated counties and municipalities for draining private industry's labor supply with public works. In words that would resound with a heavy ironic echo a decade hence, he wrote that it was "a commonplace of good economics" that public works should be carried out only "in periods of industrial depression."[94]

Occasional articles addressed the complex relationship of the labor shortage and economic class directly, though with little clarity. Albert Atwood, in "Where Have the Miners Gone?" saw the issue as "drawn between those who would let down the bars at any cost to the scum of Europe . . . and those who believe the country will be ruined by the further admission of these dregs of foreign lands." But, he admitted, the entire question of labor was "a part and parcel of the whole forward movement of American education and culture. . . . If the father has earned his living in sweat and dirt at the bottom of a ditch or mine, the son must be in business in a small way at least, and the grandson in law or medicine." Having stated the problem, Atwood could do no more than retreat to a weak admonition to employers: it was their "responsibility."[95]

To cope with the problematic issue of labor, Lorimer turned again to the dubious nonfiction he had found so useful during the war. In this case, an anonymous article, purportedly "By a Laborer," provided the credulous reader an optimistic, not to say entirely chimerical, reading on class relations in America. Thus, while the immigration issue seemed to hinge on the problem of a labor shortage, Lorimer responded with an anonymous piece, sup-posedly the work of a laboring man who suddenly had the time, the ability, and the urge to write for the *Saturday Evening Post*. The point of "Life Among the Laborers" (June 7, 1924) was to prove that the typical laboring man was well paid, independent, and pa-triotic, and that he remained a laborer because he preferred to and not because his male ancestors had failed in their manly American duty to climb up the social ladder. This was something of a tall order.

The piece opened: "Three weeks ago I quit my sixty-third job, if memory counts correctly." Although the anonymous writer had a good job with a promised promotion, an "unreasoning restlessness" seized him. The article asked readers to accept this spokesperson for labor as a representative American type, one with some quirks per-haps, but certainly no bum. The writer was walking a very thin line.

I have remained a laborer, not because opportunities for a richer life have been denied me or because I have no faith in the American hustle-and-strive doctrine, but because of my own limitations and because manual labor is agreeable to me and offers a good living. I also admit being a fellow of low taste who whole-heartedly enjoys the companionship of work-ingmen and girls.

He could have "attained" to the field of writing, but found it overcrowded; moreover, writing was harder than manual labor—no doubt an irresistible aside for the anonymous author.

The "laborer" then moved to the heart of his argument. He divided American workers into three groups: skilled union workers, alien labor, and "native common labor," and since he hated both unions and radicals, he belonged to the third, the real American group. By his example, he argued that all real American laborers remained ununionized and unradicalized, for they had pride in their work and their economic independence. And then, his peroration: "The delusion that hard manual labor is a curse is forever being voiced by articulate people whose intelligence is clouded by pity for a misery that does not exist. Millet immortalized the delusion on canvas." For himself, he made $7.50 a day, averaged $45.00 a week, and was happy in "the life that gives the most freedom and the least responsibility." As a final, decidedly weird note, he added, "I like to live where I can read either Balzac or Bugs Baer without discuss-ing them."

This representation of labor had a short shelf life, for it essen-tially subverted the basic *Post* values of hard work, ambition, and the centrality of business. Albert Atwood had been more honest when he faced the dilemma of the American dream and the prom-ised professional rise of each generation. It helped, of course, that the "laborer" that appeared in the above article was single, and childless, but a world of footloose, unmarried workingmen had no place in Lorimer's utopia. The confusion in the article is useful, though, for it helps us see how Lorimer attempted to guide the *Post* through a subject about which he had passionate beliefs, in which he had little personal experience, and for which he had no solution.

Then in 1928, in a weak attempt to gain what it could of the labor vote, the *Post* published another of its fables of life among the laboring classes, this one, "Conservative in Overalls" (September 22, 1928), signed by James Stevens. The article told the story of two workers in an Oregon sawmill, George Taylor who had found his happy way into consuming four years ago and Ed Barker who was converted only in time for the 1928 campaign. These rough laborers from the Northwest were no Wobblies; they were more like working-class Babbitts.

Back in 1924, Taylor had been intimidated by Barker, who had learned his stuff from radical pamphlets and who covered his own failure in farming by making all the men feel guilty about owning radios and automobiles. But Taylor finally rebelled, admitting that he was "a conservative in overalls," confessing to owning not only a car but to having become a real capitalist, with three houses and lots "in which his savings were invested." He had nothing to be ashamed of he insisted. "Plenty other hard-workin' men my age got more, plenty others got less. But most have some. Millions of workin' men all over this great land just about like me. Got plain jobs. Got wages above a livin'. Got homes, famblies, cars and rajo sets. Able to look any man square in the eye and tell him to go to hell. Want to keep what they got." Eventually, Taylor converted Barker, and both could now be seen as representative: "Millions more just like me. Don't want no helpin' hand from earnest, big-hearted leaders." And so, delighted with the status quo, Taylor would "vote for the old-fashioned kind of cannerdates." Sinclair Lewis could not have said it better in 1924 in "Be Brisk With Babbitt."

The leading campaign issue for the *Post*, however, was immigration—both as an independent question and as the source from which pernicious radical ideas entered the American mainstream. But the *Post* notwithstanding, immigration was not a major issue for the candidates. Still, as an editorial tirelessly argued, "In greater or lesser degree, every question before the American people is inextricably involved in our immigration policy."[96]

When Al Smith, taking a rather cautious stand himself, came out in favor of modifying the immigration law to allow separated families to reunite, the *Post* mounted its old attack. The *Post* found the family argument "hardly worthy of so astute a mind as that of the governor of New York." And an editorial responded with a smug blend of irony and twisted logic. "[Smith] knows as well as the rest of us that our immigration laws do not separate families; . . . separation . . . is almost always brought about by the immigrants themselves, who leave their families overseas and are unwilling to forego the economic benefits they find in this country by rejoining their kin in Europe. He knows that any newcomer who has his passage money can go home at will." Smith also took a stand against the system of basing immigration quotas on the 1890 census, arguing that the United States thereby discriminated against certain nationalities. Yes, indeed, rejoined the *Post*, for that was "common sense," telling us "to accept the best and reject the poorer . . . the hardest to assimilate."[97]

Hoover was elected, and he would have won without the help of the *Post*.[98] The real power of the *Post*, its commanding position among the magazines of the time, was demonstrated the following year. Starting in July, Alfred E. Smith, losing nominee of the

Democratic party, chose to publish his memoirs in the *Saturday Evening Post*.[99]

Lorimer, certainly, was delighted to print the memoirs; they were good copy and they allowed him to live up to his declared aim: "to make each issue of the publication a representative cross-section of a week in American life" and "to work for national unity under our common banner of Americanism." This was how Lorimer presented himself in yet another publication on the *Saturday Evening Post*, this one written by associate editor Frederick S. Bigelow, published by the Curtis Company, and bravely titled *A Short History of "The Saturday Evening Post"*: "An American Institution" in *Three Centuries*. The occasion was the thirtieth anniversary of Curtis's purchase of the *Post*. The audience was all of America, from advertisers to critics, and even the "historian of the future," who would be "amazed to perceive how [the *Post*] reflected the economic and social development of a nation."

Success was laid to the Americanism, perspicacity, and foresight of the editor. Under his guidance, the magazine had hewed straight to the line of Americanism: "In peace no less than war The Saturday Evening Post upholds America and American institutions first, last and always." Bigelow located the finest example of that credo in the *Post*'s fight for restricted immigration. "Years of educational work, conducted by means of authoritative articles, editorials and cartoons, finally turned the scale, and the nation as a whole emphatically went on record in favor of sane and reasonable restrictions. Legislators and publicists the country over declare that The Saturday Evening Post was the most effective single agency in bringing about this vital reform."[100]

Lorimer used the *Post*, as he said, for "national unity" under the "common banner of Americanism," but he reserved to himself the right to define both America and the American, and over his three decades as editor he had come to draw those definitions ever more narrowly. In the 1920s, for the audience who met his criteria, the *Saturday Evening Post* had indeed become the principal agency in the country for "interpret[ing] America to itself."

"There Is Nothing the Matter with America Except Damfoolishness."

The Great Depression found the *Saturday Evening Post* in fighting trim. Under economic exigency, the bloated book of the twenties was considerably slimmed down and, like a reconditioned fighter, gained new vitality. That energy was harnessed to meet the most powerful challenge Lorimer had yet faced: America, the America he believed he had created in the pages of the *Post,* was threatened at its foundations by Franklin Roosevelt and the New Deal. The times were dangerous, the economic picture dispiriting, the political outlook desperate; nevertheless, the *Post* glowed with an exhilaration lost since the days of the war. Lorimer once again had a crusade.

Even before the New Deal era, the *Post* regained some of its old spirit. While Lorimer initially treated the 1929 stock market crash as a relatively minor event, he took the occasion to celebrate anew the old financial virtues and chastise those who had too greedily pursued the new economics of consumption and speculation. All through the spring and summer of 1929, *Post* economic writers had warned readers about the volatility of the wild bull market and especially about the greed of gambling speculators. Once the crash proved those warnings correct, business writers Albert Atwood and Garet Garrett lost no time in enunciating their economic, and their moral, judgments. With some smugness, Atwood reminded readers that the shift from investment in bonds to speculation in stocks had been undertaken with open eyes and in the belief that it represented a democratic participation in prosperity; he did not remind them the *Post* itself had argued this position. Loftily, Atwood wrote that "there was an open disavowal and a deliberate thrusting aside of the older distinction between investment and speculation." The crash would teach the salutary lesson of disproving the idea, "so popular recently, that all that is required to make everybody rich is for everybody to buy common stocks."[1]

Garet Garrett lectured on greed, the "uncontrollable motive of cupidity," and rehearsed the course of the past few months when "delusion had no further to go." Moreover, he insisted upon the debilitating moral consequences of the bull market and of "the expectation of wealth without exertion." Cutting through economic ranks, affecting "brokers, speculators, corporation executives, their clerks and secretaries, artists, writers, preachers, women, college professors, wage earners, barbers, waiters," were the dream of easy money and the dire "moral effects of universal gambling." What these speculators had gained was not money but "the idea of money," a quick gain to be spent as quickly, "without knowing how ephemeral it was, and that if they spent it they would have to make it up later by work, industry and thrift."[2]

With the crash, the values the *Post* had long cherished but had allowed to become blurred and muted under the power of the new prosperity and consumerism of the boom years returned full force. Certainly, there was more for the *Post* to undertake than merely chastising the American public; it was equally important to emphasize the basic economic well-being of the country, to encourage optimism and discourage panic, to point out that economic cycles were natural "and always restore[d] sanity in the course of time." Business remained strong, argued the editorial page throughout December, as did the banks and the Federal Reserve. Prosperity, after all, should not be too closely associated with the stock market; the important thing was that "people in general earn the same wages and salaries as before, and their income from securities is the same."[3]

As business faltered, the *Post* intensified its efforts at counteracting pessimism and fear. Early in 1930, Garet Garrett did a piece on American business dedicated to proving that overproduction was not the problem. His argument rested solidly on the economics of consumption. The entire endeavor of business, allied with tech-nology, was "progressively to cheapen the satisfaction of human wants." Nor could satiety ever be reached: "Everyone is wanting something more and something better." The problem, then, lay in distribution, or more precisely in the resistance of business to sell products cheaply enough so as to keep demand "expansible." He summed it all up in an economic "law": "Since the wealth of society is increased by the downward diffusion of goods, whatever tends to hinder that process, be it cost or price, tends also to limit the total of profits, whereas whatever tends to hasten it tends at the same time to increase the sum of profits. It is a law."[4]

At the same time, Atwood did a series on the market. Although the articles provided an explanation of market forces, the overriding emphasis was moralistic. Atwood extolled the virtues of saving and of sober investment,[5] and he castigated speculation which, "like gambling at cards, or drink, or a narcotic . . . grows insidiously." Thus, all in all, the crash was not a bad thing. Those who were hurt, by and large, deserved it, for by "mathematic" demonstration, Atwood showed that "the panic hurt, for the most part, the roulette players, who have little claim on our sympathies." Moreover, these crashes are economic correctives, a fact which may have helped solace the "innocent" who " suffered": "We are living in an imperfect world and the Juggernaut of economic correction flattens out a great many undeserving victims."[6]

Meanwhile, Lorimer was keeping an editorial eye on Great Britain and the Soviet Union as diametrically opposed economic models. The Soviet Union had just announced its Five Year Plan and the *Post* was concerned to downplay its possible effectiveness, on the one hand by reporting that in Russia "conditions are not improving," and on the other by demonstrating that, the current economic situation notwithstanding, the American economy kept on improving. Marx was wrong, one article asserted, for in the United States there was a larger and richer middle class than there had been in 1909 and fewer poor.[7] Great Britain, meanwhile, was obviously in trouble, and Lorimer's first response was to show America British pluck. "Is Anything Wrong With England?" asked a February article, replying that there has always been something wrong with England. Moving from an account of the brutal conditions of medieval peasants to the unrest under the Tudors, the writer extolled the "inexhaustible spirit . . . the secret genius of its people" who had "led the way in civilization by its code of justice, its struggle for liberty, its faith in fair play." Meanwhile, the good news was that the Prince of Wales was touring the coal fields.[8]

It became clear almost immediately, however, that England was taking a wrong turn in responding to unemployment with the dole. Foreseeing a horrible example for America, Lorimer published a piece by Winston Churchill in March, a piece that upheld all the old virtues Lorimer so admired. The problem of unemployment, wrote Churchill, was a "grievous but . . . limited evil . . . artificially raised and emphasized out of all proportion to its real part in our national life and economy." This artificial emphasis was a means of discrediting the government, and worse, of proving that "the capitalist system of society has failed." The dole was not the answer; "the only remedy is hard work, thrift, faithful cooperation and good will among all classes."[9]

By May the *Post* was guardedly acknowledging the fact of large-scale unemployment at home. An editorial urged a rational examination of the facts, granting that the stock slump "had at least a temporary chilling effect." Facts were needed, "not hysterical denunciation."[10] More hard-hitting was an interview with Henry Ford. Talk of "passing laws to cure unemployment" made Ford ask, "Is it possible that this country is losing its business bearings?" Such proposals, along with the idea of raising prices to cover increased production costs due to low demand, were so dangerous that "we might as well close the book of American progress." What was needed was good business management and attention to the fundamental laws of good business practice.[11]

The clearest indication that the *Post* was beginning to take unemployment seriously was the appearance of an article offering advice for those "Hunting a Job." Reminiscent of upbeat pieces from Lorimer's first years on the *Post,* it offered exemplary anec-dotes and information on such techniques as inquiring by mail. It presented as well a list of "don'ts," culminating with "Don't get discouraged," and closing with an optimistic glow: "The industrial records of America are crowded with the names of men who made the first step toward success just as things looked darkest. What happened yesterday is finished. Today is always the threshold of the future, with all its unlimited prospects." [12]

Lorimer's intention was to keep things upbeat and to help his readers maintain a rational attitude toward the inexorable cycles of business. A July editorial called for "a moratorium on forecasting and a revival of the spirit of enterprise." Since business cycles had existed for a long time, "real alarm or even pessimism is out of place," for "the country possesses and is sure to exhibit a vital recuperative capacity." [13] An October article by economist John Maynard Keynes discovered good news by taking the long view. Keynes promised that one hundred years hence, "assuming no important wars and no important increase in population, the eco-nomic problem will be solved, or . . . within sight of solution." [14]

One solution to the unemployment problem was, from Lorimer's point of view, obvious: curtail immigration still further. An August editorial demonstrated the simple arithmetic that argued for a 50 percent cut in immigration quotas. [15] And Isaac Marcosson, conceding that "we have become reacquainted with the problem of the idle on a considerable scale," set out "to find and remove the sources of the evil." Setting aside "temporary elements," casual and seasonal work, and industrial inefficiency, he located two "permanent hazards": "technological unemployment" and "the alien worker." Since the article was titled "The Alien and Unem-ployment" (June 14, 1930), *Post* readers could identify the more serious of the two "permanent hazards"; in fact, they could do so without having to read the article.

The alien was more than a competitor for scarce jobs; he was also a putative radical. As bad times grew worse in America and radicalism flared once again, Lorimer returned to the attack. His initial response was a carefully crafted dismissal: the red menace was no menace. "That such a weird and alien thing as the Russian communist or Bolshevist or soviet idea should really cause any serious upheaval in a country like this, whose standard of living and comfort has so far exceeded that of any other nation, is pre-posterous." [16] Meanwhile, longtime *Post* contributor Julian Street had been working on a piece about John Reed, whom he had known at Harvard. His article, published in the summer of 1930, modulated the story of Reed's life with a pervasive mockery. At Harvard Reed had been "conspicuous rather than popular"; his goals had been to be a poet "and to live excitingly." He was foolhardy as a radical, with a penchant merely for provoking people. In the Soviet Union in 1917, he was "a factor though a small one" in Russia's decision to withdraw from the war. His death from typhus occurred in "the earthy paradise which he had helped to found." [17]

Lorimer continued his attack by mockery in a November piece by Will Irwin, now returned to the *Post* fold. The venue for his lead article, "The Red Ballyhoo" (November 22, 1930), was a meet-ing of communists in the Central Opera House in New York. He opened with a cruel satire on the types attempting ineffectually to hang a banner; they were a Hindu, a Japanese, and a Negro. The *Post* had long seen nearly all aliens as radicals; now Irwin's article saw nearly all radicals as aliens. Comparing the New York meeting with earlier "Red radical assemblies," he discovered an important difference. Once, the radicals had been of "only two types—the lean, dry-necked old-American and the massive Teuton. . . . But here is a potpourri of the races. . . . Hindu, Chinese, Japanese, Negro, Teuton and American. Perhaps two-thirds of the faces bear the Slavic or Slavic-Semitic marks. . . . And next in number come dark-eyed, graceful Latins."

This new "racial" distribution turned out to have major intel-lectual consequences. Thus, the typical party member was "either foreign-born or the child of recently arrived immigrants," and unlike Americans and Western Europeans, he "has a faculty for tying up abstract philosophical conceptions with personal emo-tions." That intellectual difference was, in fact, the good news in

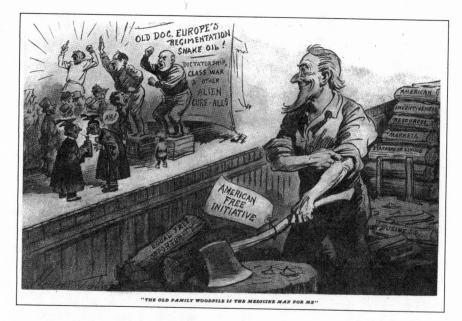

Herbert Johnson's Uncle Sam resists European ideologies.

Irwin's article. Americans were immune. "The unemployed man of America, expressing the national temperament, wants first a job and then a chance to get ahead in the world. A party which offers a workingman's heaven for his sons and grandsons after a lifetime of scorn, hardship and war for himself, has small attraction." For the moment Lorimer could dismiss the red menace as merely "Red Ballyhoo," but as the Depression deepened, mockery would give way to more savage rhetoric.

The *Post* itself felt little immediate effect from the Depression. In 1930, circulation remained high, even increasing a bit over 1929, and issues continued to run at well over a hundred pages—on March 8 reaching 224.[18] Advertising, too, remained strong, making up about 60 percent of each book. But toward the end of 1930 the *Post* began to experience difficulties; advertising, and consequently the size of the book, declined in the last two months, falling to seventy-eight pages at the end of December. By 1931 the toll the

THE HOTEL CHILD   By F. Scott Fitzgerald

ILLUSTRATED BY HENRY RALEIGH

Fifi Came, Followed by a Platoon of Young Men, and Led Them Bumpily Through the Whole Vista

IT IS a place where one's instinct is to give a reason for being there—"Oh, you see, I'm here because—" Failing that, you are faintly suspect, because this corner of Europe does not draw people; rather, it accepts them without too many inconvenient questions—live and let live. Routes cross here—people bound for private *cliniques* or tuberculosis resorts in the mountains, people who are no longer *persona grata* in Italy or France. And if that were all ——

Yet on a gala night at the Hotel des Trois Mondes a new arrival would scarcely detect the current beneath the surface. Watching the dancing there would be a gallery of Englishwomen of a certain age, with neckbands, dyed hair and faces powdered pinkish gray; a gallery of American women of a certain age, with snowy-white transformations, black dresses and lips of cherry red. And most of them with their eyes swinging right or left from time to time to rest upon the ubiquitous Fifi. The entire hotel had been made aware that Fifi had reached the age of eighteen that night.

Fifi Schwartz. An exquisitely, radiantly beautiful Jewess whose fine, high forehead sloped gently up to where her hair, bordering it like an armorial shield, burst into lovelocks and waves and curlicues of soft dark red. Her eyes were bright, big, clear, wet and shining; the color of her cheeks and lips was real, breaking close to the surface from the strong young pump of her heart. Her body was so assertively adequate that one cynic had been heard to remark that she always looked as if she had nothing on underneath her dresses; but he was probably wrong, for Fifi had been as thoroughly equipped for beauty by man as by God. Such dresses—cerise for Chanel, mauve for Molyneux, pink for Patou; dozens of them, tight at the hips, swaying, furling, folding just an eighth of an inch off the dancing floor. Tonight she was a woman of thirty in dazzling black, with long white gloves dripping from her forearms. "Such ghastly taste," the whispers said. "The stage, the shop window, the mannikins' parade. What can her mother be thinking?" But, then, look at her mother.

Her mother sat apart with a friend and thought about Fifi and Fifi's brother, and about her other daughters, now married, whom she considered to have been even prettier than Fifi. Mrs. Schwartz was a plain woman; she had been a Jewess a long time, and it was a matter of effortless indifference to her what was said by the groups around the room. Another large class who did not care were the young men—dozens of them. They followed Fifi about all day in and out of motorboats, night clubs, inland lakes, automobiles, tea rooms and funiculars, and they said, "Hey, look, Fifi!" or said, "Kiss me, Fifi," or even, "Kiss me again, Fifi," and abused her and tried to be engaged to her.

Most of them, however, were too young, since this little city, through some illogical reasoning, is supposed to have an admirable atmosphere as an educational center.

Fifi was not critical, nor was she aware of being criticized herself. Tonight the gallery in the great, crystal, horseshoe room made observations upon Fifi's entrance. The table had been set in the last of a string of dining rooms, each accessible from the central hall. But Fifi, her black dress shouting and halloing for notice, came in by way of the first dining room, followed by a whole platoon of young men of all possible nationalities and crosses, and at a sort of little run that swayed her lovely hips and tossed her lovely head, led them bumpily through the whole vista, while old men choked on fish bones, old women's facial muscles sagged, and the protest rose to a roar in the procession's wake.

They need not have resented her so much. It was a bad party, because Fifi thought she had to entertain everybody and be a dozen people, so she talked to the entire table and broke up every conversation that started, no matter how far away from her. So no one had a good time, and the people in the hotel needn't have minded so much that she was young and terribly happy.

Afterward, in the salon, many of the supernumerary males floated off with a temporary air to other tables. Among these was young Count Stanislas Borowki, with his handsome, shining brown eyes of a stuffed deer, and his black hair already dashed with distinguished streaks like the keyboard of a piano. He went to the table of some people of position named Taylor and sat down with just a faint sigh, which made them smile.

"Was it ghastly?" he was asked.

The blond Miss Howard who was traveling with the Taylors was almost as pretty as Fifi and stitched up with more consideration. She had taken pains not to make Miss Schwartz's acquaintance, although she shared several of the same young men. The Taylors were career people in the diplomatic service and were now on their way to London, after the League Conference at Geneva. They were presenting Miss Howard at court this season. They were very Europeanized Americans; in fact, they had reached a position where they could hardly be said to belong to any

Depression was taking on the *Saturday Evening Post* grew more serious. Advertising revenue was falling precipitously, and although issues were smaller, running twenty to fifty pages fewer than 1930, advertising percentages were declining markedly. Late in 1930, advertising had fallen from about 60 to about 50 percent. By the second half of 1931, percentages ran in the low forties, even with books hovering at about a hundred pages.

Although the weekly book was now half of what it had been in the prosperous twenties, averaging about a dozen pieces per issue, quality did not decline. In fact, the leaner *Post* of the thirties offered articles and stories far superior to those in its swollen predecessor. In 1931 fiction included Kenneth Roberts's first historical novel, *Lively Lady,* which began serialization in March, eight stories of F. Scott Fitzgerald's, including "Babylon Revisited," and, old quarrels forgotten, Sinclair Lewis, now a Nobel laureate, returned to the pages of the *Post.* Nonfiction was at least equally interesting, and that year featured three remarkable series. Dorothy Thompson filed first-rate articles on the situation in Germany and "Ike" Hoover, longtime White House chief usher, contributed his memoirs. But the most remarkable, and surely most surprising, nonfiction appeared on April 25, 1931, when the *Post* began serialization of Leon Trotsky's *The Russian Revolution.*

How Lorimer got hold of Trotsky's work is not entirely clear. Trotsky was preparing his manuscript for book publication with Boni-Liveright, but negotiations with Charles Boni were going very badly. In letters to Max Eastman, Trotsky continually complained about Boni. He disliked the proposed contractual arrangements; he felt Boni was stalling over the urgent business of finding a translator; he had heard that Boni was very slow to pay. Trotsky kept asking Eastman to intervene in one or another way, and in the fall of 1930, as he was completing the chapters for the first volume of *The Russian Revolution,* he wrote saying he would send these last chapters to Eastman rather than directly to Boni so that Eastman might demand payment on delivery.[19]

Money was the principal source of the trouble between Trotsky and Boni. Boris Shishkin, who translated the first volume of *The Russian Revolution* for the *Post,* claimed that Trotsky wanted $75,000 for all three volumes, but that Boni was offering less than half that amount. According to Shishkin, in the midst of these negotiations-by-cable, "The Saturday Evening Post, through an agent of the publishing house, apparently swallowed the bait they put out and decided to print the first five chapters [volume 1]." Shishkin said the *Post* paid "more than $40,000 or something of that magnitude."[20]

Trotsky was far from pleased with Shishkin's translation. In fact, some passages that Shishkin interpolated as transitions he believed necessary elicited another "furious cable" in which Trotsky accused Boni of "selling him down the river" and insisting that the publisher had hired some "wicked white Russian to distort his meaning."[21]

Trotsky continued to use Max Eastman to protect his interests. Thus, Eastman wrote to the *Post* shortly before the first installment of Trotsky's work was to appear to insist that the *Post* treat the material appropriately. Adelaide Neall replied in the coolest, most official of *Post* voices: "It has always been against the policy of the Saturday Evening Post to permit any outside censorship of the editor's functions. Past performance and reputation are the author's guarantee that they will be handled with discretion and good taste." She closed with the equally official signature, "A. W. Neall."[22]

Eastman retorted with a letter directly to Lorimer, enclosing the "extremely ungracious, not to say discourteous" letter of "Mr. Neall's." After referring to his own responsibilities in supervising the publication of Trotsky's work and citing the "sufficiently eminent, and also sufficiently unique" position of Trotsky himself, Eastman concluded: "I beg you to place my correspondence, if there must be any further correspondence, in the hands of someone who knows how to respond courteously to a courteous letter."[23]

Publishing makes strange bedfellows, as *Outlook* noted: "Leon Trotsky—Edith Wharton—I.A.R. Wylie—Nunnally Johnson— you read on the cover of *The Saturday Evening Post* for April 25. Yes, it's true, this Trotsky in the *Post* business. A discreet editor's note excuses the Communist viewpoint of the articles on the Russian revolution on the grounds of their historical importance; nev-ertheless it is true that Trotsky has done what many a staunch capitalist writer would gladly start a revolution to accomplish—he has 'made' the *Post*."[24]

Revolutionists notwithstanding, Lorimer had other matters on his mind closer to home. By the beginning of 1931, a new sense of urgency appeared in *Post* articles on the economic situation; that urgency, however, was not occasioned by the Depression itself or even by the *Post*'s own failing economic position. The crisis for Lorimer lay in the attempts of the Hoover administration to inter-vene with government programs for relief and revival. The basic theme of the *Post* in these months and in the years to follow was that projects initiated and implemented by the federal government could not ameliorate the economic picture; only American self-reliance and manly courage would win the day. In January Samuel Crowther did a long piece on various schemes to alleviate unem-ployment, schemes necessitated because our "strangely emotional" nation "has utterly refused to accept either unemployment or pov-erty as an incurable disease." The danger was that "in the rush to meet an emergency we are creating another emergency," and that we would end "in erecting unemployment into a political institu-tion in the same fashion as it has been erected abroad." In a piece essentially confused in its argument, one idea recurred: among the unemployed were many, perhaps most, who did not want to work, whose attitude toward jobs was "cavalier."[25]

By February the *Post* had intensified its criticism of new eco-nomic projects. Atwood warned readers that there was too much reliance on the federal government and asked rhetorically: "Do we really want to centralize more power in Washington and is there no danger in that course?"[26] Isaac Marcosson attacked proposals for unemployment relief that would plunge us into "a hysteria of relief."[27] And the editorial page addressed "The Dole Evil" (Feb-ruary 21, 1931), arguing that "if Congress begins to vote funds for feeding the needy, there will be no place to stop."

The editorial page took the first steps in countering proposed new methods with exhortations to self-reliance and hard work. The rallying cry was Lorimer's long cherished common sense: "It is our earnest desire," he began, "to say something which bears the earmarks of plain common sense on the subject of unemployment and how to end it." The "crazy schemes" in the air were nothing but "socialistic clap-trap" and would bear no positive results. What was needed were "courage and nerve." And a few weeks later, attacking the "professors and politicians" who fathered such schemes, an editorial warned that ideas like "compulsory unemployment reserves" were "in actual practice . . . the dole." The dole was fatal; it would act "to stifle ambition, destroy initiative and blight hope."[28]

Undermining American self-reliance was tantamount to subverting capitalism. Lorimer was "fed up" with professors who "deplore the alleged breakdown of the modern industrial system." The answer to unemployment was "hard work." Business and industry could be trusted far more than those who would offer government aid, thereby increasing the debt and encouraging inflation. In exasperation, Lorimer demanded, "How in the name of common sense are we going to work our way out of difficulties by merely thrusting ourselves deeper into the mire?"[29]

Supporting the polemics was a stream of articles and editorials that doggedly maintained an optimistic view and encouraged readers to do the same. Occasionally these took the form of promoting investments in the stock market. One editorial, half embarrassed, acknowledged, "The last thing we wish to do, or could conscientiously do, is to urge the promiscuous purchase of securities"; still, there were bargains now available in the market.[30] And an article called "Panic Profits" argued that there was no better time to buy "than at the conclusion of one of these financial storms." "Persuaded that we have scraped the bottom," the writer told the "courageous investor" he could now make money.[31] And if the promise of stock market riches was not adequately upbeat, by summer Eddie Cantor was cheering *Post* audiences with a series of Depression one-liners: "In my own case, the depression brought a strange result. Before the crash I had a million dollars, a house, three cars and four daughters. Now all I've got left is five daughters."[32]

By the end of 1931, the editorial page alternately scolded and cajoled. For the Thanksgiving issue, Lorimer turned to inspiration—and to Ben Franklin, reprinting a Franklin piece from Richardson's *American School Reader* of 1810. The editorial told a tale of the New England colony, beset by hardship and responding with prayer and fasting. When yet another fast was proposed, "a farmer of plain sense rose and remarked that the inconveniences they suffered, and concerning which they had so often wearied heaven with their complaints, were not so great as they might have expected, and were diminishing every day." This man of common sense proposed, therefore, "that it would be more becoming the gratitude they owed to the Divine Being if, instead of a fast, they should proclaim a Thanksgiving."[33]

Another November editorial hectored *Post* readers with evidence of their own cowardice. The title, "What are You Afraid Of?" (November 7, 1931), would ironically be echoed by Roosevelt's own "You have nothing to fear but fear itself." Here it became a refrain, a taunt rather than a solace. Asking if readers are afraid of their country, their bank, their leaders, their government, Lorimer assaulted them with their own guilt. Were they afraid of their banks? "Many of you have been, and a pretty mess you have made of it by your senseless runs on sound and solvent institutions. For a majority of the banks that you have closed have been just that. In pulling down your deposits you have pulled down the pillars of your bank and sent it crashing down on your own heads. You have injured yourselves, your merchants and your neighborhood." Do not look to leaders, he taunted: "The best and bravest leaders in the world cannot lead cowards in a charge." The answer lay, as always, in "courage and common sense."

Lorimer's paternalism could go no further, and he would not again assume the role of the enraged father. The 1932 election brought him and the *Saturday Evening Post* a new and dangerous enemy on whom to concentrate his rhetoric and his rage.

Lorimer had no illusions about the fate of the Republican party in the 1932 election nor about Hoover's candidacy. As a result, the

Post gave the campaign rather scant coverage, with relatively few political articles and the editorial page restricting itself to general statements in favor of optimism and equally general warnings about relying too strongly on salvation through a single leader.

While the *Post* downplayed the campaign itself, Lorimer did establish a stand on major issues, especially on radicalism and isolationism. Economically, politically, and militarily, the *Post* urged an isolationist position. The lessons of World War I were indelibly imprinted on the *Post* and the scars from that war kept inflamed by the history of the war debt incurred by our European allies. Throughout the twenties the magazine had scorned the idea that the United States should forgive the war debt. In the first place, debts between nations were like debts between honest businessmen and should be honored. And in the second place, as far as Lorimer could see, the nations that would repudiate their debts were spending money on armaments, hastening the day of the next war.

The *Post* had begun its attack on debt repudiation in 1923, supporting the position taken by Herbert Hoover, then secretary of commerce. The *Post,* along with Hoover, argued that Europe could well afford to pay its debt, and an editorial demonstrated, by the "Socratic method," that one need not take at all seriously the Allies' "contention" that they could not pay. "It all depends," the writer summed up in homely idiom, "whose ox is gored."[34] Another editorial assumed the task of disproving charges that by insisting on payment America would show that it had entered a period of "sullen and selfish isolationism." We had no duty to help Europe until such time as Europe "recognized an obligation to help herself by cutting down expenses, armies and armaments." As it was, we were simply demonstrating "amazing common sense."[35]

With increasing American prosperity, calls for repudiation grew louder. Garet Garrett spoke for the defense, arguing that with all our power we willingly broke our sword. While in the past nations "with surplus power" had turned to conquest and empire, we had engaged in a "free and voluntary act in limitation of our military power."[36] Another Garrett piece on the debt was accompanied by a Herbert Johnson cartoon portraying the domestic needs of the United States as a group of ragged children peering into the window of a bakery shop; the needs identified were airplane fields, flood relief, good roads, water power projects, grade crossings, as well as specific projects like Boulder Dam.[37]

With the Depression, Lorimer hardened his position, and when Hoover agreed to a war debt moratorium in June 1931, Lorimer responded with an editorial called "Washington Was Right" (September 19, 1931). The moratorium was a bad enough decision, the editorial argued, but worse were the possibilities of repudiation or cancellation. As for Germany and reparations, the *Post* was incredulous that anyone could attribute Germany's present economic situation to the burden imposed by reparations: "Germany's plight is not due to reparations. She has paid none."[38] As the war debt became a campaign issue in 1932, the *Post* continued to assert its position: it had warned against the moratorium; cancellation could not be considered unless there was evidence in Europe of a "will to peace."[39]

With radicalism, the second of the major issues the *Post* addressed in the election year, Lorimer abandoned his rhetoric of cool mockery in favor of more direct and heated attacks. Hard times, he explained, made communism a real threat, for "in the black muck of depression strange and poisonous seeds germinate and shoot up rankly." Still, the *Post*'s response to radicalism stumbled on an inherent contradiction, for Lorimer wished to maintain the position that American communism was an entirely alien movement with alien participants, while simultaneously arguing that Americans had been infected with the communist virus. Lorimer, therefore, insisted on the one hand that real Americans could not be communists, for they had "nothing to rebel against except themselves and their follies, for which the cures are in their own hands." But in the same editorial he went on to describe the infected American: "The deadly nightshade, skunk cabbage and poison ivy are being gathered by many of our fellow citizens in the firm belief that in combination they make fine bouquets."[40]

In an election year, the heart of the radical issue was the problem of the workingman, more precisely the unemployed workingman, a concern the Bonus March that summer only exacerbated. The *Post* line on the march was laid out by Boyden Sparkes in September. It was not possible to believe that these American men, many of them war veterans, could be "revolutionaries"; there was no question, however, that the march itself "was organized to some degree by Communists."[41] An editorial in the same vein reasserted the *Post's* faith in "the underlying soundness of the American worker," but warned against "underestimating the situation which has developed." The situation called for vigilance: "The time has passed when the activities of political demagogues, intellectual pinks and chronic malcontents, who play into the hands of the real Reds, can be viewed with toleration."[42]

Shortly before election day the *Post* published its requisite formal articles, one in favor of each candidate by someone who knew and could support him. Former President Coolidge endorsed Hoover, pointing out what his administration had managed to accomplish in bad times. Former Secretary of the Navy Josephus Daniels wrote for Roosevelt, who had served under him during the war.[43] But for the first time since Sam Blythe had joined the *Post,* he failed to travel across America and file his by now traditional campaign articles on the mood of the electorate. There could have been no clearer signal of the *Post's* essential detachment from the campaign or of its acceptance of a Democratic victory as a foregone conclusion. In October Blythe was writing about gold prospecting.[44]

With the election of Roosevelt, the *Post* editorial page assumed a statesmanlike posture, welcoming the new president, urging the country to stand behind him, but at the same time issuing a guarded warning to the new administration. "A great task and a great responsibility confront the new Administration. With House and Senate behind it and in full power, there is no alibi for a failure to measure up to its opportunity. Republicans and Democrats must back up the new Administration, but it, in turn, must back up America."[45]

A much more direct message was delivered in an article by Newton Baker, secretary of war under Woodrow Wilson. Warning against the dangers of excessive government interference and of the costs of relief, he called for a return to the American virtues of hard work and self-reliance, "the character-building agencies of America" that have maintained "the sturdiness and independence of the American character." Our real danger, he concluded, did not lie in bread lines. "Obviously, the needs of food and shelter must be first met; but no emergency can be great enough to justify us in forgetting that the thing we are proud of in America is not the mere prolongation of physical life but the enrichment of the art of living and the maintenance of the character of those who do live. Our problem reaches far beyond the bread lines."[46] With considerable uneasiness and a shaky reliance on the American character, the *Saturday Evening Post* entered the era of the New Deal.

The Hoover years had already seen the beginnings of an increased government role in mass relief and in the development of policies for federal intervention in agriculture and business. The *Post* had opposed those policies and practices under Hoover; its position under the Roosevelt administration could only harden.

But for a few months, Lorimer kept the *Post* to a course of open-minded consideration of New Deal initiatives. Shortly after the inauguration, a patriotic, if guarded, editorial urged that we all "Pull Together" (April 1, 1933). Though presidents were not "miracle men," it was "absolutely essential that the people should give their support and confidence to President Roosevelt." Certainly, "loose talk" about granting him "extraordinary additional powers" was foolish. What he needed was a nation of "self-reliance and courage" to wait and see "in a hopeful, friendly spirit," precisely the spirit the editorial, if somewhat coolly, exhibited.

In May, Sam Blythe praised the camps for jobless men, dimming New Deal luster only slightly by observing that such camps had already been established by California.[47] Garet Garrett wrote with strong appreciation of the March bank holiday, a masterful handling of panic.[48] Editorials, too, congratulated Roosevelt on the bank holiday as well as on the new federal securities bill. Editorials, however, mixed cautious praise with equally cautious criticism: the securities bill, although a step in the right direction, might well be "flawed." And after crediting the bank holiday, one editorial went on to warn against "an attempt to rebuild society at one fell swoop."[49]

As late as June, David Lawrence, now writing regularly for the *Post,* was able to support fully the administration's involvement in business, obviously a very sensitive area as far as Lorimer and the *Post* were concerned. It was a question, Lawrence wrote, of "desperate times" calling for "extraordinary measures." The point was that there was "no real inconsistency"; America had not "abandoned its idea of free opportunity for the individual business, big and little." If individual business opportunity remained "an objective still sought with unremitting zeal," the acceptance of government intervention reflected "the willingness of individuals to subordinate temporarily everything to the common interest."[50] A Herbert Johnson cartoon underlined Lawrence's message with a jaunty Roosevelt aboard the "Administration Speed Boat" steering it through the waters of "Emergency Experiments," but in John-son's cartoon some passengers register alarm at FDR's speed and uncertain destination.[51] Farm relief, however, was condemned from the outset, as it had been in the Hoover administration and indeed throughout the 1920s. The *Post* continued to believe in allowing natural business conditions to operate in agriculture; moreover, mounting federal costs horrified Lorimer.

Costs along with what seemed the reckless haste of the Roose-velt administration brought about the first stirrings of overt opposi-tion in the *Post.* Late in July an editorial marked the turning of the tide of Roosevelt's reception in its pages. While the editorial remained guarded in its criticism, giving high marks to the presi-dent's confidence, it spoke out strongly against "undue haste and extreme action." Even more to the point, it attacked those "extremists" who refused to accept criticism of any New Deal poli-cies; that, said the *Post,* was "pure Hitlerism or Stalinism."[52]

By the end of the year, the truce was over. Adelaide Neall, writing to Booth Tarkington in November, commented, "Mr. Lorimer has written a splendid editorial on present day conditions which takes up the whole page in our issue for December 9th."[53]

OUT FOR A RECORD

Herbert Johnson's ordinary citizens show some dismay at FDR's speedy course.

The Brain Trust had proved too much for Lorimer's patience and he prepared a long editorial. Lorimer had never been an admirer of "intellectuals," and their apotheosis in the Roosevelt administration seemed to spell the country's doom: the radical professor was now a policymaker.

No thoughtful man can escape the conclusion that many of the brain trust's ideas and plans are based on Russian ideology; that we are steadily being herded to the left; and that fundamental American ideas are in danger of being scrapped. . . . Somebody should tell these bright young intellectuals and professors the facts of business life. The stork does not bring profits and prosperity, and sound currency does not grow under cabbage leaves.

The answer to our problems lay in common sense, in abandoning haste for "a steady, common-sense pace," in avoiding the excesses of both capitalists and reformers for the "safe middle ground of common honesty and common sense."[54]

The final issue of the year presented another of Lorimer's full-page editorials, this one comparing the two Roosevelts: both presidents "had been given a great opportunity and both failed to grasp it." Lorimer was not, however, merely fulminating. Taking the role of the *Saturday Evening Post* with full seriousness, he was offering the second Roosevelt a chance to rescue his reputation by mending his ways, specifically by returning to the platform on which he was elected, one of "clean-cut sensible liberalism." In this editorial, Lorimer returned again to the issue that most bitterly rankled, the administration's attacks on the loyalty of those who criticized their policies: "We are in danger of making it a crime to disagree with those who hold ideas and beliefs contrary to our own."[55] If the *Post* had any function at all, it was surely to use its power to speak out. Other less powerful voices might be stifled; Lorimer's *Post* would not be.

Lorimer was not only taking on the Roosevelt administration in 1933, he was also assuming responsibility for the Curtis Corporation. In 1933, Cyrus Curtis died and Lorimer was promoted to chairman of the board. That year brought a significant weakening of the financial position of the Curtis magazines and the *Post* suffered serious losses. Circulation was not a real problem, although it fell for the first time in 1932 and again in 1933,[56] but despite a 10 percent discount in advertising rates effected in August 1932, advertising declined so far by the middle of 1933 that in one summer issue it took up only 33 percent of the book.[57] As a result, the size of the weekly issues fell dramatically; from June 1932 through all of 1933 only nine issues exceeded one hundred pages, and some fell as low as sixty. Typical issues now contained only ten pieces of editorial material—stories, articles, and serial installments.

The 1933 report to Curtis Company stockholders tried to put the best face possible on the financial situation. The year did show "a continuation of the downward trend" in earnings, but some of the loss was due to a "continually increasing tax burden" and some to the National Recovery Act, especially the "President's Reemployment Agreement," which brought about an additional $600,000 in expenses. Moreover, 90 percent of all magazines had suffered a net loss in 1933, and 4,281 newspapers and magazines had been discontinued. But the *Post,* along with the *Journal* and *Country Gentlemen,* "still occup[ied] the same preeminent positions which they held prior to the year closed."[58]

The message to the stockholders notwithstanding, the Curtis magazines had experienced a steady erosion of their "preeminent positions." The Crowell magazines, *Collier's* and *Good Housekeeping,* had made serious inroads on the share of periodical advertising previously controlled by Curtis publications. In 1941 Eberhardt Mueller prepared for confidential circulation a careful analysis of the effects of depression on Curtis publications. He wrote that while the 1921 depression had found the company strong, the situation was very different in the 1930s and particularly in 1933. Between 1929 and 1933 gross advertising revenue fell from $73,645,000 to $26,115,000, a 64 percent drop. Advertising volume fell 61 percent, and profits on advertising 94 percent, from over $21 million to $1,314,000. Even more chilling was the loss of preeminence. In the standard measure of thirty-five leading publications, Curtis magazines in 1925 controlled over 49 percent of the advertising business. In the boom years, that had slipped to just over 40 percent, and by 1933 it plummeted to 31 percent.[59]

The Curtis Company took measures to shore up its advertising position, circulating a paper to current, past, and potential advertisers. *Curtis Circulations Stand Firm* argued market strength from every conceivable angle. Advertisers could be assured that Curtis had "Sincerity of Purpose" in delivering the best "quality of circulation" for their products; "as far as is humanly possible," Curtis magazines were distributed "to people with intelligence and buying power." Moreover, the quality of circulation was maintained without "special inducements [that] lead to circulation waste." In the case of the *Post,* "Boy Retailers" continued to "produce sound circulation," especially now that a network of adult managers had been established.

Buying power was the key phrase, for the Curtis Company argument was that the circulation of their magazines was carefully restricted to an audience of potential consumers. Advertisers were reminded that despite the depression there were still 35 million employed, and Curtis had targeted that audience through a market survey conducted by its Division of Commercial Research. That survey created block-by-block maps for one hundred cities, establishing a color code for average property values, "Red for Excellent, Yellow for Good, Green for Fair and Blue for Poor." A sample analysis of the color code in Philadelphia proved its value. In that city, 62.5 percent of the relief cases came from the blue areas, only 3.6 percent from the red, and "Curtis publications go to Red and Yellow areas where few families need relief, and where many families can pay full price for a publication" and, by extension, for advertised merchandise.

The basic strength of the Curtis publications, the circular added, lay in the editorial side of the magazine, and Curtis "has not economized on editorial features." Moreover, each magazine had a "personality," "the embodiment of the ideas and convictions of its editors." *Curtis Circulations Stand Firm* echoed Lorimer's belief that in troubled times editors had a grave responsibility "for sane and stable thinking . . . to lead rather than to follow . . . to appeal to the sober judgment and not to the passions of the public." Each Curtis editor was "thoroughly grounded in his faith in American institutions and American business." Advertisers were urged to invest in such magazines, magazines convinced of "the sound sense and morality of the great American public."[60]

Taking the mission of a Curtis editor seriously, Lorimer was infused with vitality. Despite hard times at the *Post* and an administration he saw as destroying American institutions and American character, he worked with energy and a sense of excitement that pervaded the editorial offices of the magazine. Adelaide Neall's November letter to Tarkington closed with the comment that Tarkington had been right in "saying that these are stirring times, but they are mighty interesting times for any one connected with a publication such as the Post!"[61]

It was certainly true that the *Post* was not stinting on the editorial side. Although issues were smaller, Lorimer continued to

It's never too early to learn

Tiny as her hands are, dirt and smudges disappear from her play-household like magic. (She is learning to start housekeeping *right*—with Bon Ami—just as her mother learned it many years ago.)

Unskilled as her hands are as yet—no surface will suffer scratch or mar to make cleaning harder next time—(for remember she is using Bon Ami). And soft as her hands are, she need never fear that they will get rough or red. Bon Ami doesn't do that.

Bon Ami is truly the Nemesis of grime and dirt, but it won't leave scratches and it won't hurt tender hands.

THE BON AMI COMPANY . . . . NEW YORK
In Canada: BON AMI LIMITED . . . . MONTREAL

Bon Ami

cake and powder *every home needs both*

In play housekeeping or real—grime is grime, dirt is dirt, and their Nemesis is Bon Ami. Try it for cleaning and polishing BATHTUBS · TILING · MIRRORS · WINDOWS · SMOOTH PAINTED WOODWORK PEWTER · NICKEL AND AGATEWARE · ALUMINUM · BRASS · TIN · COPPER · CHROMIUM PLATE AUTOMOBILE WINDSHIELDS AND METAL TRIMMINGS · REFRIGERATORS · WHITE SHOES · THE HANDS ENAMEL STOVES · FINE KITCHEN UTENSILS · FLOORS OF TILE, MARBLE AND CONGOLEUM

An early start at women's work

buy the best material available for a popular market and to pay high prices for it. Serials in 1933 included such blockbusters as Agatha Christie's *The Calais Coach* and Nordhoff and Hall's *Men Against the Sea,* as well as novels by Oliver La Farge, P. G. Wodehouse, and Ben Ames Williams. Mary Roberts Rinehart's mystery novel *The Album* was serialized as well, Lorimer paying the considerable sum of $60,000.[62] Nonfiction included Mark Sullivan on Herbert Hoover and the Depression, Pearl Buck on Chinese warlords, Dorothy Thompson on Germany, and Bernard Baruch on inflation. Quality maintained circulation.

At the same time, there were innovations in the magazine in the interest of broadening its appeal in various ways. In an effort to attract more advertising, pages 3 and 4 were given over to ads and promotion, pushing the beginning of the editorial material to page 5. Half of page 2 was now reserved for "Next Week," a new column previewing coming *Post* features. More editorial material was added after the editorial and op-ed pages, following the Campbell's Soup ad which had a lock on the posteditorial position.[63]

The magazine was also glamorized by a color illustration for one piece of fiction each week, despite Lorimer's insistence that editorial material was best presented in black and white. Then in 1934 a double-page Norman Rockwell painting appeared in the Christmas issue. "The Land of Enchantment" showed a boy and girl reading, with romantic and adventurous figures from fiction decorating the picture. The following year Rockwell painted a Dickensian scene, "The Christmas Coach," and early in 1936 "The New Tavern Sign" showed a Revolutionary era signboard with George III deposed in favor of George Washington.[64] More humorous material was added with the weekly appearance of Carl Anderson's "Henry" and fairly regular poems by Ogden Nash. For a short time, the *Post* attempted to consolidate its anti-intellectual position with a regular book review called "The Literary Lowbrow."

The final experiment of the Lorimer *Post,* and the most lasting, was a new emphasis on *Post* writers themselves, a return to a World War I idea that had lapsed. Now with "Keeping Posted" readers were given tempting foretastes of coming attractions, al-

A Campbell's ad from the thirties

lowed familiarity with *Post* writers, and reminded of the long history of pleasure the magazine had afforded them. In the fall of 1936, "Keeping Posted" featured longtime *Post* favorites—P. G. Wodehouse, George Pattullo, Mary Roberts Rinehart, Norman Rockwell, Octavus Roy Cohen, and Arthur Train.

For George Horace Lorimer, however, the real purpose of the *Post* now went far beyond entertainment and information; the mission of the *Post* was to save America. No longer was the editorial page left, as in the twenties, to Atwood and others; it was once again Lorimer's preserve, his answer to Roosevelt, the radio, and the fireside chats. The response, as far as readers' letters indicated, was overwhelmingly positive, or so Lorimer observed in occasional letters to *Post* writers.

Post contributor Hal Evarts, for example, had written to Lorimer congratulating him on the *Post*'s political stance. "Now many who formerly considered the Post guilty of heresy are reversing their opinions and offering thanks that at least one great publishing house remained on an even keel and stood on its honest convictions instead of preaching fallacies to cater to public fancy."[65] Lorimer replied, "Hundreds of congratulatory letters are coming to the office. . . . There seems to be no question that the country is having sober second thoughts and is beginning to analyze the plans and policies that have been put forward during the past year."[66]

The editorial Evarts so much admired was Lorimer's first full-scale attack on the New Deal. It covered two full pages, addressed "The Great Illusion" (April 7, 1934) and, in what Lorimer saw as the collapse of a two-party system, assumed for the *Post* the role of the articulate opposition. From this time on, Lorimer's *Post* was no longer a recorder of events or even a commentator. The *Post* had become an actor, an agent in the unfolding of events. Asserting that the *Saturday Evening Post* was "neither a Republican nor a Democratic organ," the editorial carefully catalogued the *Post*'s position, historically, on the economic issues facing the country.

No other publication in the United States has more consistently opposed the indiscriminate sale of foreign bonds in the United States and preached as strongly, year in and year out, against the evils of speculation. . . . We have refused to take financial advertising, even from houses that we knew were reputable and honest in their dealings, because it was impossible for us thoroughly to investigate securities and guarantee our readers against loss in those stocks and bonds.

With that record, the *Post* was in a position to attack New Deal policies that "hamstring and kill our exchanges." The actions of the Roosevelt administration with regard to business were not only wrongheaded, they were un-American. The intellectuals were at work again, giving us a "government by amateurs—college boys, irrespective of their age—who, having drunk deep, perhaps, of the Pierian spring, have recently taken some hearty swigs of Russian vodka."

Editorials like this, and there were dozens in the last three years of Lorimer's editorship, not only inveighed against the New Deal but continued to rehearse the past record of the *Post* on dozens of major issues. As if the *Post* were the opposition party, it laid out its platform and campaigned for votes.

As for the traditional second party, the *Post* was hard put to find much to celebrate among the Republicans. Preparing for the 1934 congressional election, Sam Blythe wrote "A Hunt for the Republicans" (December 30, 1933). The national committee was in complete disarray, an intolerable situation since the upcoming election would be "the first nation-wide opportunity for the people to indorse or condemn the policies and practices of President Roosevelt." More to the point, "a Republican victory in 1934 would be a smashing defeat for the Rooseveltian policies." A month later, apparently despairing of the Republicans, Blythe called for the formation of a new party "that shall stand in a central ground of sane and ordered progress." Such a position, in fact the position the *Post* saw itself as occupying, would be "opposed to the decayed capitalism of the Republican Party and the radical fantasies of the Democratic Party."[67] Others might call Lorimer's magazine reactionary; he saw his position as centrist.

By the fall, Blythe took the stance that there was neither a

Republican nor a Democratic party any longer. The Democratic party had disappeared, taken over by Roosevelt and the Brain Trust. The Republican party, no more than a ghost, could hope for little more than to elect a few good men. He concluded with a bleak kind of hope—and a warning: "Also, there is a presidential election in 1936."[68] The *Post* was already campaigning.

Late in 1934, the editorial page noted wearily, "When this Administration came into power, the country had a depression to liquidate. It begins to look now as if it has both a depression and a New Deal to liquidate."[69] To that end, Lorimer had consolidated his brief against Roosevelt and the New Deal and he spent the next two years in arguing his case. That case ranged across monetary, political, and moral issues.

Economically, a spate of programs for relief and revival, exacerbated by monetary devaluation, was plunging America into debt; wasteful programs were now placing an intolerable burden of taxation on working Americans, and the debt promised to extend that burden to their children and grandchildren. "To sell all and give to the poor may be good doctrine," Lorimer noted acidly, "but it is bad economics."[70]

Politically, the Roosevelt administration mounted an intolerable challenge to the Constitution. It had destroyed the old party system, creating a new alignment of haves versus have-nots, thereby creating class antagonism in what Lorimer continued to maintain was essentially a classless America. Moreover, Lorimer charged Roosevelt with reinstituting the spoils system, subverting the civil service, and creating a cadre of New Deal loyalists. In fact, administration policies overall worked to guarantee Roosevelt's reelection, for those on the receiving end, Lorimer charged, were unlikely to vote for a discontinuation of federal largesse.

In the moral implications of the New Deal lay the greatest peril to the nation. Not only were New Deal policies un-American, borrowed from European socialism and communism, but beyond that, they threatened to undermine and even eradicate those American characteristics responsible for the building of our country.

Unemployment insurance, public works, social security—all promised subsistence without work, salary without self-reliance, security without personal thrift, without the self-sacrifice necessary, and appropriate, for insuring one's future.

And finally, the charges against the administration included the attacks it mounted on those who criticized its policies. With unprecedented control of the new media, especially the radio, Roosevelt's men treated any vocal opponent as an enemy of the people, as "tory, reactionary, cannibal, obscene, adherent to the law of tooth and claw."[71] Lorimer, his own powerful medium at his disposal, mounted the counterattack.

For over two years preceding the 1936 election, Lorimer devoted the *Saturday Evening Post* to the destruction of the New Deal and the defeat of Franklin Roosevelt. To that end, once again returning to the lessons learned during the war, he used his own most effective writers to hammer home administration abuses and re-articulate American virtues; he found notable men here and abroad to state the case against the New Deal; he opened his pages to New Deal defectors ready to speak out against the administration. And he wrote editorials, dozens of them, pungent and combative essays to reinstruct his readers in the meaning of America, in the legacy of liberty they were fast abandoning. Lorimer had no question about relative values: "More valuable than economic improvement [are] the institutions of free and democratic government."[72]

Post polemics shared the pages of each issue with fiction and entertaining articles that continued to construct a version of America unthreatened by social change. In fact, the weekly appearance of the *Post* was in itself a recurring sign of stability, order, and conservative values.

On the nonfiction side, sports now dominated, with scores of articles each year on baseball, football, and boxing. Celebrities were featured: Babe Ruth and Branch Rickey in baseball, football's great coaches like Amos Alonzo Stagg and Fritz Crisler, Jack Dempsey and Joe Louis in boxing. Celebrities were the order of the day in other fields as well, from movie stars to opera divas. As he had in the twenties, Lorimer exploited the celebrity craze, but not without some acerbity. As he noted in a letter to Kenneth Roberts, "If Mrs. Roosevelt and some of the other limelight seekers would stop writing, there might be a chance for the trained writers to live." He could hardly resist the opportunity for a jab at the Roosevelts, but his criticism went deeper than that.

It does seem these days as though the way to get an opportunity to write is to do something spectacular that has nothing to do with training for writing. If you swim the channel or if your husband figures in a spectacular kidnapping the newspapers open their arms to you. In other words the advice to the young would be if you want to write do almost anything except train to be a writer. . . . I can only imagine what your feelings must have been when you saw that Mary Pickford was a best seller! [73]

Lorimer's dismay notwithstanding, he remained an editor with a taste for big names; he not only published celebrities, he even published Mrs. Roosevelt, who took the opportunity to answer her critics in the pages of the *Post*. "In Defense of Curiosity" was published on August 24, 1935.

Fiction continued to be a major drawing card. As the mystery novel grew ever more popular, Lorimer brought preeminent examples to his audience. In 1935 he serialized J. P. Marquand's first Mr. Moto story, Rex Stout's Nero Wolfe, and two of Agatha Christie's Hercule Poirot novels.[74] The following year the *Post* carried two Mr. Moto stories and two novels by Christie, as well as another Rex Stout and a mystery by Mignon Eberhardt.[75] Among the short stories were the continuing favorites, including Arthur Train's Mr. Tutt and William Hazlett Upson's Earthworm Tractor salesman. There was as well distinguished fiction by Stephen Vincent Benét, James Gould Cozzens, F. Scott Fitzgerald, and William Faulkner.

Faulkner had been sending stories to the *Post* for a number of years, and Lorimer had accepted two of them. As early as 1927, sending the manuscript of "Christmas Tree," Faulkner had alerted the *Saturday Evening Post* to his importance: "And hark in your ear: I am a coming man, so take warning."[76] In 1931, when some stories had been returned, Faulkner responded in the persona of a disinterested outsider. The writer feared the *Post* "Publicity Engineer Himself" should be informed about "one of those mistakes which we all make at times, in the purest of intentions, and yet by which our lives are forever changed; following which, we go down, down, to be at last unwept, unsung, and worst of all, unpurchased." The facts were then laid out. Faulkner had published two stories in the *Post*. For the first, he "received five letters," including a request for inclusion in the O. Henry Prize collection. For the second, he received an English reprint request and one letter "compliment[ing] the editor on his courage in publishing such a story in an age when 'all magazines appear to be edited by and for women.'" Since that time, eight of Faulkner's stories had been turned down. "Let this be a warning," Faulkner continued, "that the Post is unwittingly in the way of falling from the high place in letters to which these fourteen people (including the aforesaid Faulkner) raised it." In case that argument was unavailing, a postscript was added.

P.S. The aforesaid Faulkner has a new baby and a new roof, both acquired on credit; hence his motives in writing you would not have been pure. Needless to say, mine are.

P.P.S. Speaking of this baby: the other day this Faulkner told a friend, an old farmer, the good news.

"How much did it weigh?" farmer says.

"Three pounds," Faulkner says.

"Well, dont feel bad about that," farmer says. "What with this Hoover prosperity and the drouth last summer, a fellow does well to get his seed back."[77]

But Lorimer continued to recognize the best; in 1934, the *Post* published "A Bear Hunt," an early version of "The Bear," and in 1936, sections of *The Unvanquished*.[78]

Lorimer was not only looking for the best in fiction; he was also carefully avoiding material that struck him as too downbeat, too depressing a response to the economic situation. Mary Roberts Rinehart sent him "The Tall Tree," a story about an out-of-work man driven close to suicide by idleness and despair. When his wife turned to fiction writing, she saved the family economically, but her assertion and her success took a permanent toll on her husband's masculinity. Adelaide Neall wrote to say that Lorimer had decided against the story. It was a delicate letter to write, for Rinehart remained among the *Post*'s most popular writers and one continually courted by competitor publications. "You have done a fine job of showing the mental workings of the unemployed husband, but it is just because you have made his despair so convincing and the wife's position so really hopeless that we feel it is not a depression time story for a publication that reaches the general public as we do." [79]

Lorimer had, however, another suggestion for Neall to send along to Rinehart. He had been looking for personal statements from his well-known writers, confessions of experiences under duress, even of moments of temporary weakness, and of the lessons these lapses had taught them. Rose Wilder Lane, a popular fiction writer, "confessed" that she had been a Communist in 1920. Of course, she had not been a card-carrying party member; she had come down with a cold the day she planned to join. Since then she had come to see the error of her ways. [80] And financial writer Will Payne told *Post* readers how he had temporarily abandoned his belief in self-reliance and individual responsibility. In 1931, his investments decimated by the fallen market, he gave up his lifelong habit of saving for spending. "But even then I knew in my heart that I was individually responsible for the mess I was in. The idea of individual responsibility, which is the inspiration of saving, is under fire from all the heavy artillery now." [81] The purpose of these confessions was clear: if *Post* readers could see that even those they admired had weakened in one way or another, had been temporarily blown off course by evil economic winds, they might be induced to reevaluate their own positions, correct their own errors.

To that end, Lorimer had Adelaide Neall write to Rinehart. He thought Rinehart might do an article on the three economic depressions she had lived through, "the experiences [she] had had under the American system, the improvement [she] had seen in the standard of living, the care and protection of the poor." But the real point was to make such an article personal. "No one knows what would have happened during that first depression after your father's death if a paternalistic government had stepped in and not only made it easy for your mother to get help, but made it very difficult for her to do anything on her own to meet her problem."[82] Since the economic situation in 1893 had lost Rinehart's father his already marginal employment, and since her father's death was, consequently, a suicide, the request was indeed preposterous. Moreover, as both Lorimer and Neall knew, Rinehart's mother had been left in desperate financial straits with two young daughters to provide for and no resources whatsoever. There was no Horatio Alger story here. Rinehart declined.[83]

As lively and entertaining as the *Post* was in the last two years of Lorimer's editorship, the greatest part of his considerable energy and acumen was devoted to his editorial mission: to save America by discrediting the New Deal and defeating the reelection bid of Franklin Roosevelt. If the Roosevelt administration would certainly gain the votes of those on the receiving end of the big giveaway, then Lorimer's strategy would be to recapture those who had temporarily fallen away in the despair and confusion of 1932, the real Americans who needed only to be reminded of their precious legacy of liberty and self-reliance. Where that meant the employed middle class, he had only to keep them informed of the growing list of un-American policies and projects of the New Deal and of the cost of those policies. Where that meant the hard-pressed worker and farmer, different tactics were required. Using all the devices and strategies learned in thirty-five years of editing the *Post,* Lorimer took up the battle, attacking New Deal policies and programs in agriculture and labor and New Deal "intellectuals" in general.

The point of view of the farmer, or of the farmer as Lorimer would have him, appeared first in 1934 when the *Post* printed an essay by Mrs. George B. Simmons called "Where Do We Go From Here?" (March 17, 1934). Writing as the wife of a Missouri farmer, Mrs. Simmons said that as she did her day's work in her farm home, she tried to think about the things she heard and read, and she could make no sense of them. In a tone that alternated between feminine diffidence and American self-assertion, Mrs. Simmons managed to articulate the entire catalogue of *Post* grievances against the New Deal. In fact, the catalogue was so satisfactory that one cannot help suspecting that Lorimer had returned once again to his World War I strategy of fictional nonfiction. The Curtis Company claimed, however, that Mrs. Simmons's article was "found . . . in the daily mail," like other "spontaneous reactions of citizens there-tofore unknown."[84]

Mrs. Simmons's essential point was how strange it was that, while she could make no sense of the claims and explanations the Roosevelt administration offered daily on the radio, "nobody ever questions its rightness and its success openly. . . . I hear what the farmers are reported to be thinking and saying, and my husband and I look at each other across the soup we are having for supper, and we say, 'We don't think those things!'" Following the artful touch of the soup for supper, Mrs. Simmons modestly sighed, "But then I am doubtless a simple soul needing governmental salvation more than I am able to realize."

As the article moved on through Mrs. Simmons's thoughts, the representation, the creation, of the "real" American farmer grew stronger and clearer, defying the Rooseveltian farmer, depicted as dependent, weak, and cowardly. She wondered how, under present conditions, children would learn to develop initiative and even "what God thinks of it all." Nor did she blame the rich: "It would, perhaps, give me the kind of fiendish glee it appears to give to some I have observed, could I think of all rich people as greedy and selfish and cruel," but she could not. "No man or woman should be limited from making any fortune that can be made honestly"; nor should anyone be punished for success with confiscatory taxes.

She was much concerned with the move toward dictatorship and the concomitant drift of the American people into "serfdom." She admitted that it seemed easier to take directions from a boss than to figure things out for oneself, "but these are not the ways expectable of the children of pioneer ancestors" who have taught us the value of "private initiative and private enterprise and personal thrift and personal desire for ownership." Despite what the newspapers and the radio said, Mrs. Simmons continued to believe in "individualism."

The war on the New Deal's agricultural policies continued with an occasional piece by one or another unknown but "typical" American farmer[85] as well as with statements by experts. In 1936, George N. Peek, first AAA administrator, printed "In and Out" in the *Post* (May 16, 1936). He had joined the Roosevelt administration and left it; he could provide the inside story. He went to Washington "to do something for agriculture and . . . something for the nation." But he eventually found he was not in "a Democratic Administration but in a curious collection of socialists and internationalists" who "could not allow themselves to be hampered by platform pledges, or by the Constitution." Finding their tactics reminiscent of Russia, Italy, and Germany, Peek left the administration and joined those who used the pages of the *Post* to press their charges.

Labor presented an even more delicate problem than agriculture, since Lorimer was not in fact addressing the unemployed worker but rather those "people with intelligence and buying power" who might be sympathetic to the claims of labor. To that end he had to create a portrait of the working man to fit the *Post's* ideal: a man whose independence and individualism would not let him accept relief and whose Americanism kept him free of the corruption of radicalism. First, however, it was necessary to prepare the ground by dismissing as much of the unemployment question as possible. Here the strategy was to link the unemployed with the alien. Typically, Lorimer discovered the real problem in U.S. immigration policy.

Martin Dies, at that time a member of the House Committee on Immigration and Naturalization, provided a polemic. Tracing the history of America from a homogeneous nation to a country made up of unassimilable immigrants from southern and eastern Europe, he argued that, without 40 million of "foreign stock," 16 million foreign-born, and 7 million aliens swelling the population, "it is reasonable to believe that the unemployment problem would never have achieved such serious and unprecedented proportions in this country." Indeed, there might well be no labor surplus at all had immigration been halted in time. The attitude of each American toward immigration and toward the dangerous aliens already here, "the gangsters, murderers and thieves," was an index of each American's patriotism; prefiguring his later role on the House Un-American Activities Committee, Dies concluded, "Either we are for or against our country."[86]

Having narrowed his subject to the native American worker, Lorimer set about depicting him as loyal to native American values: hard work, thrift, and independence. As early as 1933 the *Post* printed an article on "The Hopeful American Worker" (June 17, 1933), proving that, even unemployed, he was not at all interested in communist propaganda. The writer had spent the summer and part of the winter among the jobless and had grown convinced of their sturdy conservatism. For example, he had stood outside a body plant in Detroit while a "well-known Communist" told a "colored boy" about the failure of capitalism in the United States. The young black was up to the challenge. "Well, suh . . . if things in Russia is as you say, I reckon you-all is right, and we in America ought to do somethin' about it right heah and now. Foh mahself, Ah don't know a blame thing about what's goin' on over theah in Russia. But if you ask me, suh, Ah don't think you yourself knows such a hell of a lot!"

By 1935–1936, Lorimer had turned to arguing the labor case by inveighing against New Deal relief programs and their recipients. Again, the *Post* reader heard from both amateurs and experts. A woman who had worked four years in "volunteer philanthropy" spoke of a typical case, a man with a ninth-grade education, a wife, and children. Before the Depression, he had exercised no frugality, buying on the installment plan. Now on relief, he was angry and peremptory; he had even slapped a woman investigator who had provided one quart of milk a day rather than the two he wanted.[87] No sympathy and certainly no public monies need be expended on a man so bereft of American virtues.

The voice of business was raised in "A Businessman Looks at Relief" (March 21, 1936). The writer , after a year "as director of

Pennsylvania State's Emergency Relief Administration," could attest to great sums spent and great waste, most of which "has its roots in politics." And both political and managerial experience came with a piece by William McNair, mayor of Pittsburgh. A lifelong Democrat, he found himself "impelled to publish the facts as [he knew] them concerning the terrific waste of the people's money in the expenditure of public funds for relief." [88]

By 1936 the impending election called for more dramatic materials, materials that again raise the question of authenticity. A case in point is the story of a transient camp, purportedly written by one of the transients. The hobo in question had improved his own condition slightly and he now had some responsibility in the camp, for which he received a salary. But his case was not to be taken as representative, for "there is not a ray of hope for any man at Bayou Blue. We will leave this place just as we entered it—vagrants still." Irony and even comedy colored his account of the antics of the men in the camp, but his point was somber: public funds were being used to house and feed men who were not and never had been producers. The real purpose of the camp was simply "to improve the general looks of things by removing from public view the most ragged and vociferous victims of the depression." Meanwhile, the men loafed and drank, enjoying "this three-ringed circus of the New Deal." [89]

Well-known *Post* writers were also called on to make the case against relief. Dorothy Thompson, turning from her major series of articles on Hitler's Germany, attacked relief and work projects. She worried about their "moral effect," for it all "looks and smells very like the old-fashioned charity." [90] In a second article she addressed the costs of relief, the burden placed on the future by the mounting national debt. "The $4,000,000,000 being used this year are borrowed. That is to say that Mr. Gonzales' children's milk and their plush rabbit are being made a charge on the children to pay when they grow up. This may be helping the children now, and preparing for them another great depression." [91]

Thompson's articles, like others in the *Post*, served to oppose the position articulated by the administration itself and especially by the "intellectuals." In Lorimer's view intellectuals had for decades weakened the fiber of America and now they had invaded the government in the form of the Brain Trust. As a part of the war on the New Deal, the *Post* fired a cannonade at intellectuals and at their version of America.

In 1935 Gilbert Seldes, who had been writing for the *Post* for several years, laid bare "The America of the Intellectuals" (March 9, 1935). For twenty years "the American intellectual has sabotaged his country," he charged, importing first European art and then European political and economic ideas. Meanwhile, the country responded by paying him "as if he were a great public benefactor." How had this situation come about? For Seldes the answer was clear; it began when the idea was implanted that "the artist— painter, poet, novelist, playwright, critic—[was] the most important of all human beings." By contrast, the great Leonardo saw himself only marginally as an artist; thus "Remembering Leonardo only for his painting is like admiring Darwin only because he wrote clear English or Edison because his trousers were well pressed."

Having descended from dubious history to bizarre analogy, Seldes continued with the story of the pernicious spread of literacy. "Writing was always the privilege of the few and, less than a hundred years ago, when reading became common, the writers, in command of the press, began to build up the idea that Shakespeare was greater than Newton . . . and Edgar Allan Poe represents America more fully than Benjamin Franklin." In the nineteenth century, writers, artists and intellectuals, with their great new power, fled America for Europe; in their place came "lovers of political liberty." "We lost William Wetmore Story and F. Marion Crawford; we gained Carl Schurz and Andrew Carnegie." Then, after the war, the new expatriates vilified America and even those at home "belittled" such real American poets as Edgar Lee Masters and Vachel Lindsay. As a result, the new generation of writers was poisoned. "The simple masterpieces which Sherwood Anderson wrote about boys and horses were shrugged away by superior critics, and he was turned to floundering in psychological morasses, because it was European to wander in these swamps." Some were saved. "From the moment he wrote Arrowsmith, an American novel without the requisite dislike for America, Sinclair Lewis ceased to rank in these critical circles. . . . He was too healthy."

The principal charge against the intellectuals was their importation of the European "malady": "the misery preached by Freud . . . the fatality preached by Marx." They might, wrote Seldes with somewhat confused logic, have led us into Marxism but instead they have done something worse. Without alluding directly to the Roosevelt administration, he asserted that the intellectuals had prepared the grounds for fascism. Of course, this was not their intention, but "it is the misfortune of intellectuals that they often achieve the exact opposite of their intentions."

By 1935 the *Post* was on the campaign trail. Major *Post* contributors turned their attention to isolating the real campaign issues, as the *Post* saw them. For Sam Blythe, "The Real Issue" (November 30, 1935) was taxes and his audience "real Americans." It was for them to understand "the hard, practical basis of how much it has cost the people of this country, the millions and millions of thrifty, self-respecting and self-supporting people . . . and how much it will cost in the future." An accompanying photograph depicted relief in terms of a federally supported ballet class with students from the "Ranks of the Unemployed."

Blythe argued as well that the administration was buying the election with handouts. Any administration, he pointed out, is "a presidential campaign." Votes were needed to stay in power, and "votes are the outcome of politics, of policies advanced to secure those votes."

This plan of campaign rests entirely on the impressing of the great bulk of the people—the workers, the farmers, the labor unionists, the "forgotten men," the people in poor and moderate circumstances, the unemployed, the needy, the unsuccessful, those who need the dole—that the Government at Washington, as exemplified politically by the Roosevelt Democratic Party, is the savior, the regenerator, the almoner, the uplifter, the great hope of the submerged, all of whom have votes.

Those voters would reelect Roosevelt, for they expected a continuation of benefits. Therefore, *Post* readers were warned that the
coming years would bring benefits "increased by billions if the
prodigal source of them is not disturbed in the 1936 election."[92] A
few months later Blythe repeated this, noting the odds against the
Republicans, the handicap they faced, given "the effect and power
of the billions of dollars scattered about the country," as well as the
idealistic messages concocted by "press agents and propaganda
experts . . . employed and paid for with the people's money."[93]

Blythe continued his attack with a piece on class warfare. He
cited his own experience as a political observer for "more than forty
years" and "in every kind of national, state or local campaign,
including every presidential battle from the Harrison-Cleveland
encounter in 1888 to the Roosevelt-Hoover debacle in 1932." But
there is something new here, and he would call attention to it: "the
adroit, the incessant, and the skillful political strategy, directed at
the destruction of the fundamental American governmental principles . . . that this was not to be a country wherein one class was
arrayed against another class, where, indeed, there were to be no
classes and all men were to be free and equal under the law."[94]

Garet Garrett, meanwhile, was focusing on the American
economy and what had become, for Lorimer and the *Post,* its logical corollary—the American character. In "The Lost American"
(March 28, 1936) Garrett recounted how the current administration had revised the history of the nation's past greatness, labeling
it a "delusion," "the last phantasm of a monstrous social privilege . . . called rugged individualism [or] *laissez faire.* It was all
unreal." The effect had been that Americans had now forsaken the
"vision of their own greatness, unwilling to meet its demands upon
their courage and powers." And this was rare, even unique, for
"seldom if ever before has it happened that such a vision was
afterward dragged in the mud." As the government gave and gave
and the people took and took, Garrett saw Americans with hands
held out, "to receive something, palms up, all cupped. Americans
nobody knew."

Writing in opposition to proposals for social security, Garrett charged that such a system would abrogate American rights. "Hardly could there be a right more patent or elementary than the right of the individual to receive the whole of what he earns and to do with it what he likes. Industrial workers no longer possess that right. In the name of social security, it has been taken from them." The *Post* had long argued the virtue of thrift, but thrift was more than a virtue in itself, it was as well a sign of a man's character. Social security would create "a law of compulsory thrift."[95]

But Garrett found the ideal weapon with which to attack the Roosevelt administration when he turned to the Federal Theater Project, which, in the view of the *Post,* consolidated all the most vicious features of the New Deal: the misuse of public monies, the excesses of the intellectuals, and the triumph of radicalism. In 1936 the FTP mounted "Triple A Plowed Under," a radical attack on those who opposed the New Deal. In describing the play, scene by scene, and highlighting its radical statements, Garrett made his point over and over: that the play was "written by dramatists employed by the Government, produced in a theater rented by the Government, acted by actors hired by the Government." Moreover, the play represented, as Garrett reported, "the ideal of a militant workers'-and-farmers' alliance [which] happens to be the official program of the Communist International for the Communist Party, U.S.A." Nevertheless, "it was done with public money."

Not, he continued, that either the Treasury or the Congress was responsible for issuing the funds to support "Triple A Plowed Under." Rather, the public purse had been surrendered to Roose-velt, the "fabulous $4,800,000,000" over which the new Congress, in January 1935, had given the president control. Moreover, what had started as relief quickly became the "idea of subsidized theater for the masses," leading to the concept of "a new art of the theater that shall be aesthetically important and socially significant." Nec-essarily, then, writers had to be trained to create plays under this new aesthetic, play readers trained to select the plays, actors trained to play them, and finally the masses trained to appreciate them. And the result of all this, announced the outraged Garrett, was a project "beyond boondoggling" and a play that announced and celebrated the program of the Communist International, a play paid for by the dollars of American taxpayers.[96]

Lorimer, meanwhile, continued to use the editorial page as his political weapon, attacking the New Deal on economic, political and moral grounds. Finally, and after what must have been very careful consideration, Lorimer turned the attack on Roosevelt himself. For a long time he had cautiously evaded any such personal attack, aware of Roosevelt's enormous charm and popularity. *Post* articles, in fact, long avoided any personal comments at all on the president, Lorimer having chosen instead to whittle away at the administration with a series of articles by Alva Johnston attacking key figures like Charley Michelson and Jim Farley.[97]

But in June 1936, in the same issue that carried Garrett's piece on the Federal Theater Project, there ran a full-page editorial, "Pussyfooting About the President" (June 20, 1936). "It is the fashion among many critics of the New Deal," the editorial opened, to speak of the president as a well-meaning man who does not understand the implications of his policies." With cool irony, Lorimer demurred: "We credit the President with more brains than that." After all, "those whose minds did not meet his have walked the plank, one by one." Roosevelt should have credit for "such of his policies as are sound," and "he must accept the blame" for those that were not. In a bitter turn of phrase, Lorimer declared that we must "render unto Roosevelt the things that are Roosevelt's."

In the pages of the *Post* the 1936 campaign came more and more to seem like an election battle between Franklin Delano Roosevelt and George Horace Lorimer. The *Post* was running on its record. Moreover, unlike Roosevelt, it was not stirring up class hatreds nor engaging in invective; rather, as one editorial put it, it would review administration policies, specifically those policies with which one could agree in principle but not in practice. In the case of most of these policies, it turned out that the *Saturday Evening Post* had been there first.

For example, child labor: "More than twenty years ago, The Saturday Evening Post made a survey of child labor in the mills and presented a series of highly critical articles on it." Or conservation:

the *Post* had long fought for this, arguing for methods far superior to those now pursued. Some New Deal policies, however, were in themselves abhorrent. In relation to farm legislation, "It is difficult—except in some of the latest novels—to find words strong enough to characterize the deliberate attempts to misrepresent the attitude of industry toward the farmer and his problems."[98] Voters—Americans—could trust the *Post* because, as another editorial stated, "The Saturday Evening Post is not a partisan of any party or any individual." Such high-mindedness was a little undercut by the next statement: "It is a partisan of sound ideas, whether they are put forward by the Republican, Democratic or the Roosevelt–New Deal Party."[99]

Maintaining, if not a nonpartisan stand, at least its own tradition, the *Post* ran one pro-Roosevelt article prior to the election. Lorimer selected Harold Ickes, secretary of the interior, whose war on the slums he approved. Ickes began with measured praise: "It may be taken for granted that [Roosevelt] is neither saint nor devil, archangel nor foul fiend. A very human individual; he possesses faults as well as virtues." But his conclusion was more impassioned: "Here in truth is a great leader, a buoyant and gallant figure, tilting his lance for a cause in which he believes with all the fervor of his soul. And that cause is the cause of the great inarticulate mass of the American people."[100] The most important thing about the Ickes article, however, was how early it was published, appearing in mid-August. To be sure, the companion piece, William Allen White on Landon, appeared even earlier, but the point was that the set pieces for each party came nearly three months before the election, leaving the way clear for the *Post* to bring to a climax its campaign against Roosevelt.

Lorimer turned to his old hands. The last issue in October carried a fiery essay by George Pattullo, who had continued to write fiction for the *Post* once his days of reporting on the war and the AEF were over. Pattullo began by telling Americans how low their stock had fallen with other nations, rehearsing the story of the United States' international relations since the war, especially its softness and cowardice in allowing the war debts to go unpaid lest we lose the friendship of the debtor nations. "I have yet to hear," he wrote with scorn, "of any proposal that ranks with this for cowardice."

Meanwhile, at home he heard constantly of "rights." His attack on the Roosevelt administration began with the issue of "rights." "I marvel whence mankind derives all these newly proclaimed rights. He came into being without a stitch to his back or a right of any kind. What rights he now enjoys are such because embodied in laws and codes." Roosevelt, as a champion of these "rights," was deeply suspect. "So, when any champion of a new order begins to spout about the moral right of every man to this and that, he is talking nonsense. He is talking about privileges they hope to wrest, and when he demands more than fair play, he is merely trying to impose class tyranny." The New Deal, Pattullo warned, displayed a "heart-breaking disregard of the nation's future." Looking about him at the state of America, he said, though it hurt him to say it, that "patriotism is dead." Economically, America would come back, but recovery would mean a "final complete undoing unless with its winning is born a new spirit of patriotism, courage and self-reliance." [101]

Pattullo's sentiments were Lorimer's. It was not that they failed to see the bread lines, the Dust Bowl, the violence between strikers and police, but rather that for them those images were played against a screen of nineteenth-century convictions. Lorimer, certainly, believed he had seen worse, believed that the economic condition of America continued to improve and that the distribution of wealth continued to spread benefits to the workingman. More important, he attributed the improvement he believed in to the system of American capitalism. That system was more important, more valuable, than temporary individual hardship. It was not a question of his being altogether without compassion. For Lorimer there could be no individual success, certainly no large-scale success of individuals, if that system were undermined. Thus, business had to be left free in order to prosper, and men and women left to their own devices in order to recall for themselves the values of self-reliance and courage; these were the twin pillars that supported the system. From Lorimer's vantage point, the horror of the New Deal was that it subverted the system by undermining both pillars.

In the same issue with Pattullo's essay were two editorials. In both Lorimer continued to set the *Post*'s record against that of the New Deal. Its good objectives—the abolition of child labor, conservation, slum clearance, protection of the investor—were all things the *Saturday Evening Post* had "stood and worked for." Other objectives were simply out of date, most notably its attempt to regulate business. Once that objective had made sense; in the early days of the century when business was too powerful, the *Saturday Evening Post* "stood for a stronger political check on business." Now the situation had changed: "A democracy cannot live without a balanced check on economics and politics." The voter, Lorimer urged, must vote for the future of his country: "Eternal vigilance is the price of liberty, of safety, of personal independence, and the voter has been off the job of being vigilant." That could not continue, for "this is the most important election in the history of the country." [102]

The November 7 issue of the *Saturday Evening Post* appeared on November 3, Election Day, leading off with the first installment of a new Agatha Christie. In second place was "The Youth Document," a melancholy piece by Garet Garrett, who suddenly found himself in a new and wholly unfamiliar world. Referring to himself throughout as the "Old Reporter," Garrett returned to New York, the city he remembered from his youth now overwritten by a modern city of "steel buildings, floodlighted towers, motor traffic, sky travel, voices without bodies . . . people at ease and bored, diminished by the importance of their own externalized ideas." He recalled the old "grand, four-story, gas-lighted hotel with half a block of guest chairs and spittoons on the sidewalk in front" and himself as a young man, hungry in the city.

A young reporter came to interview him, but Garrett insisted the two merely talk. Soon they were arguing over ideas. The young reporter wanted "change," and the Old Reporter tried to make him understand the dangers inherent in exchanging one's liberty for security. The youth replied that "in a land where there is always plenty, people are entitled to economic security." And if you were out of work? asked Garrett. Why then, "I suppose I'd apply for relief or get a WPA job." But nothing so revealed the chasm between the two men, and between the two generations they repre-sented, as the moment when Garrett posed his most penetrating, if rhetorical, question: which, he asked, would make "their country richer," individual effort or guaranteed support? The young reporter did not understand the question.

Later, alone, Garrett tried to understand unemployment and its solution, but the numbers were too great. Five million youths were out of work and it was not possible to think of five million solutions. Only individual solutions were possible. Garrett grew slightly more sanguine, then, recalling a story he had recently heard. A young man bicycled from Oregon to Washington, D.C., because he wanted a West Point appointment and was determined to stay near the congressman whose backing he needed. He found a job the day after he arrived in Washington and kept the job till the end of the congressional session. Then he bicycled home to Oregon, still on the trail of his congressman. That young man needed no "solutions": "If he and his kind are let alone, they will carry the rest." But the words were braver than Garrett's spirit, and he closed with the comment that youth was "the helpless document that has received the writing of the time."

The November 7, 1936, editorial page was devoted entirely to the election. It was a dying gasp. One of the pieces identified "The Final Question," and here Lorimer rearticulated the essence of the issue. "The voter must ask himself the final question, which is whether, in his opinion, a continuance of Mr. Roosevelt's regime will tend to undermine the foundations, dissipate the substance and destroy the real spirit of the American system of representative government." And he repeated it: "But Americans have got to decide whether the essential spirit of our system is in danger." And repeated it: "What the voter must finally decide in his own mind is whether the essential spirit and direction of the New Deal regime has been American or not."

Lorimer knew, of course, that there was no question about the outcome of the election. He tried, in one of the editorial essays, to encourage split tickets, hoping to offset the enormous Democratic majorities in Congress. But resignation can be heard throughout the dignified statement that closed the third editorial.

The Saturday Evening Post, owing to its large edition and its world-wide circulation, must go to press several weeks before it is distributed to subscribers and buyers from the newsstands, so we shall not be able to comment on the election before the last of November.

But whether Landon or Roosevelt is elected, we shall continue to be nonpartisan, in the real sense of the word, and criticize the policies of either as President whenever we feel that they are unsound or unwise.[103]

When the *Post* conceded the election in an editorial that appeared on December 5, Lorimer had several points to make. He granted the fact of Roosevelt's "tremendous majority," but noted twice that 16 million voters "could not see eye to eye with the New Deal," and that "sixteen million voters are quite a lot of people." Indeed they were, perhaps more than read the *Post* each week. But the landslide victory that returned not only Roosevelt but a Democratic House and Senate could not be gainsaid, Lorimer acceded, for now "there can be no effective opposition." "For the present, at least, the future of America is in the lap of its popular god."

As for the *Post*, it would remain a nonpartisan observer, hoping that the president would keep the country's best interests at heart. "Even though The Saturday Evening Post has been a severe critic of many of the policies and tendencies of the New Deal, we shall return to the position we took when the President first came into power and suspend comment on the new Administration until its policies and purposes have been made clear by him and the Congress. We sincerely hope that during his coming term in office the President will prove to be a wise counselor, friend and leader of the whole people."[104]

The *Saturday Evening Post* would have to continue its surveillance of Roosevelt and the New Deal without George Horace Lorimer. In August he had announced his retirement, effective

For Lorimer's last issue, one of Leydendecker's Christmas covers

January 1, 1937, and had named Wesley Stout as his successor. In a formal letter to the board of directors, Lorimer "tendered his resignation" both as editor of the *Post* and as chairman of the Curtis Publishing Company. He reminded them, "This is no sudden decision," that he had "for several years past . . . been considering this action." He had been with the *Post* for nearly thirty-nine years, and for ten, vice-president and then president of Curtis. Now, he felt that he was leaving when "both the business and the editorial affairs of the Company are in good hands. . . . Need I add that I resign with regret because I have been happy in my work and fortunate in my associates. But I want a little more leisure, a little more time to attend to my personal affairs, and a chance to do some other work, including some long deferred writing." [105]

The December 26, 1936, issue of the *Saturday Evening Post* was the last edited by George Horace Lorimer. Its lead piece was the first installment of Kenneth Roberts's *Rogers' Rangers;* Lorimer wanted to end with this work of his old friend and colleague. Joseph Hergesheimer had a story too, and J. P. Marquand's *George Apley* was running. The editorial page carried a full-page Lorimer editorial; this one time the editorial was signed. Titled "Looking Forward," it was not sentimental.

Lorimer started off by making clear that the voice of the *Saturday Evening Post* was, or had been, the voice of George Horace Lorimer. "As editor of The Saturday Evening Post I have always had a free hand. Up to the hour when this number goes to press, I have formulated its policies, planned the numbers, and personally read and selected the material for them." He wanted his readers to know, moreover, where those policies arose, and in making that point, Lorimer turned his farewell editorial into his farewell political address. "My editorial policies have grown out of the conviction that the American form of government, with its system of checks and balances designed to prevent the usurpation of too much power by either the Executive, the Congress or the Judiciary, is as sound today as when it went into effect." The *Post* had always supported reasonable change, but not "cure-alls," not "change for the sake of change." Moreover, whatever a government might choose to do, "economic law . . . invariably has the last move."

Lorimer used most of the editorial to criticize, with restraint, the policies, and particularly the practices, of the New Deal, and to raise the hope, however faint, that Roosevelt's second term might be one of more careful consideration and some restraint. Toward the end, Lorimer turned his attention to business, to the theme with which he had begun the *Post* back in the final years of the nineteenth century, and he commented with satisfaction, "Through all that period, I have seen business practices and ethics growing better." And finally, there was his unfailing belief in the American character and in America itself, which "has done a pretty good job and no Ism would have done a better one."

The 1936 campaign and election had dismayed Lorimer, but the Roosevelt landslide would not have deterred him from continuing to direct what he believed to be the *Post*'s mission to guard America. And it certainly had not brought him to the decision to resign his position as editor of the *Post*. In fact, Lorimer was ill, suffering from what was soon diagnosed as cancer. Though he intended to write, hoping to do his own story of his editorship, his illness made that impossible. He traveled west in the early part of 1937 and then returned to Philadelphia where he died in his home, after a bout with pneumonia, on October 22, 1937. The *Saturday Evening Post* as he had created and guided it had predeceased him.

George Horace Lorimer,
the Boss

For the most part, this book has looked at the public Lorimer, at the expression of his public views through the medium of the *Saturday Evening Post*. But even in his role as *Post* editor, Lorimer had his private side as well, a personality expressed in his dealings with contributors and colleagues. This more private Lorimer is recalled in the memoirs and autobiographies of *Post* writers and, especially, in the correspondence that survives between those writers and Lorimer. Even the salutations in the correspondence help us to read relationships, for letters to Lorimer opened in a variety of ways, each encoding a degree of intimacy. The letter of the unknown, hopeful writer opened "Dear Mr. Lorimer." "Dear Lorimer" signaled the male bond. A few, a very few, wrote "Dear George." But for the inner circle, for those who were longtime contributors and friends, the salutation was "Dear Boss." And it is as the Boss that Lorimer is most clearly recalled in his editorial office in the Curtis Building.

"The Boss" encapsulates Lorimer's presence and editorial style, his complete authority over the contents of the *Post,* the speed and assurance with which he selected or rejected stories, articles, illustrations. "The Boss" expresses as well his mastery over contributors, his insistent need to remain in charge, to make final determinations about the materials he accepted for print—their content, length, diction, and especially their price.

Authority was the mark both of Lorimer's more private role as editor and of his public editorial credo. Authority was essential because, as Lorimer explained, a magazine had nothing to sell but ideas; moreover, those ideas *were* the magazine. A plurality of ideas amounted to an absence of identity. For the *Post,* the ideas and the identity were George Horace Lorimer's. "I believe in one-man power on a magazine, or newspaper," he told Isaac Marcosson; such a view, he said, was only common sense.

Delane of the London *Times* had it right when he said that "whatever appears in the *Times* should proceed from the initiative of whoever holds my place." That may sound like conceit, but it is simple commonsense. Editors and crowned heads are the only people in the world with the right to say "we." Editors should be the only despots. If the editor does not make good, what the public needs is a new editor, not a dozen editors. No human affair is strong enough to stand the mistakes of two men.[1]

From the outset of his career as *Post* editor, Lorimer had grasped and secured authority. When Cyrus Curtis named him acting editor and went off to Europe in search of a permanent editor, Lorimer instantly set his mark on the infant magazine, thereby winning the permanent job himself. And when *Journal* editor Edward Bok attempted to undermine Lorimer's power in the Curtis Company, Lorimer challenged Bok in a memo to Curtis from whom he received written assurance of that authority.

Even Edward Bok came to recognize Lorimer's position, though his acknowledgment rang a little sour. In *A Man From Maine,* his pious biography of Curtis, he reproduced the history of the *Post* in a chapter called "The Story of a Singed Cat." After minimizing Lorimer's role on the *Post* by attributing the idea of a magazine focused on business entirely to Cyrus Curtis, Bok did allow Lorimer some credit in relation to his concept of editorial power and responsibility.

George Horace Lorimer once gave an excellent description of the publishing business when he described it as a business purely of buying and selling brains: a business based upon having ideas and of making other men carry them out. In no other human activity may one be so absolutely sure that sins of commission will find one out, he argued. They are printed for all the world to read. On every issue of a periodical there is a plebiscite to determine its worthiness or unworthiness, whether it shall be encour-aged to continue or forced to suspend. Consequently, no business so quickly succumbs to dry-rot, to apathy, or content.[2]

As editor of the *Post*, Lorimer shaped its policies, established its tone, determined its position on all the major questions of the day. That authority was never delegated, never exercised at second hand. Lorimer read and approved everything that went into the magazine. Moreover, he read a good deal that never appeared in the magazine, read a good deal that needed reshaping and revising before it could appear in the magazine, thought up ideas for articles and stories and presented them to writers who then worked them up for the magazine. Through most of the years of his editorship, moreover, he wrote material himself for the magazine, from his Old Gorgon Graham books to the powerful, combative essays of the 1930s.

Even when the *Post* outgrew the reach of Lorimer's immediate oversight of all editorial matters, he developed a system and a style of management that was, if not exactly despotic, certainly mag-isterial. For example, starting about 1910 editor Churchy Williams was sent to New York once a week, available to aspiring *Post* contributors every Thursday, and when a submission proved par-ticularly promising, Churchy would telephone the writer to sum-mon him or her to Philadelphia for a meeting with Lorimer himself. The fortunate author would enter the imposing Curtis Building, icon of power and Americanism, ascend to the sixth floor, and enter the office where Lorimer sat at his desk flanked by windows over-looking Independence Square. There, the novice received the laying on of hands. There, too, old *Post* contributors would arrive or be called in for private editorial meetings, where the Boss would decide the fate of stories and illustrations, hear ideas for articles or series, listening only as long as it took him to get the gist of an idea and responding with a terse and final yes or no, good or bad.

From such editorial meetings came the articles and stories that shaped the weekly issues of the *Post*, the public expression of

Lorimer's authority. What was not hammered out at those meetings, what was apparently not even broached as a question, was the issue of price, for on that issue Lorimer did not negotiate. The price of a story or an article was determined by Lorimer; it was the chief expression of his private authority.

It is in matters of money that surviving correspondence allows one to hear most clearly the voice of the Boss. In a masterful series of rhetorical variations, ranging from a man-to-man heartiness suitable for contributors like Beveridge to an avuncular firmness appropriate for writers like Edna Ferber, the Boss handled the issue of price and maintained his dominance. Although the *Post* paid generously, Lorimer would not allow writers to drive up their own prices, nor would he enter bidding wars with other magazines. On the subject of money, he could not be bullied, and he could not be cajoled.

From the start, even before he had honed the rhetoric of power, Lorimer was firm on price. In 1900 he brought young Senator Beveridge to the pages of the *Post* at $1,000 an article for his series on the United States in the Philippines. But once that series was complete, Lorimer had to make it clear that such a fee was extraordinary and could not to be expected for future articles. He wanted a piece from Beveridge on the "Young Man in Politics," and he encouraged the senator to write it for the *Post*—but not at $1,000 an article. "I want, and hope, to have you for a regular contributor to the Post, but on the present basis you are, as you doubtless understand, a luxury for any publication, and we can not, at the time, when hot weather and the dull season are combining to prevent our pushing things, afford to order further material on the old basis."[3] Lorimer made his point and Beveridge lowered his price.

As Lorimer gained more confidence, and the *Saturday Evening Post* gained more power, his letters on the subject of payment grew firmer, and briefer, eliminating all special pleading about hot weather and dull seasons. By 1916, for example, when Mary Roberts Rinehart had become one of the *Post*'s most popular writers, Lorimer turned down a sentimental story, "The Confession," informing her that it was "much more calculated to appeal to your woman's magazine audience." At that time Lorimer was paying Rinehart $1,750 for a story, and Rinehart, intensely annoyed at the reference to the "woman's magazine audience," was delighted to be able to inform him that she had accepted *Cosmopolitan*'s offer of $5,000 "just in time to be obliged to refuse an offer from *McClure's* of seventy-five hundred!" Lorimer, who would not have accepted "The Confession" if it had been free, airily replied: "So glad you have taken the money away from the Philistines and have added it to your own bankroll."[4]

That same year, Edna Ferber tried to raise her price—with no success. She had submitted a story and Lorimer accepted it. But Ferber, dissatisfied with the payment, wrote back with a "Shucks," a reminder that her name itself had a certain value, and an appeal for $1,500. Lorimer remained firm: "Now with regards to this special story. It is good, but slight, and I do not feel that it is worth $1500 to us. We have no objection to paying $1500, but we do not weigh names so heavily as do some of the other magazines, and when we pay $1500, we feel that there must be quite a short story on the opposite side of the scale."[5]

Three years later, Ferber sent the *Post* a story called "Old Lady Mandle," explaining that while she was sending this piece, she usually tried to "stifle the impulse" to submit to the *Post* "because you have not, thus far, been willing to pay me the short-story price that three or four other magazines have regularly paid me. That price is $2,000." And then, as if alarmed by her own affrontery, Ferber added a comic touch: "At this juncture I see you hurling this letter into the waste basket." Neither assertion nor charm cut any ice. Lorimer replied, "We all enjoyed reading Old Lady Mandle and wish that we could use it in the Saturday Evening Post, but we feel that the price of this particular story is too high. Perhaps we imbibed some of the spirit of Old Lady Mandle in reading about her, but $1500 would be our limit on this story. That, of course, does not mean that we might not like another one $2000 worth."[6] What the Ferber letters make clear is not only that Lorimer insisted on the authority to set the price for stories and articles but that he claimed as well the right to determine that figure by some sort of private editorial calculus. Some pieces were $1,500 stories; others, $2,000 stories. Only Lorimer knew the difference.

The issue was not entirely, probably not even principally, a matter of money. Lorimer simply did not like to have his contribu-tors demand a certain price; he did not like that abrogation of his authority. He was perfectly willing to raise the amount he paid a contributor, but it had to be his own idea. For the July 23, 1927, issue, for example, Norman Rockwell painted "Pioneer," a finely executed cover with a powerful American message. On a dark blue background, surrounded by a wreath and backed by a plane in flight, a strong-jawed aviator stares into the future; in the bottom corners appear one of Columbus's ships and a covered wagon. Lorimer loved it and he sent Rockwell some good news in one of his typically terse letters: "'Pioneer' is just about high water mark for Post covers and on the strength of it we are going to raise the anti [sic] $250 per."[7]

But neither illustrators nor writers could demand that Lorimer raise the ante; the benefaction had to come from the Boss. Will Irwin had tried and failed to increase his fee; eventually, he came to understand what the control over prices represented to Lorimer.

[Lorimer] had his crotchets as an editor, however. One who runs a maga-zine on his plan must be an absolute monarch; and he had the appropriate temperament. He liked to confer bounty, not to have it screwed or wheedled out of him. Once, before I understood this peculiarity, I accom-panied a manuscript with a letter asking for a raise in prices. The manu-script came back and the letter remained unanswered. Two or three more contributions, while accepted, drew the same old fee; then without fur-ther mention of the subject, he himself raised my price to a sum in excess of what I had asked.[8]

Worse than a simple request for higher payment was such a request accompanied by the information that some other magazine had offered to pay more than the *Post*. Lorimer treated such demands as blackmail. In the first place, he simply asserted the special position of the *Post* among American magazines and dismissed the claims of any others. Thus, if a contributor like Mary Roberts Rinehart could sell at higher prices to another periodical, he coolly congratulated her. If, like Peter B. Kyne and Irvin S. Cobb, they bolted to a higher bidding competitor, Lorimer was through with them. It was a question of *his* authority and *their* loyalty.

Loyalty was, in fact, the complement to editorial authority. In his 1979 autobiography, Norman Rockwell told the story of his own loyalty test. When *Liberty* was founded in 1924, the new magazine sent an agent to offer Rockwell double the *Post*'s price for his work. After a sleepless night, Rockwell took the train to Philadelphia, asked to see Lorimer, and told his story. "Well," demanded Lorimer, "what are you going to do?" Rockwell described his response: "I looked down at the desk, waiting, but Mr. Lorimer didn't say anything. Then I noticed that he had his thumb pressed so hard down on the desk that the tip of it had turned white. I glanced at him, saw his powerful, square jaw and piercing eyes. 'I'll stay with you, Mr. Lorimer,' I said. 'All right,' he said, 'I'll double your price.'" As Rockwell noted, "He would not have given a cent more to keep me, but after I had proven my loyalty to him and to *his* magazine, after I had demonstrated what the *Post* meant to me, he showed me that the *Post* valued my work."[9]

Rockwell provided a moral fable and painted a tense picture of dominance and submission. This was no confrontation between equals, whatever the extent of Rockwell's talent and fame. He was "Norman"; the other, even in retrospect, even thirty-two years after his death, remained "Mr. Lorimer."

Lorimer did not dominate other personalities so completely as he did Rockwell, but he could still make his authority plain. In 1924, old friend and contributor George Pattullo wrote to ask the Boss's opinion about his writing some material for other magazines. Hearst had "been after [him] for some time," and Ray Long of *Cosmopolitan* was now offering $2,500 per short story, as was the new *Liberty*. Pattullo had told them all that he "had no intention whatever of leaving the Post or letting anything interfere with my friendly and loyal relations to [Lorimer]." All the competitors presented the counterargument that "a lot of [the *Post's*] first-flight men have also contributed to their publications" and, Pattullo noted, adding a subtle argument of his own, "I do have stories from time to time which are not written solely because I am convinced they would never do for [*Post*] readers." Competition, moreover, had made "the sky the limit on price." Pattullo wanted "an expression of opinion" from the Boss on his "marketing these side lines."

Lorimer responded in what was for him an unusually long letter, worth quoting in full.

I am sorry that you did not unbosom yourself fully when you saw me in Philadelphia, as it is not always possible to get one another by letter. The Post is 100% for you and your work and is quite willing to do whatever you think fair in the matter of price, but you will appreciate it is not quite fair to expect us to join in the competitive bidding of periodicals who never give a new writer a chance, never add promising men to their list of contributors, but hang on the flanks of the Saturday Evening Post and one or two other magazines and try to pick off their contributors who have definitely arrived.

We do not say that we won't use the work of men who fall for this, but we certainly do not regard them as our headliners after they have fallen for it. All the Post key men, as far as I know, submit their work first to the Saturday Evening Post and, if we turn it down, they are, of course, at liberty to offer it to anyone that they please. Naturally we prefer that they should offer it to periodicals other than the two or three that trail us.

Nowadays, there is something that resembles a revolving fund of authors in New York. Unless the Saturday Evening Post has a back-bone of men who are not in this group we begin to resemble every other popular printing press, and we do not care to be a duplicate of Colliers, Liberty, or The Cosmopolitan, to mention two or three concrete instances.[10]

Lorimer's reply was masterful, from the opening chastisement on. Pattullo was off on the wrong foot from the moment he chose not to "unbosom" himself face to face. The prices the *Post* paid, in comparison to the competition, were defended on the illogical but high-minded grounds that the *Post* found and published new writers. Publishing for other magazines would not necessarily exile

Pattullo from the *Post*, but if he fell for the blandishments of other periodicals, he would no longer be a "headliner." And as for these other periodicals, they were throughout relegated firmly to second place, appropriate publications for materials the *Post* had declined to publish. Finally, given the current state of publishing, the "revolving fund of authors," the *Post* rested its preeminence on loyalty, on the "back-bone" of its principal contributors.

Loyalty continued to have its rewards, even if they usually came in less dramatic form than they did for Rockwell, and even if they could not best be measured in money. The *Post*, after all, offered the widest and, among popular magazines, the best readership, in itself a strong incentive to publish there. Mary Roberts Rinehart, for one, recognized this. In 1931, when she wrote *Miss Pinkerton,* a novel about her popular nurse-detective, she sent it to the *Post* even though she expected Lorimer to pay only $30,000. "I think I can get forty elsewhere," she wrote to her husband, "but I want the Post audience." Her motives combined loyalty with business judgment: "It is good business and has largely put me where I am." [11]

Fame, the value of a name, had its rewards, too, whatever Lorimer's assertions to the contrary. Price *could* be open to negotiation, but only under special conditions and according to certain rigorous conventions. Will Rogers is a case in point. He had done a few pieces for the *Post* and Lorimer wanted more, but Rogers had received offers from the competition. Lorimer held out the lure of money, but he did so from the position of authority he cherished: it was not a question of Rogers's bidding him up; Lorimer had intended a raise all along. "As I wired you, we would rather that you stuck to the Saturday Evening Post and did not appear in another weekly. . . . Incidentally, though I suppose it is of no particular interest to one who is knocking them cold all over the country, we had planned to lift the ante or, as they say in literary circles, the honorarium, with the beginning of the new series." [12]

In much the same way, when Mary Roberts Rinehart found herself with two smash hits running on Broadway and Lorimer found himself without Rinehart submissions for the *Post,* he wrote to her, asking for a story and intimating the possibility of increased prices. Two months later Rinehart sent him "A Midsummer's Knight's Dream." Lorimer replied: "We have had no dealings with you for so long and you have become such a high priced soubrette, that I do not know what you think you ought to get for a story of this kind." Rinehart's answer proved she had her own kind of mastery. "I hope you will not drop dead when I tell you that I am getting four thousand dollars for a story of this length. However, I much prefer not to set any price where you are concerned, and to do, as I have always done, give you the best and trust you to give me the best price you feel I deserve."[13] Lorimer paid $4,000 for the story, double what Rinehart had received three years earlier.[14]

To the extent that a writer's fee represented the Boss's authority and the contributors' loyalty, money was a sign of Lorimer's editorial power. But the essence of that power as *Post* writers experienced it emanated from his sure editorial instinct and his decisiveness. Writers felt that he knew about writing. In the 1948 reissue and sequel to her autobiography, *My Story,* Mary Roberts Rinehart wrote that "Lorimer was in a class by himself," and what she meant by this was that "he was a reader's editor, rather than a writer's. He knew what his audience wanted and he gave it to them." Rinehart remembered him as giving "his authors a completely free hand," but that appraisal was complemented by what she considered his ruthlessness, his quickness to reject what he found unsatisfactory. "I once saw him turn down some stories by Rudyard Kipling with the brief comment: 'Not good enough.'" She recalled no such ruthlessness with her own work, at least not in this passage; instead, she created for her readers a model Lorimer letter: "Dear Mary: Story is fine. Check follows."[15]

Nina Wilcox Putnam, whose stories began appearing in the *Post* in 1917, was rapturous about Lorimer in her 1930 memoir, *Laughing Through.* Celebrating her own success, she dated it from her first formal meeting with the editor of the *Saturday Evening Post.* She had completed her first Marie La Tour story and wanted her agent to send it to the *Post.* The agent, shocked at her boldness, refused to submit: "When the time comes that you are able to write a *Post* story, I'll let you know." Nevertheless, Putnam made a Thursday appointment with Churchy Williams. The following Monday Williams called to report acceptance; moreover, Lorimer wished to meet her in Philadelphia for lunch on Wednesday to talk over future work.

Lorimer became, in Putnam's phrase, "my new patron Saint," who "had wrought a miracle for me." And she asserted, "If I were to even attempt the story of my relationship with the publishers of the *S. E. P.* I would be accused of writing slush." The Curtis Company itself is "a mountain of integrity and fair play," where she learned "the sound moral and commercial values of clean American ideals."

For Putnam, the Boss was a paternal figure. "Working for the *Post* was not like working for a machine, but like working for a strict, wise parent, who sees his own advantage in the success of his children." She credited Lorimer, properly, with the system of pay- ment on acceptance and a willingness to pay a living wage. Thus, Lorimer, "the genius" behind the *Post,* "did much toward making the author a respectable citizen with rights and earning powers in full proportion to his or her ability." Hyperbolically, she saw Lorimer as freeing the enslaved writer and declared, "A decade hence the authors of America will probably erect monuments to him something like those raised in memory of Lincoln."[16]

Will Irwin, too, recalled the speed with which the *Post* made decisions on stories and, with acceptance, paid promptly. "I would post a short story on Monday afternoon, insuring its arrival at his office in the first mail on Tuesday. Either the rejected manuscript or a pleasant letter of acceptance would reach me on the first mail Thursday. If it was accepted, the following Tuesday brought the check and the proof." And, like Rinehart, Irwin remembered Lorimer as leaving his writers' work unedited. "Seldom if ever did he ask for rewriting; and except for the change of a word here and there to conform to Victorian standards prevailing in his office, he never put the editorial pencil to the manuscript." Lorimer's policy, as Irwin recalled, was simple: "'When it's good enough to accept, it's good enough to print as the author wrote it.'"[17]

But not all writing escaped Lorimer's blue pencil. Corra Harris sent the manuscript of *A Circuit Rider's Wife* to the *Post* in 1909, and Lorimer found the story idea very promising. He wrote to tell her that her work had "possibilities provided she was willing to rewrite it 'along rather different lines.'" Encouraging letters followed throughout the summer, but when the revision reached him, Lorimer was still not satisfied, insisting that Harris allow him to edit it as he saw fit. One chapter, however, needed so much work that he gave up on it, sending it back with "orders to rewrite the whole thing, cutting out all digressions and sticking to the story."[18]

Obviously, there were writers like Corra Harris whose stories Lorimer knew would appeal to his readers but whose writing was, while good enough to be accepted, far from good enough to print unedited. In the years that followed, Harris desperately tried to gain control of her relationship with Lorimer, but he remained in charge, responding to her tactics with a superior irony. At one time, when a serial she had written was rejected, she submitted a story anonymously, but Lorimer recognized and returned it. When she threatened to publish elsewhere, Lorimer simply responded, "I think you ought to make good with all those editors you've been flirting with." Harris described him as "a bully and the best editor in the country."[19]

Working with his best writers, the ones whose work he could print as submitted, Lorimer was also prepared to make editorial decisions simply from ideas they presented him. He made such decisions with the rapid incisiveness that characterized his editorial style. Will Irwin described such a session.

When I had ideas for articles . . . I telephoned to Philadelphia for a half hour's appointment. Having arrived, I submitted my proposals. Number one—without a shade of hesitation he might say, "No—don't want that!" and he would give his reason. The same response, perhaps, to the second and the third. The fourth—

"Yes, that looks promising. Tell me a little more." Sometimes in the middle of a sentence, he would cut me off with:

"Yes, I'll take it. When can you get it in? Need any advance against expenses? All right, see the cashier!"[20]

Lorimer's decisions about art work came with the same speed and sureness. Norman Rockwell recalled, "Mr. Lorimer had a strong sense of what the public liked and accepted stories, covers, articles, illustrations according to his first impression of them."

I'd show a cover to him. He'd pace up and down before it two or three times. Then he'd stop, say, "Good," and scrawl, "OKGHL" on the side of it. That was that. The cover was accepted. He never fidgeted over a decision or told me to leave the cover so that he could decide later whether or not to accept it. That first glance, its first impact, was his criterion. "If it doesn't strike me immediately," he used to say, "I don't want it. And neither does the public. They won't spend an hour figuring it out. It's got to *hit* them."[21]

After working for the *Post* for some years, Rockwell realized that the Boss would never accept more than three covers at any one time, no matter how many Rockwell brought with him. Moreover, Lorimer had an extraordinary memory and would not accept any sketches he had previously rejected, not even when years elapsed before their resubmission. Therefore, Rockwell devised a plan to cope with this capriciousness. He now appeared each time with exactly five sketches, of which only three struck him as worthwhile. The editorial meeting would then take place with Lorimer pacing and Rockwell strenuously acting out the ideas expressed in the cover sketches, impersonating an old cowboy or dancing around in imitation of the little animals decorating a picture of spring. "'Good,' Mr Lorimer would say," sealing his decision with an "OKGHL." Then Rockwell would enhance the chances of Lorimer's taste coinciding with his own by acting out those ideas he did not like "listlessly, without running commentary." "'Bad,' Mr. Lorimer would say with a note of what I always thought was triumph in his voice."[22]

Still, Lorimer fancied himself an art critic, and as far as *Post* covers went he was probably right. But he had no taste for the modernist art schools that were beginning to influence American painting. Modernism, however, was making Norman Rockwell feel uncomfortably out of date. In 1923 he traveled to Paris and enrolled in an art school. Subsequently, he put his new ideas and modernist style into a *Post* cover and presented it to Lorimer. Lorimer "paced up and down before [the painting] for a long time," while Rockwell lectured on Paris and modern art.

Suddenly he turned about on his heel and looked at me. "No," he said. And he walked over to his desk and sat down. "Norman," he said, "we had a writer once. Did articles on subjects like county fairs, life on a farm, a town meeting in New England. Good articles; he caught the flavor of that sort of thing nicely. Then the war came along. He decided he should do articles with bigger themes, subjects that, as he put it, had a bearing on the world crisis. . . . So he did a few articles like that. They were terrible. He was out of his element." "I see what you mean, Mr. Lorimer," I said. "I'll *tell* you what I mean," said Mr. Lorimer, who didn't like to be interrrupted. "If you do something well, stick to it. . . . I don't know much about this modern art, so I can't say whether it's good or bad. But I know it's not your kind of art. Your kind is what you've been doing all along. Stay with that."[23]

Nearly forty years later Rockwell did a cover that at once respected Lorimer's point of view on modern art *and* showed that Rockwell could paint the stuff himself. On a gray tiled floor, stands a middle-aged gentleman, back to the viewer, dressed in gray, carrying his hat, gloves, and umbrella. He regards an enormous abstract canvas, painted in brilliant colors in the style of Jackson Pollock. We cannot precisely determine his reaction, but his clothing itself, somber and precise in color and style, rejects the extravagance of the canvas before him. He represents no doubt, and with some approbation, the attitude of the *Post* and George Horace Lorimer toward modernism, but Rockwell had, after all, painted the abstract.[24]

Rockwell's story of the lure of the modern had a different sequel in his autobiography. In 1936 he attempted another "quasi-modern *Post* cover," one he knew himself "wasn't very good." Again he took the work to Philadelphia, but this time the decisive Lorimer "stood before it a long time, almost ten minutes, without saying anything." And then, with his back still toward Rockwell, he said, "'I don't know, Norman. I don't know. Some of my editors tell me I should be more modern. . . . I tell you what,' he said finally, walking over to the window and looking out, 'you leave it here. Let me think it over. All right?'" Rockwell was "shocked." The Boss had never before needed to think anything over, nor had the opinions of his editors undercut his self-confidence. Anti-modernism did win out and the cover was rejected a week later. It was several months before the two met again. Lorimer summoned Rockwell to Philadelphia, but when the artist arrived he thought the office was empty.

Then I saw him. He was seated to one side of the windows, lost in thought. I was halfway across the room before he noticed me. He rose and said, "Well, Norman, I guess I won't be around much longer." . . . He walked to his desk and glanced absent-mindedly at a manuscript. "I guess I'm not the right man any more," he said. I didn't know what to say. There were tears in his eyes. He had built the *Post;* it had been nothing and he'd made it a great magazine—his magazine. . . . I mumbled something about being terribly sorry. "No," he said, "no. Perhaps I am growing old. Maybe a younger man. . . . " And his voice trailed off. "You'll be all right, Norman," he said after a minute, "Wesley Stout is going to take over."[25]

Only Rockwell, playing "Norman" to the editor's "Mr. Lorimer" and manipulating him by acceding to his needs to play his role capriciously and imperially—only Rockwell of all those who wrote of the Boss did so sentimentally. Those who tried to meet him on his own terms, those who matched his toughness with whatever of their own they could muster, never dared.

More typical of the longtime contributor is Kenneth Roberts. His response to Lorimer's retirement and death was more mas-culine, more professional. From Roberts's point of view, the retire-ment of the Boss sounded the death knell of the *Post,* Lorimer's editorial style and editorial savvy eradicated by the impersonality and indecisiveness of an editorial committee.

Roberts recalled the way he had once worked with Lorimer: "I told him my ideas, which he instantly rejected or accepted. . . . The price to be paid for a story was never discussed, and Lorimer was always generous." But on taking over the *Post,* Wesley Stout, forgetting Lorimer's first rule about the editor as despot, instituted an editorial board. Roberts found himself called to a meeting "to out-line [his] contemplated story to the assembled editors." Roberts, having previously outlined the story for Stout, had nothing to say, and the meeting proceeded awkwardly as the new editor asked those around the table if they agreed that the story would be likely to make an excellent serial.

Then Stout turned to a completed piece for which Roberts expected his usual fee of $2,000 and announced, "The editors and I decided that a thousand dollars would be the proper price for it." At first Roberts nearly laughed at this new "impersonal, indecisive board of editors, by comparison with Lorimer's warm and under-standing toughness." Then he looked around the table, at old friends like Adelaide Neall, and saw "their eyes were downcast and their faces expressionless, and realized that they were ill at ease and embarrassed." A bargaining session followed, Stout offering to go to $1,200, when Roberts discovered that his piece had been cut in half, down to some 3,500 words. In disgust, he offered the piece for nothing, "if the *Post* was really hard up," though in the end he accepted the $1,200. But the experience of the editorial committee virtually ended Kenneth Roberts's long and close association with the magazine: "It was eleven years before I found time to write anything for the *Post*."[26]

Recalling Lorimer's funeral, Roberts eulogized the Boss, whose stature "surpassed any statesman, any ruler, any prime minister, any leader of his generation." And he added, "To me Lorimer is still alive."

I can see him and hear him, as clearly as we could hear him after his funeral, when seven of us sat around a table at Adelaide Neall's—Adelaide, Mary Roberts Rinehart, May Wilson Preston, Sam Blythe, Garet Garrett, Eddie LeFevre [sic]. . . . It was what Lorimer would have liked to see: we talked about the Boss, and what he'd said to one man and what he'd done about another, and where he'd been, and what he'd thought—and we laughed till we cried, and pushed the scotch back and forth across the table, and back and forth, and I'll swear Lorimer was in the room with us.[27]

But even the scene of seven old friends celebrating his memory with laughter and scotch might have been too sentimental for Lorimer's tastes. His own style with friends ran to bonhomie and masculine humor, the complement of his editorial style—pithy, vital, edged with irony. Lorimer, too, could recall drinking the night away with friends, especially in the early years when a long day and a long night of work might end with a session of boisterous male camaraderie. Back in 1910 he had attended the Periodical Publishers' Dinner in Washington with David Graham Phillips, Bill Hibbs, and Sam Blythe. After dinner they finished off the evening in Hibbs's hotel room, as Lorimer reported to fiction writer Robert Chambers, who had attended the dinner but missed the rest of the evening.

Far be it from me, knocking or casting up, but the way in which you and Phillips threw down the crowd at the conclusion of the Periodical Publishers' Dinner was exceedingly unsportsmanlike. There was a brief session in the palm room after you retired, and then a few of us adjourned to Bill Hibbs' room where there was a very interesting and illuminating discussion of esoteric Buddhism. The argument was so interesting we were all greatly surprised to find, by looking out the windows that it was breakfast time, so we adjourned to the Shoreham for a bite. It was there that the celebrated Glow Worm quartette was formed. Its function was to radiate music and good cheer through the remainder of the day time. Though it was slightly handicapped by the fact that no member of it knew more than two lines of Glow Little Glow Worm Glimmer, the way in which our revered leader, Mr. Samuel G. Blythe, rendered those few lines brought tears to the eyes of the most thoughtless.[28]

Of course, that was the letter of a much younger Lorimer, but the wit, the energy, the feistiness of the letter to Chambers were heard again and again in Lorimer's essays on the editorial page and for thirty-seven years they had echoed through the offices of the *Saturday Evening Post* where he reigned, "lovable . . . conceited, arrogant . . . dogmatic . . . gracious . . . power-drunk . . . considerate"[29]—the Boss.

NOTES

INDEX

Notes

Introduction

1. Some biographical material and a wealth of anecdote can be found in John Tebbel, *George Horace Lorimer and "The Saturday Evening Post"* (Garden City, N.Y.: Doubleday, 1948). Tebbel was able to interview a number of Lorimer's close associates whose recollections provide a more intimate view of Lorimer at work and at play.

2. "Readers" includes literate, adult, English-speaking Americans, a number estimated at about 45 million in the first decade of the twentieth century.

3. Hegemony, understood as complex and active, as "a lived system of meanings and values," in the words of Raymond Williams, is crucial to mass culture theory for two reasons. First, it allows for a much more vigorous interaction between "practical" life and "entertainment" than did the earlier Marxist concept of base and superstructure. Second, it provides a richer analysis of the functions and uses of mass entertainment than do the coercive readings of Theodore Adorno and Max Herkheimer.

4. Stuart Hall, "Culture, the Media and the 'Ideological Effect,'" in *Mass Communication and Society*, ed. James Curran, Michael Gurevitch, and Janet Woollacott (London: Edward Arnold in Association with the Open University Press, 1977), p. 325.

5. Raymond Williams, *Marxism and Literature* (New York: Oxford University Press, 1977), p. 115.

6. Richard Ohmann argues that mass magazines arose in response to the need of capitalists to control "not output or prices, but *sales.*" The new emphasis on marketing in the late nineteenth century and the development of national markets through uniform packaging, trade names, and advertising led advertisers to seek vehicles for national campaigns. Thus, as Ohmann puts it, "It is hardly too much to say that modern magazines were an outgrowth of advertising which, in turn, was a strategy of big capitalists to deal with the historical conditions in which they found themselves." Given the mutual needs of magazines and advertisers to capture and hold a national market, magazines discovered the crucial ways in which to accomplish this, principally means by which they "helped ease the passage into industrial society for working people of moderate means" ("Where Did Mass Culture Come From? The Case of Magazines," *Berkshire Review* [1981], 85–101).

7. Editorial, "Commoner and Plutocrat," March 16, 1901.

8. Editorial, "Take Your Clothes and Go," September 5, 1903.

9. Editorial, "The New Kind of Graduates," July 18, 1903.

10. In the same way, advertising in the first years of Lorimer's *Post* served distribution. The end, of course, was consumption, but the principal issue at the turn of the century was the identification of products as national rather than local, as available in standardized form to the entire country. In general, the ads themselves made this clear with their focus on the product rather than the consumer, a focus that did not undergo significant change until after the war. Nevertheless, distribution presupposes consumption and the seeds were already sown for the dramatic emergence

of a full-blown consumer society in the 1920s. See Michael Schudson, *Advertising, the Uneasy Persuasion: Its Dubious Impact on American Society* (New York: Basic Books, 1984), and Roland Marchand, *Advertising and the American Dream: Making Way for Modernity, 1920–1940* (Berkeley and Los Angeles: University of California Press, 1985).

11. Antonio Gramsci, *Selections from the Prison Notebooks,* ed. and trans. Quintin Hoare and Geoffrey Nowell Smith (New York: International Publishers, 1971), pp. 339, 419.

12. Hall, "Culture, the Media, and the 'Ideological Effect,'" p. 325.

13. Editorial, "What Are You Afraid of?" November 7, 1931.

14. Editorial, "Washington Was Right," September 19, 1931.

15. Editorial, "From Roosevelt to Roosevelt," December 30, 1933.

16. Editorial, "Is Everybody Happy?" November 30, 1935.

17. For example, Todd Gitlin, writing of contemporary television, states that "commercial culture does not *manufacture* ideology; it *relays* and *reproduces* and *processes* and *focuses* ideology that is constantly arising both from social elites and from active social groups and movements throughout the society" ("Prime Time Ideology: The Hegemonic Process in Television Entertainment," *Social Problems* 26 [February 1979], 250–65).

Chapter 1   1897–1907: "The Greatest Weekly Magazine in the World"

1. The story of Curtis and the *Post* occurs in a number of sources, including Frank L. Mott, *A History of American Magazines,* vol. 4 (Cambridge, Mass.: Harvard University Press, 1968); John Tebbel, *George Horace Lorimer and "The Saturday Evening Post"* (Garden City, N.Y.: Doubleday, 1948); John Tebbel, *The American Magazine: A Compact History* (New York: Hawthorne Books, 1969); Edward W. Bok, *A Man from Maine* (New York: Scribner's, 1923); Frederick S. Bigelow, *A Short History of "The Saturday Evening Post": "An American Institution" in Three Centuries* (1927; rpt. and exp. Philadelphia: Curtis Publishing Co., 1936).

2. Those profits were fairly substantial by 1897; as early as 1895, net profits on the *Journal* for the second half of the year were $93,616 (unpublished minutes of the meetings of the Curtis Company Board [now in the Curtis Archives, Indianapolis], surviving in a summary version for the years 1891–1927, created in-house some years later). In December 1895 the Curtis Board minutes include the complacent comment: "Assets now definitely and finally exceed liabilities." Also see *Printers' Ink* 30 (January 10, 1900).

3. Cyrus Curtis to N. W. Ayer, December 7, 1899, and January 18, 1900, Curtis Archives; Curtis Board minutes, January 1900; at this time Curtis had placed a total of $144,319.61 worth of business with Ayer.

4. Curtis Board minutes, January 1899.

5. Curtis Board minutes, December 1897, October 1898, and September, 1899.

6. Curtis Board minutes, Annual Report, 1898.

7. Curtis Board minutes, Annual Report, July 1900, recorded the following profit and loss statement with some puzzling discrepancies:

Post Income from Advertising		$ 90,000
Post Income from Subscriptions		74,000
Post Income from Sales		96,000
	Total	$264,864
Gross Expense for Year		709,856
	Loss	$444,992
Loss to Date on Post		$923,564

At a rough equivalent of one 1900 dollar to twelve 1983 dollars, a comparable present-day figure for *Post* losses in three years is $11,082,768. ($1.00 in 1900 is calculated as equal to $11.94 in 1983, the most recent year for which these figures are available in *The Economic Report of the President*, 1984 ed., cited in Robyn E. Levine and Felicia G. Kolp, *Economic Statistics: Selected Statistics, Sources of Current Information and Historical Tables*, Report No. 84–81C, Congressional Research Service, Washington, D.C., p. 29. Calculations for 1900 come from *Historical Statistics of the United States: Colonial Times to 1970* [U.S. Department of Commerce, Bureau of the Census, Washington, D.C., 1975], 1:211.)

8. At the end of 1899, the treasurer insisted "that there [was] no possibility of showing a profit during the coming six months and a certainty of heavy losses. He urge[d], therefore, that no dividend be considered. The Board thereupon declared a dividend of 10%" (Curtis Board minutes, December 1899).

9. Edward Bok, Curtis's son-in-law as well as *Journal* editor, believed that Curtis had envisioned from the start a man's magazine devoted to the subject of business, but more disinterested sources credit that conception to Lorimer; see Bok, *A Man from Maine*.

10. Ibid., p. 164.

11. Interview with Graeme and Sarah Lorimer, August 1980.

12. George Horace Lorimer to Albert J. Beveridge, April 4, 1900, Beveridge Papers, Library of Congress.

13. Lorimer to Beveridge, March 22, 1901, Beveridge Papers.

14. Beginning January 7, 1899, and May 25 and August 24, 1901, respectively.

15. Alexander H. Revell, "The Plain Business Man," September 1, 1900.

16. January 11 and March 18, 1899; despite the series title, these articles were written in the third person; eventually the title was changed to reflect this: "How Men Make Their First $1000."

17. "Why Young Men Fail: A Clear Explanation by Shrewd Business Men," October 28 and December 9, 1899.

18. Frank G. Carpenter, "Chances for Young Men: In Japan," March 31, 1900.

19. William H. Maher, "The Clerk Who Reads," January 20, 1900.

20. J. Harry Selz, "How Trusts Affect Trade," April 21, 1900; Frank A. Vanderlip, "The Onward March of American Trade," November 10, 1900. At that time Vanderlip was assistant secretary of the treasury.

21. [George Horace Lorimer], *Letters from a Self-Made Merchant to His Son* (Boston: Small, Maynard & Co., 1902), p. 1.

22. Ibid., p. 89.

23. Ibid., pp.1–3.

24. Tebbel, *George Horace Lorimer and "The Saturday Evening Post,"* pp. 30–32.

25. Editorial, "The New Kind of Graduates," July 18, 1903.

26. Editorial, "The Professions and the Callings," May 6, 1903.

27. Francis L. Patton, Princeton University, "Should a Business Man Have a College Education?"; James B. Angell, University of Michigan, "The Choice of a Calling"; Benjamin Ide Wheeler, University of California, "Is Scholarship a Promise of Success in Life?" May 26, 1900.

28. William A. Scott, "The School of Commerce," June 22, 1901.

29. Editorial, "A Nation of College Graduates," July 13, 1901.

30. Editorial, "A Liberal Education," December 3, 1904.

31. Curtis Board minutes, October 1899. The *Post* boy plan was very new at this time; in one week of October 1899, only 1,510 copies had been shipped to boy salesmen and most of them were sent free.

32. As early as April 1900, *Post* boys were already selling an average of 13,947 copies a week; this represented about 7 percent of *Post* sales, then averaging 193,544 weekly.

33. Advertisement, July 11, 1903.

34. Extensive material on the experiences of a *Post* boy in the first years of this century is available in the Victor H. Pelz Collection at the University of Oregon; see also Jan Cohn, "The Business Ethic for Boys: *The Saturday Evening Post* and the Post Boys," *Business History Review* (Summer 1987), 185–215.

35. "CURTIS CIRCULATIONS STAND FIRM," unpublished in-house memo, the Curtis Company, 1933, Curtis Archives.

36. For example, *How to Sell a Hundred Copies Weekly* (Philadelphia: Curtis Publishing Co. 1912).

37. Mimeographed lists of prizewinners sent by the Curtis Company to boys competing for prizes, 1904; Pelz Papers, emphasis added.

38. Lorimer's move to the board came gradually; in November 1902, he was "invited to be present at meetings . . . having to do with the Post" (Curtis Board minutes, pp. 12–13).

39. Curtis Board minutes for September 1899, and February, April, and July 1900.

40. Curtis Board minutes, Annual Report, July 1900.

41. Curtis Board minutes, December 1899, and May and October 1900.

42. Cyrus Curtis to George Horace Lorimer, July 1, 1901, Curtis Archives.

43. Beveridge to Lorimer, May 16, 1903, Beveridge Papers.

44. Circulation had reached 550,000 by March 7, 1903; while the amount of advertising varied widely, some issues reflected the Curtis Company's growing success in attracting advertisers. The October 31, 1903, issue had a total of fourteen pages of advertising, 44 percent of a thirty-two-page book; Globe-Wernicke even took a double-page spread, relatively rare at a time when most companies were satisfied with quarter pages and even half columns.

45. "The Politicians," "The Brain Trust," "Swinging Round the Circle with Roosevelt," March 14, March 21, and June 27, 1903.

46. "The Shadow of the City," "The Mission of Fishing and Fishermen," September 19 and December 5, 1903.

47. Frank Norris, *The Pit*, beginning September 20, 1902; Alfred Henry Lewis, *The Boss*, beginning August 15, 1903; David Graham Phillips, *The Golden Fleece* and *The Cost*, beginning January 10 and November 14, 1903, respectively; Jack London, *The Call of the Wild*, beginning June 10, 1903; George Ade, *Tales of a Country Town*, beginning January 24, 1903; [George Horace Lorimer], *Old Gorgon Graham*, beginning October 3, 1903.

48. Beveridge to Lorimer, June 16, 1903, Beveridge Papers.

49. Robert Shackleton, "The New Senator from Indiana," September 8, 1900. For a fictionalized portrait of Beveridge's early years and college life, see David Graham Phillips's *The Cost*, beginning November 14, 1903. See also John Braeman, *Albert J. Beveridge: American Nationalist* (Chicago: University of Chicago Press, 1971).

50. Anonymous, "The Diary of a New Congressman's Wife," beginning February 24, 1900.

51. Lorimer to Beveridge, January 29, 1900, Beveridge Papers.

52. Lorimer to Beveridge, January 29, 1900, Beveridge Papers.

53. Lorimer to Beveridge, February 3 and 7, 1900, Beveridge Papers.

54. Lorimer to Beveridge, February 23 and 27, 1900, Beveridge Papers.

55. Lorimer to Beveridge, April 4 and 21, 1900, Beveridge Papers. A month later, Lorimer told Beveridge that his three articles would be reprinted in one of the little booklets the Curtis Company was using for promotion. Beveridge apparently wrote asking what he might expect to earn from these booklets, and Lorimer had to explain that they were not sold but given away "as souvenirs" (Lorimer to Beveridge, June 1 and 4, 1900, Beveridge Papers).

56. Beveridge to Lorimer, March 7, 1900, Beveridge Papers.

57. Lorimer to Beveridge, May 18, 1900, Beveridge Papers.

58. Lorimer to Beveridge, April 10, 1901, Beveridge Papers.

59. Lorimer to Beveridge, May 9, 1901, Beveridge Papers.

60. Beveridge to Lorimer, October 9, 1903, Beveridge Papers.

61. Lorimer to Beveridge, March 24 and May 2, 1902, Beveridge Papers.

62. Beveridge to Lorimer, November 10, 1902, Beveridge Papers.

63. Beveridge to Lorimer, January 17, 1903, Beveridge Papers.

64. Beveridge to Lorimer, April 2 and 18, 1906, Beveridge Papers.

65. Lorimer to Beveridge, February 5, 1907, Beveridge Papers. Beveridge sent the letter on to Roosevelt, scrawling across the bottom, "Isn't George a crackerjack?"

66. For a discussion of objectivity and disinterestedness as central tenets in American journalism from the late nineteenth century to World War I, see Michael Schudson, *Discovering the News: A Social History of American Magazines* (New York: Basic Books, 1978). Schudson argues that "the informational ideal in journalism is associated with fairness, objectivity, scrupulous dispassion," and that it is closely connected with the appeal to an audience of "the educated middle class" (p. 90). He understands this ideal as developing in response to "doubt and drift," that is, to "the relativism that followed the nineteenth century loss of faith" (p. 159).

67. Editorial, "The Unexpectedness of Teddy," July 14, 1900.

68. Owen Wister, "Theodore Roosevelt, Harvard '80," October 12, 1901; Maurice A. Low, "The President's Home," November 11, 1902; William Allen

White, "One Year of Roosevelt," "The President," "Swinging Round the Circle with Roosevelt," October 4, 1902, April 4 and June 27, 1903.

69. It is possible that Lorimer provided Bryan this opportunity, which gave the "Democracy" a kind of extra inning, in order to make amends for Alfred Henry Lewis's article about Bryan earlier in the year, an article savagely titled "The Democracy and Its Iago" (February 27, 1904).

70. John Wanamaker, the Philadelphia department store owner, and E. D. Hulbert, vice-president of the Chicago Merchants Loan and Trust Co., respectively.

71. Editorial, "Is Roosevelt a Menace?" December 7, 1907.

72. The name "Spurlock" comes from another of Lorimer's anonymously serialized novels, Jack Spurlock—Prodigal (beginning April 6, 1907).

73. Lorimer to Beveridge, November 6, 1907, Beveridge Papers.

74. Lorimer to Beveridge, December 3, 1907, Beveridge Papers.

75. Beveridge to Lorimer, December 9, 1907, Beveridge Papers.

76. Lorimer never let friendship cloud his editorial judgment. In 1907 Beveridge sent him a piece called "Habits," warning against drink and tobacco. Lorimer returned it with the comment that "Frankly, I am not for this article, though the advice is absolutely good and sound, nor will you, I think, be for it when you get back and re-read it. It seems to me that it puts you in the Ruth Ashmore class of writers, which isn't where you belong" (Lorimer to Beveridge, June 18, 1907, Beveridge Papers).

77. Isaac F. Marcosson, David Graham Phillips and His Times (New York: Dodd, Mead, 1932), p. 221.

78. Delbert E. Wylder, Emerson Hough (Boston: Twayne, 1981), p. 43.

79. There were still occasions when one or even two of these pages had to be sold in sections, but by this time the Post was able to sell full-page ads to such companies as Gold Medal Flour, Williams' Shaving Stick, Kuppenheimer, Keen Kutter Tools, and Oldsmobile.

80. Beveridge to Lorimer, May 2, 1903, Beveridge Papers.

81. Lorimer to Beveridge, May 4, 1903, Beveridge Papers.

Chapter 2   1908–1913: "More Than a Million a Week"

1. George Horace Lorimer to Cyrus Curtis, August 6, 1904, Curtis Archives, Indianapolis.

2. See, for example, the New York Times, March 25, 1908.

3. Walter H. Page to Cyrus Curtis, October 19, 1908, Curtis Archives.

4. John Irving Romer to Cyrus Curtis, October 30, 1908, Curtis Archives.

5. After 1908, Post circulation grew by about 250,000 a year, reaching 1,250,000 on October 9, 1909; 1,500,000 by March 26, 1910; and 1,750,000 by April 22, 1911. Then it stalled again, taking nearly two years to hit 2,000,000. Although the Post cover had so far announced circulation only in increments of 250,000, it changed its tactics at this time. As if to urge a team effort to raise circulation to the 2,000,000 mark, the Post headlined a readership of 1,900,000 in November 1912. Two months later, they made it.

6. Advertising revenue in 1907 was $1,266,931; in 1912, it came to $7,114,581

(Frank Presbrey, *The History and Development of Advertising* [Garden City, N.Y.: Doubleday, 1929], p. 483). During this period the Curtis Company continually raised the line rates of the *Post,* to $6 a line in January 1910, $7 in February 1911, and $8 in March 1912 (Curtis Board minutes, Curtis Archives).

7. Montgomery Schuyler and Thomas Nolan, F.A.I.A., "A Modern Publishing House: The Construction and Equipment for the New Curtis Publishing Company, Philadelphia, Pa.," pt. 1, *Architectural Record* 31 (March 1912), 281.

8. Thomas Nolan, "A Modern Publishing House," pt. 2, *Architectural Record* 31 (March 1912), 289.

9. Materials from Curtis advertising campaign, 1915, Curtis Archives.

10. Between 1908 and 1913, J. C. Leyendecker painted fifty-seven *Post* covers, Harrison Fisher forty-seven, Robert Robinson and Philip Boileau twenty-four each, Clarence Underwood twenty-three, and Sarah S. Stilwell Weber, nineteen.

11. Quoted in James Playsted Wood, *The Curtis Magazines* (New York: Ronald, 1971), pp. 66–67.

12. Michael Schudson points out that by 1920 it had become a "cliche among advertisers" that women were the "'purchasing agents' of their families," and that "trade journals cited the figure that 85 percent of all consumer spending is done by women." He quotes from an advertisement in *Printer's Ink:* "The proper study of mankind is MAN . . . but the proper study of markets is WOMAN" (*Advertising, the Uneasy Persuasion: Its Dubious Impact on American Society* [New York: Basic Books, 1984], p. 173).

13. It is important not to give the impression that anything like modern advertising research techniques were at work in 1900 or that the tendencies I am discussing reflect thoroughly worked-out policies. Nevertheless, the drift away from domestic goods to goods and services appealing to men is very clear. While some household goods continued to be advertised in the *Post* and even some goods specifically targeted for women, they represented an ever decreasing percentage by 1903 and most often appeared as small ads.

14. I am including in this number advertisements for women's and children's clothing, food, cosmetic and hygiene goods, and household furnishing; these are all small ads.

15. For a full discussion of Cyrus Curtis and the development of magazine advertising, see Wood, *The Curtis Magazines,* pp. 64–71.

16. Arthur Train, "Women as Witnesses," March 17, 1906; see also his "Women in the Courts," May 26, 1906.

17. Editorial, "Homer and the Housemaids," July 4, 1903.

18. Contents for June 20, 1908: "America's Extraordinary Envoy," "By an Expatriate": an anonymous piece by a former attaché in the U.S. diplomatic corps lamenting the lack of savoir faire among our diplomats and their staffs. "Speculation," "By Our Readers": brief, initialed anecdotes of personal experience with speculation— all, of course, demonstrating its evils. "The Eternal Question," by Bert Leston Taylor: comic love story featuring automobiles. "The Fire," by Stewart Edward White: last of a series of short stories on "life in the forest preserves." "Human Nature in Selling Goods," by James H. Collins: advice on selling; these articles by Collins were a regular staple of the *Post* at this time. "The Firing Line," by Robert W. Chambers: adventure

serial. "Failures at Forty," by William Lee Howard, M.D.: upbeat advice on starting again—and succeeding.

19. May K. Warwick, "A Woman's Rebellion" and [anonymous], "Banking Don'ts for Women," June 2, 1909.

20. James H. Collins, "The Art of Managing Women," beginning May 7, 1910; Anne Shannon Monroe, "Making a Business Woman," May 18 and June 1, 1912; Ann O'Neill, "The Woman on the Road," October 19, 1912.

21. Maude Radford Warren, "Petticoat Professions: New Women in Old Fields," November 5, 1911; "A Woman Pioneer," June 17, 1911.

22. Adelaide Neall to George Horace Lorimer, January 20, 1909, Lorimer Papers, Historical Society of Pennsylvania, Philadelphia.

23. Lorimer to Neall, March 30, 1909, Lorimer Papers.

24. Interview with Graeme and Sarah Lorimer, August 1980.

25. "A Woman Editor and Her Work," *Brooklyn Eagle,* p. 13, undated clipping in Wesley Stout Papers, Library of Congress.

26. Editorial, "A Woman as School Superintendent," August 21, 1909.

27. Editorial, "A Woman's Sphere," July 19, 1913.

28. Covers by Sarah S. Stilwell Weber, October 3, 1908, April 9, June 11, and August 20, 1910, April 15 and October 14, 1911.

29. Covers by J. C. Leydendecker, April 10 and November 13, 1909, March 26 and July 2, 1910.

30. Covers by Robert Robinson, July 9 and November 26, 1910, January 21, 1911, January 11 and May 17, 1913.

31. Examples include Mary Roberts Rinehart, "Three Pirates of Penzance," August 20, 1910; Peter Kyne, "The Log of the Courtney Ford," August 6, 1910; and Montgomery Glass, "Sympathy: Its Use in Business as Demonstrated by Morris Perlmutter," October 15, 1910.

32. Mark Claw, "The Theatrical Syndicate From the Inside," April 3, 1909; J. J. Schubert, "The Theatrical Syndicate From the Outside," August 14, 1909; [anonymous], "Making a Living by Literature," November 11, 1911; B. B. Johnson, "The Business End of Baseball," July 19, 1913; Issac Marcossen, "The Business Side of the Circus" and "What the Circus Costs," May 15, 1909, and April 9, 1910; James H. Collins, "The Business Side of the Church," beginning February 1, 1913.

33. Beginning September 5, 1908, August 27, 1910, and November 9, 1912, respectively; October 2, October 16, and November 6, 1909.

34. See, for example, Isaac Marcosson, "A Curb on Corporation Abuses" and "Safeguarding Securities," January 11, 1908 and April 16, 1910; Forrest Crissey, "Neglected Opportunities" and "Every Man His Own Merchant," February 11, 1911 and September 20, 1913; Edwin Lefevre, "Stock Manipulation" and "The Panic of the Lion and the Pessimist," beginning March 20, 1909 and November 16, 1912, respectively.

35. Roger W. Babson, *Actions and Reactions: An Autobiography* (New York: Harper and Bros., 1935), pp. ix, 213–15.

36. "Boys Who Made Good," in "Thrift," August 14, 1909.

37. [Isaac Marcosson], "The ABC of Investment," in "Your Savings," March 30, 1907.

38. Uncle Bill Spurlock [George Horace Lorimer], "The ABC of Confidence," November 30, 1907.

39. April 20 and June 8, 1907, August 1 and August 15, 1908.

40. Editorial, "Mr. Taft and His Party," April 2, 1910. Beveridge supplied an article, "Political Parties," February 26, 1910, taking the same approach to the subject.

41. Editorial, "The Indiana Election," September 24, 1910.

42. Editorial, "An Insurgent Gain," December 3, 1910.

43. Correspondence from the Periodical Publishers' Association of America, March 17, 1910. Curtis wrote to Frank Munsey and Charles Scribner in 1911 urging them not to resign from the association lest "a defection from our organization of so well known a magazine as yours weakens our strength." Apparently those publishers who did not wish to dissociate themselves from the conservative Republicans in the Senate were anxious about allying themselves with the stand the Organization was taking. Thus Curtis noted that he hoped "our association may have all the strength possible from its conservative members," fearing that any "defection in our ranks" would hurt their cause (Curtis to Frank Munsey, Curtis to Charles Scribner, October 20, 1911, Curtis Archives).

44. George Horace Lorimer to Albert J. Beveridge, January 18, 1910, Beveridge Papers, Library of Congress.

45. Newspapers, on the grounds that they carried a lesser amount of advertising, were to be exempt from the new second-class rate.

46. Editorial, "Twentieth-Century Pioneers," February 5, 1910.

47. "The Popular Magazines and Their Advertising," December 17, 1910. See also Marion Butler, "That Postal Deficit," and Thomas H. Carter, "The Postal Deficit and How to Cure It," February 19 and March 12, 1910. The series on popular magazines ran weekly from December 10 through December 31, 1910, and covered the subjects of magazines and the post office and magazines and the postal deficit.

48. Beveridge to Lorimer, May 1, 1912, Beveridge Papers.

49. Editorials, "Dangerous Primaries" and "What Will Progressives Do?" May 4 and 18, 1912.

50. Lorimer to Beveridge, June 27, 1912, Beveridge Papers.

51. Editorial, "The New Parties," July 20, 1912.

52. Robert H. Davis, "Interesting People," *American Magazine*, 1910, p. 325.

53. Beveridge to Lorimer, December 9, 1907, Beveridge Papers.

54. "The Fortunes of the Sun: An Experiment in Printing All the News," September 2, 1911; this was subsequently published as *The Making of a Newspaper Man* (Philadelphia: Henry Altemus Co., 1912).

55. Samuel G. Blythe, "A Mere Matter of Figures: But are You Sure Your Arithmetic is Straight?" October 5, 1912.

56. Samuel G. Blythe, "Before the Battle: A Final View of the Struggle That Will Come in November," October 26, 1912.

57. Woodrow Wilson, "Cut Out Privilege," October 26, 1912. The *Post* played still another role in the 1912 election; that year the Republican party adopted magazine advertising and whatever the political leanings of the *Post*, it was the right magazine to reach a mass audience. A series of full-page ads began late in September. The first displayed a line drawing of two prosperous-looking men in a Pullman car

discussing the election with a black porter. The headline that captioned this fatuous illustration asked, "Are You Doing Your Own Thinking?" and the text narrated the edifying story of how the porter, a victim of radical propaganda, was set straight (Advertisement, September 21, 1912). Eventually, the Democrats advertised too, though only once, offering "Woodrow Wilson's Message to the American People" and providing a coupon to clip for sending contributions (Advertisement, October 26, 1912).

58. Lorimer to Beveridge, October 1, 1912, Beveridge Papers.

59. Editorial, "The Old Parties," November 30, 1912.

Chapter 3   1914–1918: "A Great Social Influence"

1. As early as 1912 a *Post* editorial addressed the situation in the Balkans, satirizing "preparedness for war" with its exorbitant costs in money and men. "We think poorly of 'preparedness for war' among men. It is much like going to enormous trouble and expense to secure preparedness for biting among dogs. When Montenegro, with the area of a trans-Missouri county, the population of a New York City ward, and the wealth of one medium-sized coal mine, puts thirty thousand men in the firing line, it is time to talk preparedness for peace." Editorial, "Food for Balkan Powder," November 9, 1912.

2. Editorial, "Strange Alliances," August 22, 1914.

3. Editorial, "When War Shall Cease," October 3, 1914.

4. In 1904 Lorimer had sailed to France to see his ailing father, but Dr. Lorimer died before his son arrived; Lorimer returned to New York with his father's body.

5. George Horace Lorimer to Albert J. Beveridge, [n.d.], Beveridge Papers, Library of Congress.

6. Certainly, neither the *Post* nor America was unique in the defensive conservatism espoused in those years. See Charles S. Maier on Western Europe and "the survival and adaptation of political and economic elites, and the capitalist order they dominated," in the postwar decade (*Recasting Bourgeois Europe: Stabilization in France, Germany and Italy in the Decade After World War I* [Princeton, N.J.: Princeton University Press, 1975], p. 3).

7. Editorial, "Our National Defense," October 17, 1914.

8. Editorial, "You Will Win the War," June 1, 1918.

9. Will Irwin, *The Making of a Reporter* (New York: Putnam's, 1942), p. 153.

10. Samuel G. Blythe, "London in War Time," September 19, 1914.

11. Samuel G. Blythe, "The Toll," November 7, 1914.

12. Irvin S. Cobb, "Music," July 13, 1912.

13. Newspaper clipping reporting on a speech by George Horace Lorimer to the Franklin Society in Philadelphia, May 17, 1918, Curtis Archives, Indianapolis.

14. Irvin S. Cobb, *Paths of Glory: Impressions of War At and Near the Front* (New York: Grosset & Dunlap, 1915), p. 51. Cobb's pieces, beginning with "A Little Town Called Montignies St. Cristophe," October 10, 1914, were collected in book form in 1915 and reissued two years later to include his prowar *Post* article, "Thrice is He Armed," April 21, 1917.

15. Irwin, *The Making of a Reporter*, pp. 203–04.

16. Ibid., p. 184. For examples of Poole's immigrant stories, see "Up from the Ghetto: From a Dweller to a Speculator in Slums" and "Getting That Home: Told by Jan, the Big Polish Laborer," March 16 and July 7, 1906.

17. Ernest Poole, *The Bridge: My Own Story* (New York: Macmillan, 1940), p. 216. See also Truman Frederick Keefer, *Ernest Poole* (New York: Twayne, 1966).

18. George Horace Lorimer to Mary Roberts Rinehart, August 18, 1914, Rinehart Papers, Univeristy of Pittsburgh Library.

19. George Horace Lorimer to Corra Harris, August 3, 1914, quoted in John E. Talmadge, *Corra Harris: Lady of Purpose* (Athens: University of Georgia Press, 1968), p. 74.

20. [Corra Harris], *A Circuit Rider's Wife*, beginning January 22, 1910.

21. Talmadge, *Corra Harris*, p. 48.

22. Ibid., pp. 75–77.

23. Will Payne, "War and Business" and "War and the Home Market," October 3 and November 7, 1914; Corinne Lowe, "Talking the Cure" and "Will America Dress Herself?" October 3 and October 24, 1914; A. Woods Hutchinson, "Following the Red Trail," October 10, 1914.

24. Irwin, *The Making of a Reporter*, p. 204. Lorimer also wrote to Mary Rinehart that he planned to taper off on "war stuff" (Lorimer to Rinehart, September 25, 1914, Rinehart Papers).

25. Lorimer to Beveridge, May 4, 1915, Beveridge Papers.

26. Lorimer to Beveridge, June 11, 1915, Beveridge Papers.

27. Lorimer to Beveridge, June 15, 1915, Beveridge Papers.

28. Lorimer to Rinehart, December 31, 1914, Rinehart Papers.

29. For Rinehart's war experiences in 1915, see Mary Roberts Rinehart, *My Story* (New York: Farrar and Rinehart, 1931), and Jan Cohn, *Improbable Fiction: The Life of Mary Roberts Rinehart* (Pittsburgh, Pa.: University of Pittsburgh Press, 1980).

30. While Rinehart's articles were running, Lorimer wrote congratulating her and crediting the magazine's rising circulation in part to her work: "We have come through the war in such bully shape, with an increase of 50,000 weekly in the circulation over peace times, and the advertising beginning to run ahead of last year almost every week. . . . Your articles have been fine and have helped a lot" (Lorimer to Rinehart, June 17, 1915, Rinehart Papers). Rinehart's articles were collected as *Kings, Queens and Pawns* (New York: Doran, 1915).

31. Rinehart, *Kings, Queens and Pawns*, p. 336.

32. Ibid., pp. 336–37.

33. Ibid., pp. 367–68.

34. Editorial, "The Barbarisms of Warfare," June 5, 1915.

35. When the *Titanic* sank in 1912, Lorimer explained to Beveridge, "From our point of view, as well as that of the survivors, the Titanic is a dead one. Before we could present anything about it, every magazine and newspaper in the country will have sickened the reading public on the subject" (Lorimer to Beveridge, April 26, 1912, Beveridge Papers).

36. Owen Wister, "The Pentecost of Calamity," July 3, 1915; quotes are taken from the Macmillan publication, 1916, p. 18.

37. Ibid., pp. 61, 86.

38. Ibid., p. 148.

39. Editorial, "Why an Embargo?" August 28, 1915.

40. Editorial, "Our National Defense," October 17, 1914.

41. Editorials, "Another Preparedness" and "The War Talk," December 18, 1915, and May 20, 1916.

42. Will Irwin, "Common Sense About Preparedness," January 1, 1916.

43. Harry Merrill Hitchcock, "Men Wanted for the U.S. Navy," June 3, 1916; [anonymous], "Learning to Fly: The Observance of a Military Aviator," June 3 and August 5, 1916; Herbert Quick, "The Average Man and the Army," March 4, 1916.

44. Editorial, "Vox Populi," November 18, 1916.

45. Lorimer to Beveridge, March 16, 1917, Beveridge Papers.

46. Editorial, "In Safe Hands," March 3, 1917.

47. Rinehart later deeply regretted "The Altar of Freedom," haunted by her own success in having encouraged mothers to send their sons to war; see Rinehart, My Story, pp. 220–21; and Cohn, Improbable Fiction, pp. 108–09.

48. Woodrow Wilson to George Horace Lorimer, April 9, 1918, Lorimer Papers, Historical Society of Pennsylvania.

49. Editorial, "Approved," May 5, 1917.

50. J. C. Leydendecker covers, May 19, June 30, September 22, October 6, and December 22, 1917, and July 27 and November 30, 1918.

51. J. C. Leydendecker covers, December 30, 1916, and December 29, 1917.

52. Booth Tarkington, "Captain Schlottermerz," January 26, 1918.

53. Michael Schudson locates the end of "objectivity" as the prime value in journalism in the experience of World War I. While I am arguing here for a more overt and self-conscious form of deception, his analysis helps establish the larger moral environment in which the Post could print fictitious accounts as fact: "Nothing could have been more persuasive than the war experience in convincing American newspapermen that facts themselves are not to be trusted. Reporters had long taken pride in their own cynicism, but this expressed itself in a love of being close to, and conversant with, the 'inside story' of political and economic life. Their cynicism had sneered at popular illusions while relishing hard, stubborn, and secret facts. But in the war and after, journalists began to see everything as illusion, since it was evidently the product of self-conscious artists of illusion" (Discovering the News: A Social History of the American Newspapers [New York: Basic Books, 1978], p. 142).

54. Eric Fisher Wood, "The British Censorship," April 28 and May 5, 1917.

55. Samuel G. Blythe, "Our Pet—Villa," April 22, 1916.

56. Editorials, "The Slav at the Gate," May 8, 1915; "Undeveloped Russia," June 26, 1915; "The Russian Case," June 16, 1917.

57. Editorial, "A Show-Down in Russia," October 13, 1917.

58. Editorial, "The Great Gold Brick," April 6, 1918.

59. Poole, The Bridge, p. 268.

60. Ibid., p. 321.

61. Ernest Poole, "A Vast Friendship," December 8, 1917; see also his "The City of Chaos," December 22, 1917.

62. Ernest Poole, "What the Russian Peasant Wants," March 2, 1918.

63. William T. Ellis, "Broken Icons," February 2, 1918.

64. Editorial, "The Scum of the Melting Pot," May 4, 1918.

65. Editorial, "Free Speech," August 11, 1917.

Chapter 4 1919–1922: "The Foolish Ideas We Have Imported"

1. George Horace Lorimer to Julian Street, May 23, 1919, Street Papers, Princeton University Library.

2. Irvin S. Cobb, "George Horace Lorimer: Original Easy Boss," *Bookman*, December 1918.

3. Isaac Marcosson, *Adventures in Interviewing* (1919). This is from chapter 3, "A Great American Editor," from typescript of published version, Curtis Archives.

4. Editorial, "Poor Richard Says," February 4, 1922.

5. Editorials, "The Habit of Work," March 6, 1920; "The Doctrine of Sweat," July 17, 1920.

6. [Anonymous], "Home From the Wars," May 10, 1919.

7. Editorial, "Come Clean," October 16, 1920.

8. Editorials, "Miracles," November 20, 1920; "The Younger Set," September 4, 1920; "To Bewildered Parents," November 20, 1920.

9. Editorial, "Fiddling," May 22, 1920.

10. Corra Harris, "Taking Over Our Problems," May 31, 1919.

11. Editorial, "The Russian for Quitter," March 15, 1919.

12. Will Payne, "The Socialists' Koran," January 25, 1919.

13. [Anonymous], "A Reminiscence," May 31, 1919.

14. Editorial, "Policies," January 11, 1919; Forrest Crissey, "New Feet Under the Table," October 4, 1919.

15. Editorial, "Striking Thirteen," October 18, 1919; George Pattullo, "The National Crisis in Boston," November 15, 1919.

16. J. E. McKenzie, "Syndicalism Strikes," November 29, 1919.

17. Delbert E. Wylder, *Emerson Hough* (Boston: Twayne, 1981), p. 43.

18. Emerson Hough, "The Great American Steer," beginning September 22, 1906; "The Price of Beef," beginning February 9, 1907; "Made in America," beginning April 3, 1915; "Traveling the Old Trails," beginning July 5, 1919. See Wylder, *Emerson Hough,* for a complete bibliography.

19. Emerson Hough to Samuel Merwin, June 19, 1908; quoted in Wylder, *Emerson Hough,* p. 30.

20. Editorial, "A Word of Explanation," June 18, 1921.

21. Floyd Parsons, "The Coal Outlook," February 18, 1922.

22. Ellis Searles, "The Coal Miners' Case," April 1, 1922.

23. Editorial, "Sanctuary," February 7, 1920.

24. Editorial, "Self-Preservation," February 7, 1920.

25. Editorial, "No Admittance," January 8, 1921.

26. Kenneth Roberts, *I Wanted to Write* (Garden City, N.Y.: Doubleday, 1949), pp. 78, 126.

27. Kenneth L. Roberts and Robert Garland, "The Brotherhood of Man," August 30, 1919.

28. Roberts, *I Wanted to Write,* p. 133.

29. George Horace Lorimer to Kenneth L. Roberts, October 31, 1919, Roberts Papers, Dartmouth College Library; also quoted in Roberts, *I Wanted to Write,* pp. 134–35.

30. Roberts, *I Wanted to Write,* p. 145.

31. "According to W. W. Husband, then Commissioner General of Immigration, the articles by Roberts were responsible for the passage of the restrictive Immigration Act of 1924" (James Playsted Wood, *Magazines in the United States* [New York: Ronald Press Co., 1949], p. 159). See, for example, Kenneth L. Roberts, "The Existence of an Emergency," April 30, 1921.

32. Editorial, "The Burbanks of the People," April 30, 1921.

33. Editorial, "The Great American Myth," May 7, 1921.

34. George Horace Lorimer to Julian Street, June 28, 1922, Street Papers.

35. Editorial, "Business is Business," January 17, 1920.

36. Editorial, "Con or Coalition," February 21, 1920.

37. Editorial, "New Men for a New Era," April 24, 1920.

38. Editorial, "Compromise," May 29, 1920.

39. Editorials, "Hoover, Wood, Lowden Also Ran," "The Hard-Boiled," "Hoover," July 24 and July 31, 1920.

40. Samuel Blythe, " 'W. G.,' " September 25, 1920.

41. Samuel Blythe, "Jimmy," October 2, 1920.

42. Editorial, "Come Clean," October 16, 1920.

43. Cartoons, Herbert Johnson, "The Noisy Neighbor" and "Circulation Stuff," October 30, 1920.

44. "Lorimer Assails Cox as Unethical," October 26, 1920, newspaper clipping, Curtis Archives, Indianapolis.

45. Editorial, "To Our Subscribers," July 2, 1921.

46. Editorial, "Better Than Bucket Shops," April 29, 1922.

47. Edward G. Lowry, "A Post-Mortem on Cock Robin," November 1, 1919.

48. Curtis Company advertising campaign, January 29–June 15, 1915, Curtis Archives.

Chapter 5   1923–1929: "This Niagara of Print"

1. Leon Whipple, "SatEvePost," *Survey,* March 1, 1928, pp. 691–703, 714–20.

2. James Playsted Wood, *The Curtis Magazines* (New York: Ronald, 1971), p. 105.

3. Whipple, "SatEvePost," p. 714.

4. Frank Luther Mott, *A History of American Magazines* (Cambridge, Mass.: Harvard University Press, 1968), 5:696.

5. Curtis Company minutes, Curtis Archives, Indianapolis.

6. Whipple, "SatEvePost," p. 714.

7. "It has been estimated that 10,000,000 people read [the *Saturday Evening Post*] and the Lord knows how many people look at it" (Benjamin Stolberg, "Merchant in Letters," *Outlook* 173 [May 21, 1930], 82–86, 115–17).

8. Frank Presbrey, *The History and Development of Advertising* (New York: Doubleday, Doran, 1929), p. 483.

9. Whipple, "SatEvePost," p. 699.

10. Stolberg, "Merchant in Letters," p. 117.

11. Mott, *A History of American Magazines,* pp. 698–99, citing *Time* 34 (December 4, 1939), 78.

12. Frederick S. Bigelow, *A Short History of "The Saturday Evening Post": "An American Institution" in Three Centuries* (Philadelphia: Curtis Publishing Co., 1927), pp. 35–36, 9.

13. John B. Kennedy, "Nothing Succeeds Like Common Sense: An Interview with George Horace Lorimer," *Collier's,* November 27, 1926, pp. 8, 47–48.

14. Walter Tittle, "The Editor of The Saturday Evening Post," *World's Work,* January 1928, p. 307.

15. Leon Whipple tried to calculate the actual *Post* readership in 1926. "In 1926 it was figured that if from our population of 105,710,620 you subtracted the children under fourteen, illiterates, foreign language readers, the criminals, insane and paupers, the residual possible market for publications in English was 60,782,577. Divide that by 2.94 adults over 14 per family, and you have 20,674,346 families. More than one in ten of these took The Post" ("SatEvePost," p. 699).

16. Ibid., pp. 700–01.

17. Ibid., p. 699.

18. Ibid., pp. 714–15.

19. Ibid., p. 717.

20. Ibid., p. 720.

21. Stolberg, "Merchant in Letters," p. 84.

22. Ibid., p. 84.

23. Ibid.

24. Ibid., pp. 115, 85.

25. Ibid., p. 117.

26. Upton Sinclair, *Money Writes* (New York: Alfred and Charles Boni, 1927), pp. 18, 68–69.

27. Ibid., pp. 70, 85, 88, 94.

28. Ibid., pp. 67–68.

29. Ibid., p. 50.

30. Albert W. Atwood, *These Eighty Years* (n.p.: 1961), p. 180.

31. Will Irwin, *The Making of a Reporter* (New York: Putnam's, 1942), pp. 298, 386.

32. George Horace Lorimer to Will Irwin, August 29, 1921, Stout Papers, Library of Congress. Lorimer nearly always took this position with his authors. In 1921 Ring Lardner wrote asking how Lorimer felt about his doing some work for *American Magazine.* Lorimer replied: "If you have time to write two or three pieces for the American, why not do them for The Saturday Evening Post? We are far from being over-stocked with your stuff" (Ring Lardner to George Horace Lorimer, April 11, [1921]; Lorimer to Lardner, April 13, 1921, Stout Papers).

33. Irwin was in fact getting good prices for his *Post* material. In the first half of

1921 he was paid $1,000 apiece and, after July, $1,200. The problem was that fewer pieces were accepted.

34. Will Irwin to George Horace Lorimer, February 13, 1923, Lorimer Papers, Historical Society of Pennsylvania, Philadelphia.

35. Lorimer to Irwin, February 14, 1923, Lorimer Papers.

36. Kenneth Roberts, *I Wanted to Write* (Garden City, N.Y.: Doubleday, 1949), p. 148.

37. Quoted in Wood, *The Curtis Magazines*, p. 105.

38. George Horace Lorimer to E. N. Brandt, March 22, 1937, Lorimer Papers.

39. Editorial, "Albert J. Beveridge," June 4, 1927.

40. "A Latin Cromwell," February 24, 1923.

41. Sir Basil Thompson, "The Spread of the Fascist Movement in Europe and Italy," March 10, 1923.

42. "The Ambush of Italy," August 25, 1923.

43. "The Fight of the Black Shirts," September 8, 1923.

44. Isaac F. Marcosson, "After Mussolini—What?" May 29, 1926.

45. Roberts, *I Wanted to Write*, p. 153.

46. Quoted in ibid., p. 171.

47. See John Tebbel, *George Horace Lorimer and "The Saturday Evening Post,"* (Garden City, N.Y.: Doubleday, 1948), pp. 151–55; and Roberts, *I Wanted to Write*, pp. 176–79.

48. Roberts's figure; Tebbel says McClure's fee was $15,000 (ibid.).

49. Benito Mussolini, "New Paths," September 8, 1928. Contemporary observers watched the Lorimer-Child alliance with some amusement. In his 1930 piece in *Outlook*, Stolberg could not resist a comparison between Blythe and Child: "There seldom was a more intelligent and charming observer of public affairs and political monkeyshines . . . than Samuel G. Blythe, undoubtedly the best special writer the *Post* ever had. His partial retirement is a real loss. For a while it seemed that ex-Ambassador Richard Washburn Child was to be his successor. Barkis was willin', but he just wouldn't do, it seems. Mr. Lorimer might have put up with either his Boy Scout philosophy or his prep school style, but their happy fusion was probably a little too much" (Stolberg, "Merchant in Letters," p. 86). Child continued to weave a tissue of deception in the preface he wrote for the Scribner's publication of *My Autobiography* (1928): "So [Mussolini] began. He dictated. I advised that method because if he attempts to write in longhand he corrects and corrects and corrects. So he dictated. The copy came back and he interlined the manuscript in his own hand" (quoted in Laura Fermi, *Mussolini* [Chicago: University of Chicago Press, 1961], p. 286).

50. Lothrop Stoddard, "Racial Realities in Europe," March 22, 1923; James Davis, "The Immigration Laws are Working," October 9, 1926; George S. Dougherty, "The Criminal as Human Being," March 15, 1924; S. W. Stratton, In Collaboration with Frank Parker Stockbridge, "Robots," January 21, 1928; Major General J. G. Harbord, "Shall America Lead in Radio?" June 1, 1929.

51. There is evidence that the *Post* had for some time occasionally used the names of experts to glamorize and authenticate articles written by unknown or less well-known professional writers. As early as 1916 David Belasco agreed to having his name signed to a piece on play production; the article had been constructed out of talks with

Louis De Foe, who had subsequently written it (David Belasco to Louis De Foe, 1916, Stout Papers).

52. James J. Corbett, "The Roar of the Crowd," beginning October 11, 1924; Fanny Brice, "The Feel of the Audience," November 21, 1925; John Philip Sousa, "Keeping Time," October 31, 1925; Luther Burbank With Wilbur Hall, "The Harvest of the Years," beginning August 14, 1926; Paul Whiteman and Mary Margaret McBride, "Jazz," beginning February 27, 1926; Eddie Cantor, As Told to David Freedman, "My Life Is in Your Hands," beginning October 6, 1928; Harold Lloyd, Directed by Wesley Stout, "An American Comedy," beginning March 24, 1928; Sir Harry Lauder, "Roamin' in the Gloamin'," beginning January 7, 1928.

53. Barney Oldfield, Reported by William F. Sturm, "Wide Open All the Way," beginning September 19, 1925; Samuel C. Hildreth and James R. Crowell, "Down the Stretch," beginning May 20, 1925; Henry Ford, As Told to William A. McGarry, "Prosperity—What is It?" April 10, 1926, and "Man and His Machines," May 1, 1926; Coach Amos Alonzo Stagg, As Told to Wesley Winans Stout, "Touchdown!" beginning September 19, 1926; David Sarnoff, As Told to Mary Margaret McBride, "Radio," August 7, 1926.

54. Prince Christopher of Greece, In Collaboration with Mary Margaret McBride, "This King Business," beginning May 12, 1928; Dr. George Frederick Kunz, As Told to Marie Beynon Rey, "Trailing Gems in Europe," March 10, 1928; Geraldine Farrar, As Told to John Jay Whitehead, Jr., "Coming Back and Looking Back," beginning April 14, 1928; J. C. Penney, As Told to Joseph Faus, "The Bible in Business," beginning September 22, 1928; Eddie Cantor, As Told to David Freedman, "My Life Is in Your Hands," October 6, 1928; Harold Lloyd, Directed by Wesley Stout, "An American Comedy," March 24, 1928; [Anonymous], As Told to Earl Chapin May, "Reinsmen Still Reign on Fast Dirt Tracks," September 15, 1928; [Anonymous], As Told to Myron M. Stearns, "For Metal Only," September 8, 1928.

55. Some celebrities appeared second-hand, their stories being told by someone who had an inside chance to observe. If the *Post* could not get the real thing, and if the celebrity were really star quality, second hand was good enough. In 1927 Helen Kay Schunk wrote about the history of aviation; she had been Former Secretary to Anthony Fokker ("Getting Into Aviation," November 5, 1927). In 1928 a series on Lindbergh was printed, by the man who had served as Lindbergh's "Aide on his United States Tour" (Donald E. Keyhoe, "Flying With Lindbergh," beginning May 19, 1928).

56. Jan Cohn, *Improbable Fiction: The Life of Mary Roberts Rinehart* (Pittsburgh, Pa.: University of Pittsburgh Press, 1980), pp. 278, 280.

57. Stolberg, "Merchant in Letters," p. 80.

58. Bigelow, *A Short History of "The Saturday Evening Post,"* p. 22. In 1929 Lorimer turned down a story by long-time contributor Julian Street "because we do not care editorially for the mistress situation in our fiction" (George Horace Lorimer to Julian Street, October 2, 1929, Street Papers, Princeton University Library). Whipple, in *Survey*, commented that "On the physical side of sex morals The Post's pages are pure; no adolescent sex delinquency ever started in them." Pointing out that Puritan morals are undoubtedly good business, Whipple conceded that "the decency of The Post . . . is no less praiseworthy for that" ("SatEvePost," p. 718).

59. George Horace Lorimer to Thomas Costain, June 24, 1929, Lorimer Papers.

60. Tittle, "The Editor of The Saturday Evening Post," p. 305.

61. Editorial, "Alas, the Poor Artist!" July 7, 1923.

62. Editorials, "The Box Office" and "The Off-Color Line," March 21 and April 25, 1925.

63. George Horace Lorimer to Kenneth Roberts, April 2, 1925, Roberts Papers, Dartmouth College Library.

64. Sinclair Lewis, "Be Brisk With Babbitt," *Nation* 119 (October 15, 1924), 441.

65. George Horace Lorimer, "The Unpopular Editor of the Popular Magazine," *Bookman*, December 1924, from original typescript, Curtis Archives. Lorimer also got in his licks at the little magazines that so irritated him: "For every story that the popular magazine rejects there is a place somewhere. There are magazines that make a cult of dulness [sic]; thin little refuges for pink and pallid verse; expensive and degenerate, as well as cheap and nasty, periodicals that cater to the prurient minded; not to mention those reviews and magazines whose brahmans beat their breasts and proclaim their literary and artistic quality."

66. Kenneth Roberts continued to write on the subject of immigration ("Lest We Forget," April 18, 1923); and Issac Marcosson joined in ("Checking the Alien Tide," May 5, 1923). Elizabeth Frazer visited "Our Foreign Cities" (September 8, 1923); Edward Filene, the retailer, warned that all progress would be impeded in America should the Johnson anti-immigration bill fail ("Immigration, Progress and Prosperity," July 28, 1923); James Davis, secretary of labor, revealed that convicted criminals in Europe were given the choice between jail and emigration ("Jail—or a Passport," December 1, 1923).

Lorimer argued for the passage of the Johnson bill in the spring of 1924, in one editorial citing a list from the *Congressional Record* of all organizations in Massachusetts opposing the bill. Even after the Johnson bill was enacted on July 1, 1924, the *Post* maintained its vigilance. In September 1925, an editorial alerted readers that the Johnson bill was soon to run out; it needed to be reenacted and made stronger. Throughout 1926 readers were continually reminded of this, in one instance by references to the high cost of deportation, in another by commentary on the crime situation in Chicago (Editorials, "They Want Unrestricted Immigration," "Putting the Bars Up Higher," "The Dearest Way the Worst Way," "More Deportations Needed," April 5, 1924; September 26, 1925; February 27 and April 3, 1926).

67. Lothrop Stoddard, "Racial Realities in Europe," March 22, 1924.

68. Editorial, "The Crime School," November 14, 1925.

69. George Horace Lorimer to Mary Roberts Rinehart, October 31, 1929, Rinehart Papers, University of Pittsburgh Library; quoted in Cohn, *Improbable Fiction*, p. 187.

70. Albert W. Atwood, "Corporations and People," February 27, 1926. Even the workingman could prosper through investment. In 1927, Cyrus McCormick of International Harvester wrote about the 70 percent of his employees who were participating in a stock ownership plan (Cyrus McCormick, Jr., "Partners on the Payroll," October 15, 1927).

71. Will Payne, "High Tide in Speculation," February 18, 1928.

72. Editorial, "Thrift and Living Standards," November 22, 1924.

73. Editorial, "Saving or Spending," October 19, 1929.

74. Floyd W. Parsons, "The Civilization of Business," February 23, 1924.

75. Garet Garrett, "An American Book of Wonder," December 10, 1927, and January 7, 1928.

76. In 1926 articles by Henry Ford and Elbert Gary celebrated prosperity as the combination of more production with more consumption, or as the system of produc-ing for consumption, and asserted the "growing conviction" that business was no longer subject to cycles (Henry Ford, As Told to William A. McGarry, "Prosperity—What is It?" and Elbert H. Gary, "Cycles Versus Common Sense," April 10 and December 18, 1926). The next year staff writer Samuel Crowther told Post readers that it was no more than an "outworn cliché" to believe prosperity must end ("To Make Prosperity Permanent," November 19, 1927).

77. Whipple, "SatEvePost," p. 714.

78. Following are a few examples: James H. Collins, "The Beauty Business," November 22, 1924; Katherine Sproehnle and Jane Grant, "Commerce in Amenities," September 13, 1924; J. R. Sprague, "The Lure of the Paris Label," November 1, 1924; Olive Chapin Lawson, "Selling Style," June 12, 1926; Maude Parker Child, "The Social Atlantic" and "Diplomatic Entertaining," April 25 and May 16, 1925; [Anonymous] (As Told to Mara Evans), "Profits, in Pets," March 17, 1928; Donald Culrose Peattie, "Orchid Extravaganza," August 4, 1928; George Frederick Kunz (As Told to Marie Beynon Rey), "Trailing Gems in Europe," March 10, 1928; Maude Parker Child, "Princely Hospitality: How to Entertain and Be Entertained," August 8, 1925; Edward Longstreth, "The Art of Party-Throwing," July 27, 1929; Kenneth L. Roberts, "Florida Loafing," May 17, 1924; Richard Connell, "A Weekend at Atlantic City," May 22, 1926; Frank Ward O'Malley, "Random Thoughts on the Riviera," May 22, 1926.

79. Lorimer had become an enthusiastic collector, along with Post contributors and friends Kenneth Roberts, novelist Joseph Hergesheimer, and illustrator M. L. Blumenthal. Lorimer's sense of male camaraderie, once elicited by evenings of drinking and hijinks with men like Blythe and Phillips, now emerged most powerfully in letters about his victorious antiquing. Lorimer's letters to Roberts were filled with comments on his recent finds. Returning from Europe in 1925, he sent off a quick note reporting on his purchases abroad: "I didn't buy much abroad but what I picked up was first chop and included a little old silver, a little old china, a set of unusually fine ladder-back chairs, a Queen Anne settee, a pair of very fine oblong shaped Gothic tapestries, which ought to help the toute ensemble of my library, as they say in Paris." And in the spirit of competition, he would send off a line, a single sentence, to report a success: "It causes me much pain to notify you that I have just found and purchased in Princeton, New Jersey, the best Sheraton sofa in America, not excepting that in the Metropolitan Museum" (Lorimer to Roberts, August 18, 1925 and June 14, 1926, Roberts Papers). Joseph Hergesheimer, too, received bulletins from the antiques front: "On Sunday I annexed a Lowestoft tea set and twelve of the finest Lowestoft plates" (George Horace Lorimer to Joseph Hergesheimer, June 10, 1924, Stout Papers).

80. These articles appeared on February 12, 1927, August 4, 1928, November 17, 1928, March 17, 1928, and September 24, 1927, respectively.

81. Editorial, "What's the Hurry?" March 8, 1924.

82. Samuel G. Blythe to George Horace Lorimer, September 4 and 24, 1924, Stout Papers.

83. Quoted in Tebbel, *George Horace Lorimer and "The Saturday Evening Post,"* p. 189.

84. Quoted in ibid., p. 190.

85. April 14, June 23, July 21, and September 22, 1928.

86. Tebbel, *George Horace Lorimer and "The Saturday Evening Post,"* p. 190.

87. Blythe to Lorimer, July 26, 1928, Lorimer Papers.

88. Samuel G. Blythe, "The Fundamentals of This Campaign," September 15, 1928.

89. Evangeline Booth, "Some Have Stopped Drinking," January 28, 1928.

90. Editorials, "The Wrong Kind of Sympathy" and "Impounding Wheat," May 12 and September 1, 1923.

91. Garet Garrett to George Horace Lorimer, September 19 [and 27 or 28, 1924]; Lorimer to Garrett, September 29, 1924, Stout Papers.

92. In his article in *Outlook,* Stolberg records Lorimer's "laughing remark": "I have a seven-hundred acre farm near Philadelphia, and I guess I know something about the troubles of the farmer" ("Merchant in Letters," p. 718).

93. Editorial, "Farm Prices and Elections," October 20, 1928.

94. Editorials, "Do We Want Coolie Labor?" and "Ruinous Competition," February 24 and April 28, 1923.

95. Albert Atwood, "Where Have the Miners Gone?" March 10, 1923. See also Elizabeth Frazer, "Our Foreign Cities," September 8, 1923; Edward A. Filene, "Immigration, Progress and Prosperity," July 28, 1923; James J. Davis, "Jail—or a Passport," December 1, 1923.

96. Editorial, "High Percentages," November 3, 1928.

97. Editorial, "Governor Smith on Immigration," October 13, 1928.

98. Although the *Post* had waged a strenuous campaign for Hoover, Lorimer "resented even the implication that the *Post* had been hand in glove with Hoover" (Tebbel, *George Horace Lorimer and "The Saturday Evening Post,"* p. 191). Just before the election, he asserted in a letter to Mabel Walker Willdbrandt that "whatever I have done in The Saturday Evening Post has been done on my own initiative" (quoted in ibid., p. 192). Hoover offered Lorimer the ambassadorship to the Court of St. James but the editor declined.

99. Alfred E. Smith, "Up To Now—An Autobiography," beginning July 27, 1929.

100. Bigelow, *A Short History of "The Saturday Evening Post,"* pp. 10–11, 21.

Chapter 6   1930–1936: "There Is Nothing the Matter with America Except Damfoolishness."

1. Albert Atwood, "Investment and Speculation," December 7, 1929.

2. Garet Garrett, "Wall Street and Washington," December 28, 1929.

3. Editorials, "Economic Soundness" and "Reforming Wall Street," December 7, 1929.

4. Garet Garrett, "The Wild Wheel in the Business Machine," January 18, 1930.

5. Albert Atwood, "Old-Fashioned Savings," January 11, 1930.

6. Albert Atwood, "The Appetite for Stocks," April 19, 1930.

7. Sylvester Viereck, "Pyatiletka," January 18, 1930; and George Soule, "What Do We Earn?" February 2, 1930.

8. Philip Gibbs, "Is Anything Wrong With England?" February 8, 1930.

9. Winston Churchill, "The Dole," March 29, 1930.

10. Editorial, "Unemployment," May 3, 1930.

11. Samuel Crowther, "The Way to Wealth, an Interview with Henry Ford," May 17, 1930.

12. Kenneth Coolbaugh, As Told to Charles Gilbert Reinhardt, "Hunting a Job," September 13, 1930.

13. Editorial, "Business Revival," July 12, 1930.

14. John Maynard Keynes, "Economic Possibilities for Our Grandchildren," October 11, 1930.

15. Editorial, "Arithmetic and Unemployment," August 2, 1930.

16. Editorial, "The Communist Menace," September 27, 1930.

17. Julian Street, "A Soviet Saint," July 13, 1930. In care of the *Post*, Street received a furious letter in response to his Reed article. Essentially, the writer demanded to know Street's motive "for such slipshod and obviously insincere treat-ment; . . . do you think that the persistent ignoring and distorting of what actually takes place is going to save you and your class?" But before attacking Street personally, the writer took one of the three pages of his letter to rationalize his own action in having even read the *Saturday Evening Post*. He came to buy the magazine only after having seen a man on the streetcar reading the article about John Reed. He knew, of course, "that it would be folly to expect the truth in such a paper. . . . A person with but half a dozen red corpuscles in his veins other than bovine, or one ounce of brain in quality above that of a moron, does not read the stuff that is poured without limit by the respectable magazines of our day, lest the half dozen red human corpuscles or the ounce of brain run riot with impotent indignation and apprehension at the sowing of the wind—and the headlong plunge into the ripening whirlwind that will surely engulf these false apologists of a dying age" (A. J. Lipshitz to Julian Street, September 19, 1930, Street Papers, Princeton University Library).

18. In 1929 circulation averaged 2,865,996; in 1930 that rose slightly to 2,891,773 (Curtis Archives, Indianapolis).

19. Leon Trotsky to Max Eastman, October 27, 1930, Eastman Papers, Lilly Library, Indiana University.

20. *The Reminiscences of Boris Shishkin,* Oral History Research Project, Butler Library, Columbia University.

21. Ibid.; Max Eastman translated the remaining two volumes for the book pub-lication of *The Russian Revolution* (William L. O'Neill, *The Last Romantic: A Life of Max Eastman* [New York: Oxford University Press, 1978], p. 310, n. 4).

22. Adelaide Neall to Max Eastman, n.d., Eastman Papers.

23. Max Eastman to George Horace Lorimer, n.d., Eastman Papers.

24. *Outlook,* May 6, 1931, pp. 6–7.

25. Samuel Crowther, "Let Us Take Stock," January 10, 1931.

26. Albert Atwood, "Let George Do It," February 14, 1931.

27. Isaac Marcosson, "Guaranteeing the Job," February 28, 1931.

28. Editorials, "Everyman's Job" and "The Great Fallacy," January 10 and March 21, 1931.

29. Editorials, "Calamity Janes" and "Enemies of the People," May 24 and March 28, 1931.

30. Editorial, "Bargain Days," February 28, 1931.

31. Frederick Van Wyck, "Panic Profits," August 1, 1931.

32. Eddie Cantor and David Freedman, "Yoo-Hoo! Prosperity!" August 15, 1931.

33. Editorial, "Thanksgiving," November 21, 1931.

34. "Can Europe Pay Her Debts?" September 21, 1923.

35. Editorial, "Sullen and Selfish Isolationism," December 15, 1923.

36. Garet Garrett, "The Apologetic American," September 18, 1926.

37. Herbert Johnson cartoon, March 10, 1928.

38. Immediately after the announcement of the moratorium, Lorimer and Garet Garrett sailed to Europe, "where they compiled material for a Post series on the German and general European debt situation. Hundreds of thousands of copies of these articles were printed and distributed at private expense" (John Tebbel, *George Horace Lorimer and "The Saturday Evening Post"* [Garden City, N.Y.: Doubleday, 1948], p. 196).

39. Editorial, "Whose Capacity to Pay?" August 13, 1932.

40. Editorial, "Reds, Blues and Yellows," June 18, 1932.

41. Boyden Sparkes, "Seeing Red," September 10, 1932.

42. Editorial, "The Roots of Unrest," September 3, 1932.

43. Calvin Coolidge, "The Republican Case," and Josephus Daniels, "Franklin Roosevelt as I Knew Him," September 10 and September 24, 1932.

44. Samuel G. Blythe, "The Argonauts of '32," October 15, 1932.

45. Editorial, "Roosevelt's Opportunity," December 10, 1932.

46. Newton D. Baker, "Beyond the Bread Lines," December 17, 1932.

47. Samuel G. Blythe, "Camps for Jobless Men," May 27, 1933.

48. Garet Garrett, "Why Some Banks Fail and Others Don't," May 20, 1933.

49. Editorials, "Let the Seller Beware" and "Turmoil," May 13 and 27, 1933.

50. David Lawrence, "Uncle Sam Becomes a Partner," June 10, 1933.

51. Herbert Johnson, "Out for a Record," June 10, 1933.

52. Editorial, "Providence and the President," July 29, 1933.

53. Adelaide Neall to Booth Tarkington, November 15, 1933, Tarkington Papers, Princeton University Library.

54. Editorial, "The Excesses of Reformers," December 9, 1933.

55. Editorial, "From Roosevelt to Roosevelt," December 30, 1933.

56. Average weekly circulation had increased by some 700 copies in 1931 to 2,892,406. In 1932 it fell to 2,850,401, and in 1933 to 2,768,301. In 1934 it held just about steady at 2,769,862.

57. Summer was always slower for the *Post;* still, 33 percent of a seventy-two page book on July 22, 1933, was a very poor showing indeed.

58. "To the Stockholders, Curtis Publishing Company," April 18, 1934, Curtis Archives, Indianapolis.

59. Eberhardt Mueller, "Our Company Through the Next Boom and Depres-sion," 1941, Curtis Archives.

60. *Curtis Circulations Stand Firm* (Philadelphia: Curtis Publishing Co., 1933), Curtis Archives.

61. Neall to Tarkington, November 15, 1933, Tarkington Papers.

62. Jan Cohn, *Improbable Fiction: The Life of Mary Roberts Rinehart* (Pitts-burgh, Pa.: University of Pittsburgh Press, 1980), p. 282.

63. The position of the Campbell's ad had become an index to the size of the issue. In Mueller's 1941 analysis of the effect of economic depressions on Curtis publications, a projection of plans to meet future depressions suggested the possible necessity of decreasing "the size of the text body": In *Post* lingo, that "means putting Campbell's soup further forward" (Mueller, "Our Company Through the Next Boom and Depression").

64. December 22, 1934, December 28, 1935, and February 22, 1936.

65. Hal G. Evarts to George Horace Lorimer, April 11, 1934, Evarts Papers, University of Oregon.

66. Lorimer to Evarts, April 16, 1934, Evarts Papers. Lorimer also told Julian Street about the favorable response to his editorials: "We have been having a wide response both from my recent editorials and from Garrett's article" (George Horace Lorimer to Julian Street, September 29, 1931, Street Papers, Princeton University Library).

67. Samuel G. Blythe, "A Clear Call to the Center," January 1, 1934.

68. Samuel G. Blythe, "New-Deal Politics," September 22, 1934.

69. Editorial, "Smilin' Through," September 22, 1934.

70. Editorial, "Human Rights and Lefts," September 29, 1934.

71. Editorial, "Smilin' Through."

72. Editorial, "Government Spending," February 24, 1934.

73. George Horace Lorimer to Kenneth Roberts, August 29, 1935, Roberts Papers, Darmouth College Library.

74. J. P. Marquand, *No Hero*, Rex Stout, *The Frightened Men*, Agatha Christie, *Death in the Air* and *Murder in Mesopotamia*, beginning March 30, June 15, February 9 and November 11, 1935, respectively.

75. J. P. Marquand, *Thank You, Mr. Moto* and *Think Fast, Mr. Moto*, Agatha Christie, *Cards on the Table* and *Poirot Loses a Client*, Rex Stout, *The Rubber Band*, and Mignon Eberhardt, *Danger in the Dark*, beginning February 8, September 12, May 2, November 7, February 29, and June 20, 1934, respectively.

76. William Faulkner to the Editors of the *Saturday Evening Post*, December 21, 1927, Stout Papers, Library of Congress.

77. William Faulkner to the *Saturday Evening Post*, January 1, 1931, Stout Papers.

78. William Faulkner, "A Bear Hunt," "The Unvanquished," "Vendee," Febru-ary 10, 1934, and November 14 and December 5, 1936.

79. Adelaide Neall to Mary Roberts Rinehart, December 11, 1934, Rinehart Papers, University of Pittsburgh Library; Crowell's *Good Housekeeping* bought the story for $4,000.

80. Rose Wilder Lane, "Credo," March 7, 1936.

81. Will Payne, "A Common-Sense Confession," March 30, 1935.

82. Neall to Rinehart, March 6, 1936, Rinehart Papers.

83. Cohn, *Improbable Fiction, passim.*

84. Frederick S. Bigelow, *A Short History of "The Saturday Evening Post": "An American Institution" in Three Centuries* (1927; rpt. and exp. Philadelphia: Curtis Publishing Co., 1936), p. 57.

85. For example, Victoria Hazleton, "Work Relief," March 2, 1935; and Jay E. House, "Saga of a Family Farm," January 25, 1936. Hazleton wrote that she was "glad [her] father died in 1931. It would have disturbed the very foundations of his soul to have observed this country today."

86. Martin Dies, "The Immigration Crisis," April 20, 1935.

87. Priscilla Wayne, "Does the World Owe John Doe a Living?" May 4, 1935.

88. William N. McNair, "The Waste of People's Money," November 30, 1935.

89. John Benton, "Rest for Weary Willie," September 5, 1936.

90. Dorothy Thompson, "Dream Your Own Millions," August 10, 1935.

91. Dorothy Thompson, "Vitamins and the Green-Plush Rabbit," August 24, 1935.

92. Samuel G. Blythe, "Grass Roots or Withered Tops?" September 7, 1935.

93. Samuel G. Blythe, "No Plumed Knight Needed," April 18, 1936.

94. Samuel G. Blythe, "A Letter to the Candidate," June 6, 1936.

95. Garet Garrett, "Security," September 19, 1936.

96. Garet Garrett, "Federal Theater for the Masses," June 20, 1936.

97. Alva Johnston, "Hundred-Tongued Charley, the Great Silent Orator" and "Big Jim Farley; He Gets the Blame," May 30 and June 27, 1936.

98. Editorial, "The Big Barrage of Invective," February 8, 1936.

99. Editorial, "Recessional," August 1, 1936.

100. Harold L. Ickes, "Roosevelt as I Knew Him," August 15, 1936.

101. George Pattullo, "Our Sentimentalists," October 31, 1936.

102. Editorials, "The Pious Pre-Election Politician" and "Are You Ready for the Question?" October 31, 1936.

103. Editorial, "'Pride and Prejudice,'" November 7, 1936.

104. Editorial, "The New Administration," December 5, 1936.

105. George Horace Lorimer to the Board of Directors of the Curtis Publishing Company, August 28, 1936, Lorimer Papers, Historical Society of Pennsylvania, Philadelphia.

Epilogue: George Horace Lorimer, the Boss

1. George Horace Lorimer, quoted in Isaac Marcossen, *David Graham Phillips and His Times* (New York: Dodd, Mead, 1932), pp. 220–21.

2. Edward W. Bok, *A Man From Maine* (New York: Scribner's, 1923), p. 193.

3. George Horace Lorimer to Albert Beveridge, May 18, 1900, Beveridge Papers, Library of Congress.

4. Mary Roberts Rinehart to George Horace Lorimer, December 13, 1916;

Lorimer to Rinehart, December 4 and 15, 1916, Rinehart Papers, University of Pittsburgh Library.

5. George Horace Lorimer to Edna Ferber, February 3, 1916, Stout Papers, Library of Congress.

6. Edna Ferber to George Horace Lorimer, July 24, 1919; Lorimer to Ferber, August 11, 1919, Stout Papers.

7. George Horace Lorimer to Norman Rockwell, June 30, 1927, Stout Papers.

8. Will Irwin, *The Making of a Reporter* (New York: Putnam's, 1942), p. 186.

9. Norman Rockwell, as told to Thomas Rockwell, *Norman Rockwell: My Adventures as an Illustrator* (Indianapolis: Curtis Publishing Co., 1979), p. 82.

10. George Pattullo to George Horace Lorimer, October 22, 1924; Lorimer to Pattullo, October 31, 1924, Stout Papers.

11. Mary Roberts Rinehart to Stanley M. Rinehart, September 25, 1931, Rinehart Papers; Lorimer, in fact, paid $50,000 for the serial on the condition that it be lengthened to six installments (Jan Cohn, *Improbable Fiction: The Life of Mary Roberts Rinehart* [Pittsburgh, Pa.: University of Pittsburgh Press, 1980], p. 196).

12. George Horace Lorimer to Will Rogers, February 1, 1927, Stout Papers.

13. Lorimer to Rinehart, October 21, 1921; Rinehart to Lorimer, October 26, 1921, Rinehart Papers.

14. Cohn, *Improbable Fiction,* pp. 144, 276.

15. Mary Roberts Rinehart, *My Story: A New Edition and Seventeen New Years* (New York: Rinehart and Co., 1948), p. 509.

16. Nina Wilcox Putnam, *Laughing Through: Being the Autobiographical Story of a Girl Who Made Her Way* (New York: Sears Publishing Co., 1930), pp. 300–05.

17. Irwin, *The Making of a Reporter,* p. 185.

18. John E. Talmadge, *Corra Harris: Lady of Purpose* (Athens: University of George Press, 1968), pp. 41–43.

19. Ibid., pp. 72–73, 94.

20. Irwin, *The Making of a Reporter,* pp. 185–86.

21. Rockwell, *Norman Rockwell,* p. 81.

22. Ibid., p. 81.

23. Ibid., pp. 104–05.

24. Norman Rockwell, "The Connoisseur," January 13, 1962.

25. Rockwell, *Norman Rockwell,* p. 147.

26. Kenneth Roberts, *I Wanted to Write* (Garden City, N.Y.: Doubleday, 1949), pp. 344–45.

27. Ibid., pp. 345–46.

28. George Horace Lorimer to Robert W. Chambers, March 24, 1910, Lorimer Papers, Historical Society of Pennsylvania, Philadelphia.

29. Quoted from an interview with *Post* editor Marione Derrickson, Curtis Archives, Indianapolis.

Index